HOPE 365

A DAILY DEVOTIONAL FOR TEENS

HOPE 365

A DAILY DEVOTIONAL FOR TEENS

DEAN SIKES

30TH YEAR COMMEMORATIVE EDITION

ISBN # 978-0-692-20097-1

POST OFFICE BOX 8915
CHATTANOOGA, TENNESSEE 37414
THE UNITED STATES OF AMERICA

ORIGINAL PRINTING: 2014
2ND EDITION: 2021

ALL SCRIPTURE REFERENCES IN THIS BOOK ARE FROM
THE NEW KING JAMES VERSION OF THE BIBLE.

DEDICATION

At present, there are approximately **1.3 billion** teenagers alive today. This book is dedicated to every single one of you. Irrespective of your country of origin and despite what might be happening in your world today, I want you to know the truth: God loves you; He's got a plan for your life; and because you're breathing, YOU MATTER.

When I wrote this devotional book, I did so with one goal in my heart: create a resource that would inspire and motivate teenagers around the world to have a daily relationship with the Lord through the written Word.

And so, every one of our 365 daily devotionals in this book were written with you in my heart. Each page has a story that is wrapped in a biblical principle, principles that offer hope and point you toward faith in the Word of God.

As you turn the page and begin your daily walk, we hope you'll enjoy the journey.

JANUARY 1

ALL THINGS NEW

Happy New Year. What a time to be alive in God. What plans He has for you.

Today, all over the world people from all walks of life and from every imaginable social class are, to some degree or the other, writing down "New Year's Resolutions." Statistics tell us however that most of these resolutions will not be accomplished. There are many reasons for this but suffices to say, life just keeps on moving with or without our accomplishing resolutions.

Got something for you to consider today. What if instead of being consumed with a list, what about instead being consumed with a promise? A promise from The Lord.

The bible tells us in the book of Revelation that Jesus makes all things new.

Why not kick start this New Year in a brand-new way. Ask The Lord to give you a clean slate, a fresh beginning, and then maybe consider making one serious commitment versus a bunch of resolutions.

Consider committing to The Lord that every day this year, you'll visit with His Word; not because you have to, but because you want to.

Today is the first day of the New Year. Thanks to Jesus, He's made all things new for you and me. As we move forward throughout this year, let's give the Word of God first place in our lives.

As we do, watch as the Word leads us to and through a committed lifestyle to Him.

Today's Word is Revelation 21:5

"Then He who sat on the throne said, "Behold, I make all things new." And He said to me, "Write, for these words are true and faithful."

JANUARY 2

SMILE

Do you ever notice what happens when you do something kind for someone else? Ever seen the smile come across the face of a family member or boyfriend or girlfriend when you've given them a gift? Usually, on the other side of kindness or giving a gift, you'll be met with a smile.

A smile oftentimes shows us that something we've said or done has pleased someone else.

It's no different with your Heavenly Father. Want to please God and make Him smile? Live a life of faith based on the Word of God.

Today's Word is Hebrews 11:6

"But without faith it is impossible to PLEASE Him, for he who comes to God must believe that He is, and that He is a rewarder of those who diligently seek Him."

JANUARY 3

PRAYER

Many years ago, I learned something very interesting about prayer: sometimes the answers to my praying did not come in the form I most expected.

For example, when I would pray that a girl liked me in high school, the Lord would oftentimes put me in a position to sow the seed of kindness to someone who didn't seem very likable.

When I would pray for patience, many times He would allow me to experience situations that required me to be patient.

To me, prayer isn't just about always getting something I want or think I might need; maybe prayer is simply talking with and listening to my Heavenly Father - after all, He is God.

Perhaps today you can take a few minutes and just hang out with the closest Friend you'll ever have - talk with Him. He's ready to listen.

Today's Word is Jeremiah 29:12

"Then you will call upon Me and go and pray to Me, and I will listen to you."

JANUARY 4

SECRET GIVER

One of my favorite verses in the Bible talks about how we are to give to others. Let me explain what I'm talking about.

Ever been around people who talk, talk, talk about all they do for others? It's all that's going on in their life, and they seemingly want or maybe even need you to hear them, because telling you all about what they "do" brings them validation.

Now, contrast that person with the guy or girl who never talks about all they do and are otherwise seemingly more interested in others than themselves. Oftentimes, we never, ever know what this person does for other people, but the Word tells us that their Heavenly Father will reward them.

Maybe today we can each be willing to be a "secret giver"; and as we are, perhaps the Lord will give us an opportunity to quietly do something for someone else.

Today's Word is Matthew 6:3-4

"But when you do a charitable deed, do not let your left hand know what your right hand is doing, that your charitable deed may be in secret; and your Father who sees in secret will Himself reward you openly."

JANUARY 5

FRUIT

How do you really get to know people? Let's say you see someone at lunch or maybe in a math class, and you have a desire to get to know him or her.

Certainly, you could ask others about this new interest that's come across your radar screen, and you could always just go up and introduce yourself. But, beyond the surface introductions of life, is there any way to really know someone?

The answer is ABSOLUTELY YES. One of the ways to know others comes directly from the best-selling Book of all times - the Bible teaches us to simply watch and listen. Watch their life and listen to the words they speak.

What do I mean? Maybe you can think of it like this: an apple tree produces apples; an orange tree grows oranges, and a rose seed results in roses. It's all about the fruit of what's been planted.

It's the same in life. How can we really get to know others? Take a look at the fruit of their life.

Today's Word is Matthew 7:20

"Therefore by their fruits you will know them."

JANUARY 6

A CLOUD & A FIRE

Ever felt like the enemy was chasing you - maybe even relentlessly chasing you?

Thousands of years ago, the Children of Israel had left Egypt and were en route to their Promised Land. On their journey, Moses, their Leader, was led by the Lord to keep walking away from the enemy, literally day and night.

Ever wondered how Moses knew where to lead six million people? He knew, because God gave him direction – He literally led him with a cloud by day and fire by night.

What's that got to do with you? Maybe today the enemy is chasing you, and maybe, just maybe, you're not too sure which way to turn or where to go.

If that's you, I've got good news for you to consider: God is still in the "leading" business - invest time in his Word, talk with Him, and then take time to listen. As you do, be ready to experience your very own CLOUD BY DAY and FIRE BY NIGHT.

Today's Word is Exodus 13:21

"And the Lord went before them by day in a pillar of cloud to lead the way, and by night in a pillar of fire to give them light, so as to go by day and night."

JANUARY 7

OBEDIENCE

I've been in fulltime ministry since January 1, 1993. Over these decades of working for the Lord, one of the most important lessons the Holy Spirit has ever taught me is the lesson of OBEDIENCE.

So many times, I've been instructed by Him to do something that simply made no sense to me whatsoever. On those times I ignored my reasoning and obeyed, we won. On those times I chose to ignore His instructions and do things my way, well, let's just say that I wish I had been obedient.

Maybe today you're being led by the Lord to do something for someone or maybe say something to someone, or maybe He's just leading you to take time to be with Him. Whatever you might be experiencing, I encourage you to trust your heart and obey.

Thousands of years ago a Leader named Joshua received what I can only imagine must have been the strangest battle plan any military leader had ever been instructed to initiate: march around a city for a set number of days in complete silence. Then, on the next day, when you hear a trumpet, everyone in your army should shout; and when this happens, the walls will fall down, and the city will be yours.

Can you imagine? Joshua not only could imagine it, but he also chose to be obedient. As he obeyed, the walls fell, and victory was his.

Today, obey God and watch the walls fall down.

Today's Word is Joshua 6:20

"So the people shouted when the priests blew the trumpets. And it happened when the people heard the sound of the trumpet, and the people shouted with a great shout, that the wall fell down flat. Then the people went up into the city, every man straight before him, and they took the city."

JANUARY 8

AVAILABLE

One of the neatest aspects of living a life of faith is, to me, the opportunity we have every day to see an opportunity that the Lord has placed in our lives and then do something for Him about that opportunity.

Opportunities don't always come in seemingly grand ways. For example, you might be led to push a grocery cart back into the store that someone else has left in the parking lot. Maybe you see an elderly person sitting by themself in a mall, and you are led to sit down and chat for a couple of minutes.

Could be that you're eating lunch at your favorite restaurant, and you suddenly feel the need to buy the person next to you his or her lunch - all of these examples are possible in everyday living.

Through the years, I've learned that we don't have to be known by everybody, we don't have to have a recognizable face, and we don't even have to have a lot of money to be used by the Lord in the lives of others. Maybe, we just need to be AVAILABLE.

Today's Word is Matthew 25:37-40

"Then the righteous will answer Him, saying, 'Lord, when did we see You hungry and feed You, or thirsty and give You drink? When did we see You a stranger and take You in, or naked and clothe You? Or when did we see You sick, or in prison, and come to You? ' And the King will answer and say to them, 'Assuredly, I say to you, inasmuch as you did it to one of the least of these My brethren, you did it to Me."

JANUARY 9

HISTORY

Can you imagine what it must have been like for a teenage boy to purposefully come face-to-face with a giant - a literal giant who was threatening to destroy anyone and everyone who got in his way?

This giant had so frightened an entire army that no one was willing to go out and stand their ground, defend their family, and protect their country. No one, that is, until a teenage boy was led by the Lord into the presence of King Saul.

At first, King Saul had no belief that David had any business even talking about going out and fighting that giant named Goliath. Then something interesting happened. As David talked with King Saul, he let the King in on his source of confidence:

As a shepherd, David knew the importance of protecting his sheep. Those sheep were his responsibility, and he knew their worth. So, when a lion and a bear came against those sheep, David chose to trust God as His deliverer and protector - his confidence came in his trusting God.

You see, David had history with God, and he knew in Whom he trusted. You know when I believe David won the battle against Goliath? Not when he slung a rock toward his forehead; no, I believe David won the instant he RAN toward the enemy.

Having history with God will build our faith and cause us to run towards our challenges rather than away.

Today's Word is 1 Samuel 17:47-49

"Then all this assembly shall know that the Lord does not save with sword and spear; for the battle is the Lord's, and He will give you into our hands." So it was, when the Philistine arose and came and drew near to meet David, that David hurried and ran toward the army to meet the Philistine. Then David put his hand in his bag and took out a stone; and he slung it and struck the Philistine in his forehead, so that the stone sank into his forehead, and he fell on his face to the earth."

JANUARY 10

LISTEN

Have you ever gone through a season in life and just not known what to do, where to go, or even whom to trust?

I have, and I believe that just about anybody who has walked with the Lord for any length of time has also. What do you do in times like these?

I'll share with you what I've done, and it's always worked. I've gotten really quiet on the inside and just listened for the still, small voice of God.

When you go through something and all around you is evidence that the enemy is coming against you, it can be tough to get quiet and listen. Even so, that's the time to exercise your faith, to stand on the Word, and to receive direction from the Lord.

Teenagers often ask me how they can know the voice of God for themselves. My response is always the same. If you invest time with someone, you'll begin to recognize that person's voice. It's absolutely no different with knowing God's voice: invest time in His Word and in prayer. As you do, you can be like Elijah when he stood on a mountain and encountered God - no matter how much is going on around you, take time to listen and He'll show up.

Today's Word is 1 Kings 19:11-12

"Then He said, "Go out, and stand on the mountain before the Lord." And behold, the Lord passed by, and a great and strong wind tore into the mountains and broke the rocks in pieces before the Lord, but the Lord was not in the wind; and after the wind an earthquake, but the Lord was not in the earthquake. After the earthquake came a fire, but the Lord was not in the fire. And after the fire came a gentle whisper.

JANUARY 11

A FISH STORY

Sometimes students ask me why they don't seem to be hearing anything from God. When they pray, it feels as if their prayers hit the ceiling; and when they try to read their Bible, it's like trudging through mud.

When asked, unless the Lord gives me specific instructions to do otherwise, my response is always a question:

"What's the last instruction the Lord gave you that you haven't yet completed?"

When God gives us an assignment/instruction, He intends on us getting the job done. If we choose to ignore or blow off the leading of the Holy Spirit, then we get the opportunity to "go around that mountain" one more time, until we choose to obey what He's instructed us to do.

Remember Jonah? He got an all-expense paid, multiple-day stay in the belly of a big fish - all because he refused to obey his assignment.

Let's be mindful that God does not change. So today, it might be a profitable idea to take a minute and ensure that you're obeying what He's told you to do - otherwise, like Jonah, you might be heading for the belly of a fish.

Today's Word is Jonah 1:2

"Arise, go to Nineveh, that great city, and cry out against it; for their wickedness has come up before Me."

And Jonah 3:2

"Arise, go to Nineveh, that great city, and preach to it the message that I tell you."

JANUARY 12

FEAR

At the core of every single attack or assignment that the enemy dreams up, conspires against, and attempts to deploy in your life, there is always one word at the core of his motivation: FEAR.

You've probably heard or maybe seen the word fear broken down, one letter at a time:
F.E.A.R. = False Evidence Appearing Real.

If you are dealing with fear or maybe a more appropriate way of saying it: if you have not yet discovered how to deal with fear, I have the solution for your consideration.

How do you and I get rid of fear? One word: LOVE.

You see, as much as faith activates God's Word, fear activates the enemy. The Bible teaches us that faith works by LOVE.

So, do you want to see fear flee from your life? Live by the LOVE of God.

Today's Word is 1 John 4:18

"There is no fear in love; but perfect love casts out fear, because fear involves torment. But he who fears has not been made perfect in love."

JANUARY 13

THE HEART

One of my favorite verses in the Bible is in the fourth chapter of Proverbs. In this chapter we're instructed with absolute clarity to keep, to guard, our heart, as out of it come issues that we face along this journey we know as life.

Not only are we to just keep our heart; we are to guard it with all diligence. I looked up the word diligence, and here's what I discovered:

To keep something with diligence is to do so with "constant and earnest effort to accomplish what is undertaken".

Did you see that? Constant and earnest effort. With that definition of diligence in place, can you see why God places such a high value on our being diligent to protect or keep our spiritual heart? He knows that whatever gets into our heart in abundance will eventually flow right out of our mouth in words. He also knows that words create worlds.

Not long ago, someone said to me, "the heart of the human problem is the problem of the human heart." As I have thought about that sentence, I have done so being ever so aware of just how important it is for me to guard my heart. As I do, I believe God will lead me by His Word to have a HEART after Him.

Today's Word is Proverbs 4:23

"Keep your heart with all diligence, for out of it spring the issues of life."

JANUARY 14

FORGET IT

As I continue traveling into high schools, I'm again and again meeting teenagers who feel compelled to share with me the many things they've done wrong in their past. I'm all for confessing our sins to the Lord and even to one another. But, once I've asked for His forgiveness, He expects me to move on, having been justified by the price He paid for my sin on the cross.

They ask me how they can move on without feeling guilty and condemned. My response is always the same: Jesus doesn't condemn you, so why would you condemn yourself?

Part of living by faith is learning to receive forgiveness and grace from our Heavenly Father. As we do, we soon learn that the enemy is the one who tries to pull us backwards. God is always moving forward.

Maybe it will help you to think on this truth:

The sins that the devil seemingly won't let you forget; once you've asked for and received forgiveness, God cannot remember.

Today's Word is Romans 8:1

"There is therefore now no condemnation to those who are in Christ Jesus, who do not walk according to the flesh, but according to the Spirit."

JANUARY 15

HE'S LOOKING

Maybe one of the most taught passages of the Bible is the account of the Prodigal Son.

You might remember that this young man left his father and brother, took his inheritance, and went out on his own. After living a life that he thought he wanted, he soon realized that he'd missed God. The Bible teaches us that when this young man came to himself and realized what he'd done, he figured that those who worked for his dad had it better than him, so he decided to go back home and ask his dad if he could return as a servant, not a son.

The part of this story that most moves me is when we find that the father was looking for his son to return. If you read what the Word says, you'll see that it's as if the father was constantly looking for the return of his son.

It's no different with our Heavenly Father and us. No matter how far we might be away from Him or what we've done that might cause us to wrongly believe we could never again be His child, right now at this very moment, God the Father is sitting on His throne, looking intently across the earth to see which of His sons and daughters are on the horizon, coming home.

Today's Word is Luke 15:20

"And he arose and came to his father. But when he was still a great way off, his father saw him and had compassion, and ran and fell on his neck and kissed him."

JANUARY 16

GRASSHOPPERS

How do you see yourself? Do you like you? Do you understand you? These are some important and, hopefully, thought- provoking questions for you to consider.

Think of it this way: if your hand is a mirror, what do you see when you look into it?

If you would only allow yourself to see what God sees when He looks at you, you'd be sitting there right now with a big smile on your face. Why? Because if you're a Believer, God sees you through His Son; and as such, your life is hidden in Him.

How we see ourselves in light of how God sees us is a big deal.

In the Bible, we see where twelve guys were sent to look at the land that had been promised to them by God. Ten of these men came back to the people with a report of fear - there was no way they could take the land, because there were giants there. These ten went so far as to say that they saw themselves as little grasshoppers in comparison to the giants they'd seen.

But among the twelve Spies, there were two who refused to buy the lie, and instead encouraged the people with the truth. They saw themselves as victorious.

The Bible teaches us that as we think in our heart, so are we. In other words, how you think about yourself in light of what the Gospel says about you makes a big difference in how you live your life.

So today, it might be a good idea to take a moment and look in the mirror. As you do, do you see what God sees?

Today's Word is Numbers 13:33

"There we saw the giants (the descendants of Anak came from the giants); and we were like grasshoppers in our own sight, and so we were in their sight."

JANUARY 17

HARVESTS

Have you ever wondered what makes successful people, successful? Have you ever taken the time to study the life of a person whom you deem successful? What is one of the qualifiers that separate successful people from all others?

I've taken quite a bit of time over the years to come up with an answer that, I believe, is a universal commonality among the truly successful. THEY ARE GIVERS.

The Word of God makes a clear case for those who give: they'll also receive.

The Bible teaches us that seeds produce after themselves, so whatever we sow (give), that's what we can expect to harvest (receive).

Want to have friends? Then sow the seed of kindness. Want to be healthy? Then sow the seed of taking care of your body. Want to have financial increase in your life? Then sow financial seeds where you are led to do so.

You see, if you plant a tomato, you're not going to get a potato. If you plant a rose, you're not going to get a daisy.

The entirety of God's Word is founded on the principle of sowing and reaping: God had a Son, but He wanted a family. So, He gave His Son in order that you and I could become His children.

Today, if you have a harvest on your mind, maybe it's time to start planting the seed.

Today's Word is Genesis 1:11

"Then God said, 'Let the earth bring forth grass, the herb that yields seed, and the fruit tree that yields fruit according to its kind, whose seed is in itself, on the earth'; and it was so."

JANUARY 18

PERSISTENCE

Want to get more results in your life? If so, I'd like to share with you what someone shared with me:

Be persistent.

Let's say, for example, that you are really believing God for something to happen in your life.

Once you have prayed about this certain area or circumstance, and after you have a Scripture that you're confessing and believing as it relates to that area or circumstance, have a dogged persistence to receive what you're believing for and make the quality decision to refuse to quit.

What do I mean? Persistence is defined as, "the act or fact of persisting". In other words, you just don't quit until you see results.

I know from very personal experience that being persistent in faith gets the attention of God and produces results.

Maybe today if you're ready to give up, don't. Instead, consider ramping up your persistence, increase your time with the Lord, and then say what His Word says about your situation.

Today's Word is Luke 11:8

"I say to you, though he will not rise and give to him because he is his friend, yet because of his persistence he will rise and give him as many as he needs."

JANUARY 19

WWJD

Years ago, I began noticing that students were wearing bracelets that had four letters imprinted on the fabric of the bracelet. The four letters were WWJD and represented a thought-provoking question:

What Would Jesus Do?

It seemed that in every school I'd go into to speak, I'd encounter those bracelets and that question.

In more recent years, I've seen fewer and fewer of the WWJD bracelets; but today, it might be helpful for each of us to ask God to imprint those four letters and that question deeply into our hearts.

You see, if you read Matthew, Mark, Luke, and John, you'll see exactly what Jesus would do, because you'll see what Jesus did.

So many times, we see that before Jesus did anything, He was first moved with compassion. His love for people motivated Him to go the extra mile to forgive, to heal, to listen; and in the end, it was His compassion that caused Him to save.

What Would Jesus Do? He'd show compassion. We should, too.

Today's Word is Matthew 14:14

"And when Jesus went out He saw a great multitude; and He was moved with compassion for them, and healed their sick."

JANUARY 20

EVERLASTING LIFE

If I were to ask what the most familiar Verse in the Bible is, I'd imagine you would probably say, "John 3:16." And you'd be correct. Ask anyone, anywhere who has any knowledge of the Word of God this same question, and more times than not, the response would be the same: "John 3:16."

"For God so loved the world that He gave His only begotten Son, that whoever believes in Him should not perish but have everlasting life."

If I were to then ask you a follow-up question pertaining to John 3:16, the response might not be quite so universal. Let me explain.

At the end of this verse, we're promised something called everlasting or eternal life. Here's my question: what is everlasting (eternal) life?

Most people say that it's Heaven. And while Heaven certainly is reflective of eternity, eternal life, everlasting life, is something else.

We find the answer on over in the book of John - eternal life (everlasting life) is defined as you and I knowing God and His Son Jesus. To me then, eternal, everlasting life is all about our having a RELATIONSHIP with Him, right here, right now.

Do you know Him?

Today's Word is John 17:3

"And this is eternal life, that they may know You, the only true God, and Jesus Christ whom You have sent."

JANUARY 21

TREASURE

What's valuable to you? Is it your stuff? Your relationships? Your dreams? Your accomplishments? Your popularity?

I'd imagine that we all have something in our life that we genuinely treasure, something that's very valuable to us. But here's a question to consider:

Do we have it, or does it have us?

I meet a lot of teenagers who share with me that they have big dreams, legitimate dreams. But as I listen to them tell me about their hopes and dreams and why they want to accomplish them, I realize that for some of these students, their dreams have them.

If you find yourself discovering that maybe your dream, your treasure, has you instead of you having it, I believe that it might be a great idea to check your heart. Examine your motivation for not only what you want to do, but also why you want to do it.

You see, where your heart truly is, there you'll find your treasure.

Today's Word is Luke 12:34

"For where your treasure is, there your heart will be also."

JANUARY 22

PROMOTION

Have you ever taken the time to consider the system by which we advance in God's Kingdom?

To the natural mind, God's system makes no sense.

Consider this:

If I want to really live, I must die (to my selfish desires).
If I want to go higher, I first must go lower.
If I want to receive, I first must give.
If I want to be a great leader, I first must be a humble servant.
If I want to increase, I must first decrease.

You see, God takes the seemingly foolish things of this world and blows the minds of those who try to get ahead without Him.

Today, maybe it's worth considering that His system really does work and it's a system He put in motion with us in mind.

Remember, God loves you so much - He gave you a system that'll protect you and when followed, will promote you in His Kingdom.

Today's Word 1 Corinthians 1:27

"But God has chosen the foolish things of the world to put to shame the wise, and God has chosen the weak things of the world to put to shame the things which are mighty;"

JANUARY 23

ASSIGNMENT

One of the most asked questions I get from teenagers who come from all walks of life is, "Do you think God has a plan for my life?"

I always smile and with absolute confidence I respond, "Yes, I know He does."

My confident response usually triggers another set of questions, not the least of which is, "But how do you know He does?"

Here's how I know - the Bible tells me so.

I believe that when God put His breath into our lungs and gave us life, He also created us with purpose - an assignment, a calling - something that we were uniquely created to fulfill in the Kingdom of God.

If today you're wondering about this purpose, I encourage you to take some time, get with God, and be willing to be led into the journey of a lifetime.

After all, along with all of eternity, we're all waiting on YOU to fulfill YOUR assignment.

Today's Word is Romans 11:29

"For the gifts and the calling of God are irrevocable."

JANUARY 24

TRUST

As you walk with Him for any length of time, you'll be given the opportunity to move from one level of relationship with the Lord to another.

One of these transitional moves with God is when we change from simply believing God to trusting Him. There is a difference. The enemy believes in God, he just chose to not trust Him. That's what got him in trouble. When we're self-reliant, we're putting our trust in us, not Him. That NEVER works - it's called pride, and it leads to destruction.

After decades of working fulltime for God, I've learned what I believe is a difference between believing and trusting God - maybe this will help you:

We believe with our mind; we trust with our heart.

No matter what's going on in your life, God's Spirit will always be in your heart. Learn to trust Him more and more. After all, He knows the answers before we know the questions.

It truly is all about whom we trust.

Today's Word is Proverbs 3:5-6

"Trust in the Lord with all your heart, and lean not on your own understanding; in all your ways acknowledge Him, and He shall direct your paths."

JANUARY 25

A THIEF

Through the years, I've been asked to share our message of hope with students and faculties who have experienced what most of us never have or, hopefully, never will: school shootings.

When I've spoken at those schools that have received national and international media coverage because of a student opening fire on classmates, one question I have always been asked:

"Why do bad things happen to good people?"

That's a legitimate question deserving of a legitimate answer. Here's what I've learned:

We live in a fallen world. In it, we have good and evil. Good God, bad devil.

God loves, the devil hates. God is the giver of life; the enemy is the stealer of life.

God loves us with such a deep love that He gives each of us the freedom to choose whom we will serve and how we will live out our days. Some choose to follow God and live a life of faith, while others choose to serve the enemy and bring pain into their environment.

Next time you see evil on the loose, remember, the devil is a thief whose mission is to steal, kill and destroy.

Today's Word is John 10:10

"The thief does not come except to steal, and to kill, and to destroy. I have come that they may have life, and that they may have it more abundantly."

JANUARY 26

FRUIT TREES

Because I invest my life hanging out with teenagers, I have opportunity to talk with lots of them in varying circumstances and situations.

Students who have a working knowledge of the Bible will sometimes want to chat about what the Bible refers to as the "fruit of the Spirit". This is an interesting topic to me, because if you read what the Word says, you'll see that to live a life governed by the fruit of the Spirit, you do so by first and foremost living a life of LOVE.

All the remaining characteristics of the fruit of the Spirit flow out of this life of love.

So, when we love God and then love others, we have taken the first steps, huge steps, to living a life full of the fruit of the Spirit.

Here's something for you to think about: if your life was a fruit tree that had been planted in a garden, today, what kind of fruit would people see that your life is producing?

Want a life full of fruit? Begin by living the love life.

Today's Word is Galatians 5:22

"But the fruit of the Spirit is love, joy, peace, longsuffering, kindness, goodness, faithfulness, gentleness, self-control. Against such there is no law."

JANUARY 27

WALKING WITH GOD

When you're dating someone, isn't it fun to just hang out with that person? The more time you invest with someone you care about, generally speaking, the more you get to know that person. You know what he or she likes, what they dislike; and if you really spend quality time together, you can easily become best friends.

It's no different with your relationship with God.

The Bible tells us in the first chapter of the Word that God created us in His image. We even have His characteristics. Understanding this helps us to better receive the truth that God is our friend.

Thousands of years ago there was a guy named Noah, and he knew the voice of God, because he had a relationship with Him. One day, God spoke to Noah to build an ark, because He was sending rain. Can you imagine what Noah must have thought: "What's an ark? For that matter, what's rain?"

Despite his questions and the ridicule he received from his "friends", Noah trusted God and built an ark. When he did, his obedience saved the life of his family and a bunch of animals.

Now, come forward thousands of years to today. God hasn't changed at all - He still speaks.

Want to be friends with God? He's right there with you, right now.

Take a step of faith ... go for a walk with your Heavenly Father and listen for His voice of instruction.

Today's Word is Genesis 6:9

"This is the genealogy of Noah. Noah was a just man, perfect in his generations. Noah walked with God."

JANUARY 28

ATMOSPHERE CONTROLLER

When I first started out in ministry, I did so by working for three and a half years with a Grammy-winning Christian Artist who has literally traveled the world making music for the Lord. I was his Road Manager; and over the course of my time with this ministry, I was in over six hundred and fifty worship services.

I learned a lot about faith and the power of music during this time in my life. It was also during this time that I again and again saw how music is a spiritual force - an atmosphere controller.

Music is built just like God; it has three parts: while in God, there's God the Father, God the Son, and God the Holy Spirit; in music, we have melody, rhythm, and harmony. Each part makes up the whole.

Music, I believe, was created by God to penetrate our heart. It is a force to be reckoned with.

Next time you have heaviness weighing you down in your heart and you just can't seem to find God in the circumstances of life, I've got a suggestion for you to consider: Go to your music library or go online and search for truly anointed music that takes you into the presence of the Lord. Turn that music up and watch His presence invade your life.

Music really is God's atmosphere controller.

Today's Word is 1 Samuel 16:23

"And so it was, whenever the spirit from God was upon Saul, that David would take a harp and play it with his hand. Then Saul would become refreshed and well, and the distressing spirit would depart from him."

JANUARY 29

REMEMBER ME

Do you ever feel like you've blown it so badly that there's just no way God could ever use you? I have, and that's a horrific feeling.

On the road, I meet a lot of teenagers who share with me some of their life experiences that they've not shared with anyone else at any other time. They talk with me because I'm safe to talk with. They know that I'm leaving their school that day and heading off to another school to meet more students.

When they share with me that they feel like they're not good enough for God, my heart goes out to them because I realize they haven't yet received something called righteousness consciousness. Our righteousness (right standing with God) has absolutely nothing to do with our actions - it instead has everything to do with what Jesus has already done for us.

Two thousand years ago there were two criminals being crucified next to Jesus. No doubt these two men were being punished for choices they had made in their lives. One of these men lashed out at Jesus while the other asked for mercy.

Hearing the call for mercy, Jesus did not turn His back on the criminal; instead, He gave the man what I like to call words of hope.

Today, maybe you've really messed up. If so, don't run from Him; run to Him, and as you do, ask Him to remember you. He will.

Today's Word is Luke 23:41-43

"And we indeed justly, for we receive the due reward of our deeds; but this Man has done nothing wrong. Then he said to Jesus, "Lord, remember me when You come into Your kingdom. And Jesus said to him, "Assuredly, I say to you, today you will be with Me in Paradise."

JANUARY 30

DRY BONES

Do you have a favorite book of the Bible? A Book that may mirror certain aspects of your life? If not, I'd encourage you to invest some time reading the Bible with a purpose in mind: finding yourself in the Word.

For me, it's unquestionably the book of Ezekiel. As I read this Book, the words jump off the page and into my heart. Ezekiel speaks to me.

For example, in the 37th chapter of Ezekiel, we see where the Lord had placed the Prophet Ezekiel in a valley of dry bones. As we read the first ten verses of chapter 37, we also see where the Lord gives clear instructions to His Messenger - simply put, the Lord told Ezekiel to speak to the dry bones.

Now to you and me, that instruction probably sounds as ludicrous as I imagine it sounded to Ezekiel. But, irrespective of how it sounded, Ezekiel knew the power of obedience.

By verse 10 of chapter 37, we see the results of Ezekiel's obedience: he was no longer standing in a valley of dry bones; instead, standing before him was an exceedingly great army.

What's the point? Take some time to find yourself in Scripture; as you do, be listening for instructions from Heaven that may very well sound bizarre now but produce amazing results.

God's Word is our instructional manual - it's time to get to work.

Today's Word is Ezekiel 37:1 & Ezekiel 37:10

"The hand of the Lord came upon me and brought me out in the Spirit of the Lord, and set me down in the midst of the valley; and it was full of bones."

"So I prophesied as He commanded me, and breath came into them, and they lived, and stood upon their feet, an exceedingly great army."

JANUARY 31

ANGELS AMONG US

I remember driving to church by myself on a Sunday morning when I was 16 years old. I drove past a man who was walking toward an interstate. As I passed him, I heard the Word of the Lord on the inside of me say, "Go back and give him a ride."

I turned around, pulled up beside him and instead of offering him a ride, I offered him some cash. I drove off feeling good; and as I did, I heard the Lord say, "That was nice Dean, but he didn't need cash, he needs a ride. Go back and offer him a ride."

Reluctantly, I turned around and this time, before I got back to him, I stopped at a market and bought him some water and some snacks. I got back in my car, drove back to the man who was still walking toward the interstate, pulled up beside him (I think at this point I was freaking him out), and very religiously offered him the food and water.

I again drove off and again, the Lord said to me, "That was kind of you Dean, but he didn't need food, he needs a ride."

So, I again turned around, pulled up beside him, and offered him a ride. He was so relieved. He sat down in my car; and as we drove toward the interstate, he told me about his life.

As we drove, he noticed I had a red Gideon Bible in my car. He asked about my little Bible; and as he did, I heard the Lord say, "Offer the Bible to him." And so, I did.

This man got so excited. He told me that he'd believed God for a small Bible to have with him on his journey. The instant I gave him my Bible, it was time to let him out of my car.

As I drove off, I never saw him again.

Today's Word is Hebrews 13:2

"Do not forget to entertain strangers, for by so doing some have unwittingly entertained angels."

FEBRUARY 1

DEAL WITH IT

You know what one of the major issues I encounter on the road is? Teenagers who are hurting but have yet to deal with the emotional pain in their lives.

Over the years, I've learned from very personal experiences that our emotions are real; and left to themselves, can cause enormous challenges in day-to-day living.

When God created us, He did so knowing that we would need emotions. For that matter, He has emotions. That might surprise you; but as you read the Word, you will see where at times He was angry, He was sorrowful, He had joy. God, through Jesus, knows how we feel.

And you know what? I believe He wants us to feel. It's what we do (or not do) with our feelings that can get us into trouble. For example, in Ephesians 4:26 we're instructed to, "Be angry, and do not sin": do not let the sun go down on your wrath..."

As teenagers, you have emotions. Want something to consider from someone who's been there and spoken with millions of people your age: deal with them.

If you do not deal with your emotions, they will eventually deal with you.

Today's Word is Genesis 1:27

"So God created man in His own image; in the image of God He created him; male and female He created them."

FEBRUARY 2

FACING THE UNEXPECTED

For years now, our ministry has owned an airplane. Our plane is literally a time machine that allows us to go further, to reach more students, and to then return home faster.

Because I'm in the plane more than a lot of people are in their cars, through the years, I've encountered some moments in the air that have caused me to trust God like never before.

Several years ago, there were ten days in October that changed my life. Over the course of these ten days, I lost two airplane engines on two different airplanes while in flight.

On both flights, I was sitting in the back, minding my own business, when suddenly, we were in serious, emergency situations.

At those moments, I did not have time to try and remember what the Word says about my safety. I instead had to declare in faith exactly what the Word declares about the circumstance I was in.

And you know what? God responds to His Word coming out of our mouth in faith!!

On both flights, we landed safely. Sure, those were two very uncomfortable flights ... but God.

If you find yourself in unexpected circumstances, that's not the time to plant the seed of His Word. Instead, that's the time to call in a harvest from His Word.

Not sure what to pray? Ask Him. He'll answer.

Today's Word is Jeremiah 33:3

"Call to Me, and I will answer you, and show you great and mighty things, which you do not know."

FEBRUARY 3

GET SPECIFIC

It might surprise you to know how many teenagers ask me to pray with them about having a relationship with a boyfriend or girlfriend. I appreciate the fact that teenagers are asking for agreement in prayer - especially about a relationship.

I enjoy having the opportunity to pray with teens - teenagers make me smile. But before I pray, I ask them a question: What are you believing God for in this person?

After hearing this question, they often have this bewildered look come across their face.

I am then often led to introduce them to my story about my wife, Lori. You see, I too wanted a relationship, and thankfully, the Lord used a friend of mine years ago to ask me what today I ask teens.

I wanted to get married but had not yet gotten specific about the person I wanted to spend the rest of my life with - I had not made a list.

The more I prayed about my wife, the more I was led to make a list and to then ask Him to bring this person into my life. I did, and He did.

I share with teenagers all over the world a life lesson I learned through believing God for my best friend who is now my wife:

Nothing in life will ever become dynamic, until it first becomes specific.

Get specific and ask God. He's listening ... right now.

Today's Word is 2 Chronicles 1:7

"On that night God appeared to Solomon, and said to him, Ask! What shall I give you?"

FEBRUARY 4

BE STILL

Do you ever get so busy that you find you're too busy to have time with the Lord?

I remember one time in particular where our ministry had so much going on. I had overcommitted and there seemingly were not enough hours in the day to get everything done that I thought had to be accomplished. The result? I was worn out, frustrated, and according to my family, not a lot of fun to be around.

After several weeks of this, I heard the Word of the Lord down deep in my heart. He said, "Let's go take a ride together."

And so, I drove up to a lake, got in a boat, and was led to go by myself out to the middle of this massive body of water. Once I got out on the water, I was led to turn off the motor.

Sitting there in the warmth of the sunshine with absolutely no one around and with no technology distracting me from the mission of the moment, I heard the Lord say this to my heart:

"I had to get you in a quiet place so you would hear My voice."

Oh, I was so very grateful. During my time with the Lord on the water, I realized where I'd missed it, and He gave me a special time of being refreshed. Here's what I learned:

If the enemy can't slow you down, he'll try to speed you up.

Today, maybe you can relate to being too busy. If so, you might want to get real still; and as you are, prepare for a meeting with the Creator of the Universe.

Today's Word is Psalms 46:10

"Be still, and know that I am God; I will be exalted among the nations, I will be exalted in the earth!"

FEBRUARY 5

MARVEL

The word marvel means to be filled with wonder or astonishment.

If you read in the New Testament, you'll see that there are two instances where Jesus marveled. He marveled at a person's faith, and he likewise marveled at people's unbelief.

Want to consider something that you might find of interest? Because we know from what the Word tells us in Hebrews 13:8, "Jesus Christ is the same yesterday, today, and forever," we can be confident that He never changes. Understanding this truth brings revelation that every single day, you and are causing Jesus to marvel, either through our faith, or lack of it.

So, here's my question for you to consider: right here, right now, are you living a life of faith or one of unbelief?

Either way, He's marveling at you.

Today's Word is Matthew 8:10 and Mark 6:6

"When Jesus heard it, He marveled, and said to those who followed, "Assuredly, I say to you, I have not found such great faith, not even in Israel!"

"And He marveled because of their unbelief..."

FEBRUARY 6

BELIEVING IS SEEING

When you give your heart to the Lord, your life changes. Suddenly things that once brought you joy and/or fulfillment don't seem to have the same effect on you. Maybe you change the people you hang out with, or maybe you don't go to all the same places you used to go. Simply put, new desires come with your New Life.

As my faith continues to grow (our faith should never stop being developed), one of the most interesting personal transitions that I've recognized has to do with living a life of faith with the Word of God as my foundation.

In the Bible we're taught to call those things that be not as though they already are - in other words, by faith, we can see into our future and by speaking the Word, we can bring our future into our present. We can do this only if what we're believing God for is His will and in His timing.

How's that possible? By changing how we used to live. The world has a principle by which people by the millions live everyday: seeing is believing. That's not God's plan for His kids; His way says:

Believing is seeing!

Today's Word is Matthew 21:22

"And whatever things you ask in prayer, believing, you will receive."

FEBRUARY 7

MEASURED FAITH

Several years ago, our ministry's airplane was at a private airport to have maintenance done.

At this airport, there were several planes in the hangar; and during that day, because one of those airplanes was going to be flown, several of the hangered planes, including ours, needed to be re-positioned on the tarmac.

As the flight department re-positioned the planes, a dear friend of mine and I stood back and watched as a large jet was positioned next to our plane.

Without even considering what I was saying, I heard myself ask my friend this question: "How do you go from our plane to that jet?" Without any hesitation whatsoever, my friend immediately asked me, "How do you go from my truck to your airplane?"

I do not think I will ever forget what I next heard deep down in my Spirit: "In My Kingdom, you go from faith to faith and from glory to glory."

I went to my Bible and saw where God has given every single person a measure of faith. So how do some people seem to have such great faith and others have anemic faith? I learned that faith is like a muscle - to become stronger, it must be exercised.

By the way, my friend at that airport exercised his faith and has since moved from his truck into a jet.

Today is a great day to start exercising your faith.

Today's Word is Romans 12:3

"For I say, through the grace given to me, to everyone who is among you, not to think of himself more highly than he ought to think, but to think soberly, as God has dealt to each one a measure of faith."

FEBRUARY 8

DO YOU SEE WHAT HE SEES

When you fly a lot, you tend to see things from a different perspective. At higher altitudes, what looks large on the ground doesn't always have the same appearance up in the air.

Jesus routinely experienced life from a different perspective while He was here. Remember, when Jesus walked the earth, He did so as the Son of Man, not the Son of God. Because of His relationship with His Father, though, He was able to see things from another perspective.

You might remember that there was a day when He'd been teaching an audience of about five thousand men (not to mention the ladies and the children who were in the crowd). As He finished teaching, His staff asked Him to send the crowd away so they could find food for themselves.

Instead of sending them away, Jesus had the people sit down, and He blessed five pieces of bread and two small fish which one of His disciples had obtained from a little boy who was there.

Here's where this story gets interesting to me. As the disciples did a quick calculation of the food in the hands of Jesus, one of the disciples saw the need, another disciple saw the lack, but Jesus, operating from a higher perspective, saw the miracle.

Today, that same perspective is available to you and me. To get there, here's the question: Do you see what He sees?

Today's Word is John 6:9-11

"There is a lad here who has five barley loaves and two small fish, but what are they among so many?"

Then Jesus said, "Make the people sit down." Now there was much grass in the place. So the men sat down, in number about five thousand. And Jesus took the loaves, and when He had given thanks He distributed them to the disciples, and the disciples to those sitting down; and likewise of the fish, as much as they wanted."

FEBRUARY 9

REACH OUT & TOUCH

I encounter many teenagers on the road who wrongly believe that constant suffering is God's plan for their lives. Maybe they're in abusive relationships, or perhaps their norm is constantly feeling oppressed and/or depressed. Once they hear and see the Truth, however, the mindset of many of these students begins to change.

To me one of the most dramatic instances of this type of change occurred in the life of a lady in the Bible who had suffered for twelve years with a bleeding issue in her body. She went to Jesus, saw Him as her Healer, and sure enough, her faith touched His healing power. In an instant, she was totally and completely healed.

If you take the time to read on for several more verses, you'll see one more miracle that happened for this lady.

In the beginning of this story, this person is referred to as "a certain woman". After having a faith encounter with Jesus, this same lady was called, "Daughter."

Want to be transformed from a certain somebody to that of a son or daughter? Reach out and touch Jesus with your faith.

Today's Word is Mark 5:25 and Mark 5:34

"Now a certain woman had a flow of blood for twelve years ..."

"And He said to her, "Daughter, your faith has made you well. Go in peace, and be healed of your affliction."

FEBRUARY 10

STICKS & STONES

Growing up, did you ever hear or maybe even say the childhood rhyme, "Sticks and stones may break my bones, but words will never hurt me?"

I did and so many others did as well.

But you know what? That rhyme is a lie. To me, words are the most powerful force on the earth.

If you go over to the very first chapter in the Bible, you'll see that God's creative force was and is His Word. Read it for yourself. Every single time God wanted to change His world, He first spoke. And each time He spoke, what He said, He then saw.

If you continue reading down to Genesis 1:27 & 28, you'll also see that you and I were created in His image.

So, since God created His world by His Word and then created you and me in His image, I can assure you that today, your words are likewise creating your world.

Next time you're tempted to say something hurtful or mean to someone else, it might be a good idea to remember that your words are creative forces that can create real feelings in the lives of others.

It's true, sticks and stones can cause outward bruises, but words go deep into our heart and, once there, will either wound or heal.

Today's Word is Proverbs 18:21

"Death and life are in the power of the tongue, and those who love it will eat its fruit."

FEBRUARY 11

FREEDOM

One of the saddest moments for me on the road is when I come face-to-face with a student who is noticeably bound up with regret, remorse, and resentment.

How could all those emotions be tied to one person, especially a teenager? Well, left undealt with, our emotions have a way of eventually dealing with us. Maybe not today or tomorrow; but please believe me, emotions are real, and they must be dealt with.

How do I know this? Well, not only have I seen so many bound up people at events on the road, but I was also one, too.

You see, I've ministered to thousands of people who have been bound by addiction, sin, and shame. And each time God places me in these situations, I realize that we all need freedom. True freedom.

Maybe you're wondering how you can be free. Freedom begins with a choice. God loves us so much that He gives us the freedom to choose (I believe His love for us is why He instructs us in His Word to, choose you this day ...).

If you choose life, that'll take you down one direction. If you instead choose death and the things of death, you'll be heading down another direction all together.

Jesus is the Giver of life, while the enemy, the devil, is the taker of life.

Want to begin to experience the kind of freedom that only comes from your loving Heavenly Father? Choose Jesus - when you do, freedom is en route to you.

Today's Word is John 8:36

"Therefore if the Son makes you free, you shall be free indeed."

FEBRUARY 12

HE GETS IT

I meet a lot of teenagers who come to me after one of our events and with total sincerity say to me that no one understands them; and as such, they feel all alone.

When this happens, I usually wait for a few seconds and then smile and ask if I can share a verse with them.

I then talk with them about the closest friend they or I or you will ever have.

When Jesus was in the earth, He was so as a baby, a little boy, a teenager and then as a man. Throughout His life, He had every opportunity to miss the mark and fall short of God's best for His life.

The Bible tells us that even though He was tempted, He did not give into any temptation. How is that possible? There's only one answer: His relationship with His Father was so special that even though He was tempted, just like you and I are, His desire to please God kept Him from sinning.

Like so many other teens, you may relate to feeling as if no one understands you or that you're all alone. If so, look no further than Jesus - He gets it.

Today's Word is Hebrews 4:15

"For we do not have a High Priest who cannot sympathize with our weaknesses, but was in all points tempted as we are, yet without sin."

FEBRUARY 13

THOUGHTS

When God created us, He gave us a mind.

The mind is a force to be reckoned with. Medical science has long ago proven that your mind is like a muscle - the more you use it, the stronger it becomes.

What you put into your mind is also of tremendous importance. Here's something to consider: garbage in, garbage out. Faith in, faith out - it really is your choice.

Whatever thoughts enter your mind do so as seeds. These seeds drop down from your mind and into your heart. While in the soil of your heart, these seeds are growing; and one day, with no advance warning, these seeds grow into words that come out of our mouth.

Why is that important? You'll remember that when God created the earth, He did so with words. He then created you and me in His image - our words create our world.

Today you might want to consider your thoughts ... your very world is a result of what you think.

Today's Word is Proverbs 23:7

"For as he thinks in his heart, so is he..."

FEBRUARY 14

LOVE IS A PERSON

Today is a day that the world sets aside to celebrate love. All over the Internet today you'll see postings and emailed messages in all different languages, but the messages posted will all have to do with an emotion called love.

But you know what? Love is more than just an emotion; it's so much more. Maybe more than any other description of love, the one that most ministers to me is that love prefers others.

When you as a student look to the life of Jesus, I wonder what and whom you see. The Word teaches us that there's no greater love than to lay down your life for someone else. That's exactly what Jesus did for you on an old rugged cross.

While today is a day that society sets aside to celebrate love, God doesn't just relegate His love to a day. No, much, much more, He gave us the gift of His Son; and when He did, it was with no strings attached.

The decision relating to how you respond to His love for you is in your court. Think about it and remember, love is much more than an emotion, love is a Person.

Today's Word is 1 Corinthians 13:4-7

"Love suffers long and is kind; love does not envy; love does not parade itself, is not puffed up; does not behave rudely, does not seek its own, is not provoked, thinks no evil; does not rejoice in iniquity, but rejoices in the truth; bears all things, believes all things, hopes all things, endures all things."

FEBRUARY 15

WHO'S YOUR DADDY

Ever think about where you came from? A lot of students wonder about this.

Almost every day that I get to speak and minister in high schools, and at some point during my time, I talk with them about this subject and do so by referring them to Job 33:4.

If you're a teenager and find yourself today considering where you came from, I'd like to offer you a visual to consider:

Let's say your name is Joe. When God created you, He did NOT gasp, put His hand over His mouth, and franticly declare, "Jesus, get over here...You won't believe what I just did. Oh, what a mistake!" No indeed.

Much to the contrary. When you were created, I firmly believe that God smiled and as only a loving Father full of joy can and may have said something like this: "Jesus, come look at what I've done - Joe is now in the earth. I'm so excited."

Do you see the difference? Here's the bottom line as I see it: God, the Creator of the universe, has never ever made a mistake ... as such, you're created by the Creator of purpose, you're here on purpose, and you're here to fulfill His purpose.

Next time you wonder about where you came from, I'd encourage you to stop, look in the mirror, and smile ... because your Father, the giver of your life, is smiling at you.

Today's Word is Job 33:4

"The Spirit of God has made me, and the breath of the Almighty gives me life."

FEBRUARY 16

FEARFULLY & WONDERFULLY MADE

Have you ever noticed the teenager who is oftentimes by himself, a loner, someone who just doesn't seem to fit in? Every single day that I'm on the road, I see these teens, and my heart really goes out to them.

I try to make a little more effort to meet the loners that I encounter in schools; and when I do, more times than not, these are the very young people who most want to be heard.

And so, when I get to meet a young person who spends a lot of time by himself, I get to do a lot of listening. Maybe you can relate to the loners, or perhaps the person I'm describing as a loner is in fact, you.

If so, I want you to consider the truth that's in the Word: just because you're perhaps different from everyone else, that's not a negative. Truth is, we each have been created with qualities and characteristics that come straight from the very image of God.

Understanding this truth, I ask teenagers to make a choice. Instead of making fun of, isolating, or ridiculing people who don't seem to fit in, choose instead to celebrate what makes each of us unique. For you see, you, me, and yes, the loners, are all fearfully and wonderfully made.

Today's Word is Psalms 139:14

"I will praise You, for I am fearfully and wonderfully made; marvelous are Your works, and that my soul knows very well."

FEBRUARY 17

NEVER ALONE

Have you ever been bullied? Ever been made fun of? Someone ever walked by you and knocked your books out of your hands? Have you ever had someone post something mean or embarrassing about you online?

If so, then no doubt you probably also know that it's nothing short of God's grace that causes you to be able to keep it together, at least until you're in a safe place and free to let the emotional pain be emptied out of your heart and mind.

If you've experienced some of what I described above, then I hope you will receive some truth that I'm about to share with you: hurting people hurt people.

That doesn't make what's happened to you right or even fair, but, maybe just maybe, understanding why some people hurt others may help you navigate through some bottled up and/or buried pain of your own.

One thing is for sure, no matter what you go through or experience, no matter how alone you may feel at this very moment, there's One who has promised to never, ever leave your side.

It might be helpful if right here, right now, you take a brief minute and get quiet before the Lord. As you do, give Him the pain in your heart and watch as this Friend makes His comforting presence known to you.

Remember, He's closer than a brother and He's promised to never, ever leave you.

Today's Word is Proverbs 18:24

"A man who has friends must himself be friendly, but there is a friend who sticks closer than a brother."

FEBRUARY 18

DADS & FATHERS

As a teenager, do you ever feel like there's just something missing in your life; something significant that you instinctively know should be there but isn't?

Many, many students have come to me at our events and as they've begun to share some of their stories with me, this something missing becomes the topic of our brief encounters.

After decades of talking with and listening to teens, I've discovered that one of the missing ingredients in the lives of so many young people isn't an ingredient at all; instead, it's a person.

This person is their father.

In what God has called me to do, I get to meet hundreds of thousands of teenagers on the road, and many of them, way too many of them, are going through life without a father. Sure, they might have a dad but man, is there a difference.

While a dad may give you what you want, a father gives you what you need.

I believe this is why God is our Heavenly Father - He's promised to meet all our needs.

What if you don't have an earthly father in your life? Begin to exercise your faith for God to bring a spiritual father to you - someone who will pour love, time, and truth into the very core of your heart.

Want to see this void in your heart begin to disappear? Believe God to turn your heart to your father and your father's heart to you.

Today's Word is Malachi 4:6

"And he will turn the hearts of the fathers to the children, and the hearts of the children to their fathers, lest I come and strike the earth with a curse."

FEBRUARY 19

SIN

Ever wonder where sin comes from? You're going along in life and then suddenly, seemingly out of nowhere, you find yourself in sin. How'd that happen?

It happened through a process that is clearly outlined in the Word of God - this process has everything to do with desire.

When you and I desire something, we think about it. What we think about, we see in our mind's eye. Our vision comes alive when we talk about it, and what we talk about will one day play out in our lives (remember that our words create our world).

So, based on the above process, sin is birthed by a thought. This thought develops into a desire. And once it's a desire, it takes on the form of a vision that ultimately can produce words.

How do you stop sin from taking up residence in your life? Yield your mind to the Word of God and watch the Word transform your thought life.

My spiritual father taught me that I'd never beat thoughts with thoughts. I beat thoughts with words, and Words in red always win!

Want to beat sin? Get immersed in the Word.

Today's Word is James 1:15

"Then, when desire has conceived, it gives birth to sin; and sin, when it is full- grown, brings forth death."

FEBRUARY 20

JUST DO IT

For many years now, NIKE has had a seemingly very successful marketing campaign built around a three-word phrase ... Just Do It.

Someone sitting down and reading the Bible could very easily have discovered that campaign. Yes, the Bible. It's full of creative genius.

As a Christian teenager, you're not called to just read your Bible; much, much more, you're called to do what your Bible says.

It's one thing to sit around and read a few scriptures and move through life knowing what you think the Word says. It's something altogether different to actually take what the Word says from the written page and do it.

I meet so many teens that are not interested in religion. Me either. I want the real deal.

Want to see the Bible come alive in your life? Want this to be real to you? Here's a suggestion ... Don't just read it, do it.

Today's Word is James 1:22

"But be doers of the word, and not hearers only, deceiving yourselves."

FEBRUARY 21

FAITH IN ACTION

I remember speaking at a convention in Valley Forge, Pennsylvania, and when I had finished ministering that day, several people hung around to chat before the event ended.

As I was getting ready to head back to the plane and fly home, a man stopped me and asked to talk. He had tears in his eyes, and it was obvious to me that he not only wanted to talk, he needed to talk.

A long time ago the Lord taught me an important lesson: He gave us two eyes, two ears, but only one mouth - maybe He did so in an effort to remind us that we should talk less and listen more.

Anyway, I listened. As I did, this man shared with me that he and his 16-year-old son were best friends and that they really enjoyed hunting together. That past summer they'd gone on a hunt and sometime during that day, something had gone horribly wrong. This dad told me that while they were hunting, he had accidentally shot and killed his son.

Oh, the pain in his face. He then asked me a question: "How can I ever forgive myself?"

What I shared with him in response to his question is something I was led to share with you: forgiveness is faith in action; even when we need to forgive ourselves.

Next time you find yourself needing forgiveness, don't run from God, run to Him. Take a step of faith and receive all the forgiveness you need - remember, He's full of compassion and mercy.

Today's Word is Psalms 145:8

"The Lord is gracious and full of compassion, slow to anger and great in mercy.

FEBRUARY 22

WHAT'S BETWEEN YOUR EARS?

One of the greatest prayer requests students have these days has to do with their thought life.

Many years ago, the Lord taught me the value of renewing my mind with His Word. As I understand it, the mind is the battleground where the enemy comes to fight. If he can get you to consider a thought, then the battle has truly begun. Here's why:

Remember, thoughts from your mind drop down into your heart and then, out of the abundance of your heart, you speak. Words then create worlds and so, maybe now you have a better understanding of just how important what you think about is as it relates to the world you live in.

If your focus is on the flesh, you'll live a fleshy life. If, however, your mind is focused on pleasing God, you'll live a life led by the Spirit of God. Remember, He really does know what's best for us.

Bottom line: the biggest battle most people ever fight happens between their two ears. What's your mind on?

Today's Word is Romans 8:5

"For those who live according to the flesh set their minds on the things of the flesh, but those who live according to the Spirit, the things of the Spirit."

FEBRUARY 23

YOUR GREATEST CHEERLEADER

Ever felt ganged up on? Ever felt like everyone was against you? Maybe you know what it's like to feel all alone. In addition to all of this, have you ever felt like you've blown it so badly that God wasn't even close by?

If so, I've got some good news to share with you today.

In His Word, God has promised that He'll never leave you, He won't walk out on you, and no matter how horrible the sin that you or I have ever committed, nothing, and I do mean nothing, can ever separate you from the love of God. That's good news!

The easy lie to fall for is that because of something we've said or done, we've disqualified ourselves from relationship with our Father. But because of what Jesus did for us on that cross, He's already paid the supreme price for our free access to God. Relationship then is a choice for you and me to make.

Instead of focusing on who might be against you, maybe today you'll be better off by being mindful of the greatest cheerleader you'll ever have.

Today's Word is Romans 8:31

"What then shall we say to these things? If God is for us, who can be against us?"

FEBRUARY 24

DOUBTING

Do you know one of the aspects of the Bible that I've grown to appreciate the most? God always says what He means and always means what He says.

Understanding this, the Bible comes alive fast.

The other day I was led to read some verses in the book of James; and as I did, I was immediately reminded of God meaning what He says. Here's what I saw -

If you or I choose to live a life that is full of doubt and unbelief, we're promised that not only will we be tossed around and live in instability, but we will also receive absolutely nothing from the Lord.

Now that's serious stuff. You see, unbelief is to the devil what faith is to God.

Want to please God and live in His blessing? Starve doubt and feed your faith.

Today's Word is James 1:6-8

"But let him ask in faith, with no doubting, for he who doubts is like a wave of the sea driven and tossed by the wind. For let not that man suppose that he will receive anything from the Lord; he is a double-minded man, unstable in all his ways."

FEBRUARY 25

MEANT FOR YOUR GOOD

I remember getting a call to speak at a high school where there had been a shooting. At this school, three young ladies had been shot and killed, and five other students shot and wounded.

Early on the morning of my assembly with the remaining students, the principal of the school walked me down the hallway to the vestibule of the school lobby where the shooting had taken place.

As we stood in that area, he told me what it was like to hear the first shots, how he watched students fall, and how he put himself in the line of fire between the gunman and the remaining students.

One of the miracles of this story, however, has to do with what happened 24 hours after the shooting. You see, on the morning of the shooting, there were 32 students standing in a circle, holding hands, and praying - this was the group of teens that the gunman fired into. Twenty-four hours later, in that same lobby vestibule, over 300 students stood in a circle, held hands, and prayed.

No matter what you're going through right now, God has a way to turn what was meant for your harm into your good. Trust Him. Love Him. Obey Him.

Today's Word is Genesis 50:20

"But as for you, you meant evil against me; but God meant it for good, in order to bring it about as it is this day, to save many people alive."

FEBRUARY 26

WHAT CAN BE

After I finish speaking in a school, students always want to talk, and I always enjoy listening to what's going on in their hearts and minds.

One of the sentences I most often hear from young people goes something like this: "I just can't seem to see how to ever get through ..."

I share with them that one of the reasons they can't see the answer is because their focus is on the challenge. What you and I magnify in our lives is what we see.

If you choose to walk by sight alone, you will always see the challenges of life.

If, however, you choose to invoke faith into your daily experiences, guess what? Where once all you saw were the challenges of life, through the eyes of faith you'll begin to see how to overcome anything that comes against you.

Faith is a substance. It's real. And it's powerful. Stop giving the challenges of your life all your attention. Give attention to the Word; and as you hear what the Word has to say, your faith will have no choice but to grow.

Faith, growing in your life, will cause you to stop living in what you see and will instead cause you to begin living in what can be.

Today's Word is 2 Corinthians 5:7

"For we walk by faith, not by sight."

FEBRUARY 27

JESUS IS THE WHO

Have you ever gone through something and had no peace? Maybe it seemed that on every corner something else was going wrong in your world. I know all too well what this feels like; but because of some lessons learned, I also know how to overcome this lack of peace.

To me, trust is the key. It's not just what we trust, much more importantly, it's WHO we trust.

Jesus is the Who. He has the answer to every challenge that comes our way. He has the solution to every obstacle. He has the joy for depression. The healing for sickness. The finances for lack. But most of all, Jesus died so we can live.

All that He's already done for us can be ours; but, to receive it, we must trust Him.

Peace will come to your mind as you focus on Him and on His promises. The only way that I know of that will cause you to really keep your focus on Him is to trust Him and trust the love He has for you.

Want peace? Trust Him.

Today's Word is Isaiah 26:3

"You will keep him in perfect peace, whose mind is stayed on You, because he trusts in You."

FEBRUARY 28

AIR IN YOUR TIRES

When I was in high school, I didn't really enjoy mathematical equations that required me to think about comparable objects. That said, I've got something for you to think about today in a comparative sense:

Love is to faith what air is to a tire.

Without air, a tire on your car can never carry the load it was created to carry. The air gives substance to the tire.

It's no different in faith. The Bible teaches us that our faith works by love. So, if you and I are not living a life of love, guess what? Our faith cannot carry the load it was created to carry. Remember, faith is a substance.

Our faith comes by our hearing the Word. Love comes as we yield to what the Word teaches us.

A good place to start on this love walk is to love God and love people. The more love you have in your heart, the more faith will be in your life.

Maybe today's a good day to check the air in your tires.

Today's Word is 1 John 5:3

"For this is the love of God, that we keep His commandments. And His commandments are not burdensome."

MARCH 1

BLINDED BY THE LIGHT

Can you imagine how weird it would be if you and some of your friends were out walking down a dusty road; and while talking with each other, a bright light from the sky suddenly shined down so brightly that your eyes were blinded.

And then, to make things a little more intense, while you're rolling around in the dust, trying to get your eyes to open, you and those with you suddenly hear a voice also from up in the sky, and this voice starts asking you why you're persecuting Him.

What would you do? While you're considering this, I'd like to share with you that this really happened to a guy named Saul.

Saul was the church's biggest nightmare. He was vehemently against the church and all that it stood for. Despite all that he'd done against God, God still had a plan for him. Three days after he was blinded by the light, Saul's eyes opened; and when they did, he was a new man. Soon after, Saul became Paul and ended up writing two-thirds of the New Testament of the Bible.

Maybe today you, too, know what it feels like to not want to have much if anything to do with God. That's ok. He still has a plan for your life.

Be ready. There's a time coming when God, the Creator of the universe, may very well send a blinding light into your life. If He does, remember that only Jesus can open the blind eyes.

Today's Word is Acts 9:3-4

"As he journeyed he came near Damascus, and suddenly a light shone around him from heaven. Then he fell to the ground, and heard a voice saying to him, "Saul, Saul, why are you persecuting Me?"

MARCH 2

THE TEN-SECOND RULE

The Bible tells us that it's ok to get angry; we're just commanded to not sin in that anger.

Many, many years ago the Holy Spirit instructed me to do something very specific when I got angry: walk away and count to ten.

Sounds simple, doesn't it? When I obeyed His ten-second rule, I was fine. When I chose not to obey and instead gave into my desire to get the last word, that's when I found myself wishing I had adhered to His instruction to walk away and count to ten.

In the Bible, there's a guy named Balaam, and Balaam had a donkey. One day Balaam was out riding his donkey, and trouble and danger were ahead. For whatever reason, God showed the donkey the danger, but Balaam could not see it.

The donkey, in an effort to protect Balaam, went in different directions, crushed Balaam's foot against a wall, and in the end, in an effort to ensure that Balaam did not run right into death itself, the donkey just sat down.

Balaam became so angry that he repeatedly beat his donkey, and then he ended up having a conversation with him. The Bible tells us that God opened the mouth of the donkey and the two of them talked.

Next time you get so angry that you're not even thinking right and maybe you're not seeing danger or disaster up ahead, instead of God having to send you a talking donkey, you might consider invoking the ten-second rule.

Today's Word is Numbers 22:28-30

"Then the Lord opened the mouth of the donkey, and she said to Balaam, "What have I done to you, that you have struck me these three times?" And Balaam said to the donkey, "Because you have abused me. I wish there were a sword in my hand, for now I would kill you!" So the donkey said to Balaam, "Am I not your donkey on which you have ridden, ever since I became yours, to this day? Was I ever disposed to do this to you?" And he said, "No."

MARCH 3

REAL MEN CRY

My favorite time of ministry is when I give an invitation for students to publicly respond to what the Lord is doing in their hearts.

For decades I've stood on stages and seen hundreds of thousands of students walk aisles to altars where I've watched the Lord do what only He can do - touch hearts and change lives. Every time I see this happen, tears come to my eyes.

Almost without fail, however, somewhere at the altar I make eye contact with a young man or young lady who is doing everything within their power to fight off tears from streaming down their face.

I usually walk over to this young person, put my hand on their shoulder, and let them know that regardless of what they think, it really is ok to cry. Tears are not a sign of weakness; tears help us heal.

You want to know how I know it's ok to cry? My role model cried. When one of His very close friends died, the Bible tells us that Jesus wept.

Please understand this: Jesus was a real man who experienced real emotions. So, if He cried, we can, too. Maybe today, if you have tears welling up in your eyes right here, right now, go ahead and cry.

Remember this: Jesus is our example. Real men cry.

Today's Word is John 11:35

"Jesus wept."

MARCH 4

MATTERS OF THE HEART

Let's say, for the sake of example, that your name is Mike, and you're 15 years old. Let's also say that when you hit the teenage years, something strange happened to you, especially in your heart.

Suddenly, Mike, you started noticing young ladies you never before noticed. You began having feelings for a girl. One day, the young lady who has been your best friend is somehow, now someone you find yourself wanting to date.

What happened? Where'd all these feeling come from? Simply put, your heart woke up.

Every teenager I've ever met has, at some point and at some level, experienced a change of heart.

Your heart is such a powerful force. Into it flow emotions, from it flow words, and through it blood is pumped. Your heart has several functions but, spiritually speaking, the Word of God teaches us that above everything else, your heart is to be guarded. There is nothing more valuable in your life than your heart.

Guarding your heart does not mean that you cannot nor should not get close to people - we all need relationship. As you are led into and out of relationships, do yourself a big favor when it comes to matters of the heart. Pray, use wisdom, and above all else, guard it.

Today's Word is Proverbs 4:23

"Keep your heart with all diligence, for out of it spring the issues of life.

MARCH 5

NO SUCH THING AS AN UNLOVED TEEN

One of the saddest comments I ever hear from a teenager is the lie that they believe no one loves them.

As I listen to these students share with me what's going on in their lives, it doesn't take long to realize why these students are tempted to buy that lie. But the truth is, they are loved. And for that matter, each of us is loved.

But maybe you, too, know what it feels like to seemingly have no one in your life who loves you for you; not for what you can do or what you can provide; not because you can spend time or money with or on someone; not even because you look great 24/7.

No matter what lie the enemy has thrown in your direction, here's the truth: there is Someone who loves you just because. He loves us when we're not very lovable; He loves us when we blow it; He loves us when we're tracking and when we're not. This someone is God, and He loves you because ... He is love.

Next time you're perhaps tempted to open the door to the lie that you're not loved, shut that door, and embrace by faith this truth: God is love and love never fails.

Today's Word is 1 John 4:8

"He who does not love does not know God, for God is love."

MARCH 6

OUT OF FEAR

Some time ago, there were ten days in the month of October that radically shook me to my core, caused my faith to be put to the test, and I was drawn closer to The Lord than ever before at that point in my life.

Two occurrences took place in private airplanes. Over the course of these ten days, I lost an engine in flight on two separate planes. Think about that: two engine failures on two planes in ten days.

What happened to me next however was more challenging than my coming out of the skies twice with a dead engine. Fear gripped me and did not want to let go.

You may not have ever lost an airplane engine but perhaps you've gone thru or are going thru something, and now fear has gripped you. If so, I've got Good News.

Got fear? Want to get rid of it? Go to the Word of God and ask Him to give you a Scripture that you can confess - as you speak that Word in faith, fear will split.

About two months after we lost those engines, we were flying in another airplane from Nashville, Tennessee, to Douglas, Georgia, where I was ministering that night at a youth service. We were at 16 thousand feet right over the city of Atlanta and without any warning, the Spirit of God gave me a Scripture that immediately brought peace to my heart and mind.

When I read this verse out loud over and over, my confidence in Him grew stronger each time. I realized He had given me a weapon. I was now attacking that which earlier had been attacking me.

Today's Word is Psalms 94:19

"In the multitude of my anxieties within me, Your comforts delight my soul."

MARCH 7

FOLLOW THE LEADER

I don't recall ever meeting a teenager who enjoyed losing. Be it in sports, academics, or even relationships, losing is never really the objective.

What if I could show you a truth in the Word of God that, from the moment you choose to live by it, you will never lose again? Interested? Good, because I can.

In the simplest of terms, we win when we follow the Leader.

The Word promises us that God always leads us in triumph in Christ. No matter how you look at it, always means always. Triumph means victory and being in Christ gives us the yoke- destroying, burden-removing power of God.

Want to win? Follow the Leader.

Today's Word is 2 Corinthians 2:14

"Now thanks be to God who always leads us in triumph in Christ, and through us diffuses the fragrance of His knowledge in every place."

MARCH 8

PRAY & OBEY

How many times can you remember being led to do something you just did not want to do; and yet, deep, deep down in your heart, you knew you were supposed to do it?

I meet a lot of teenagers who share with me how they wish they'd obeyed what their heart was leading them to do; but, for whatever reason, they disobeyed the leading of the Holy Spirit and instead did what they wanted to do.

I know from very personal experience that those selfish choices never lead to long-term, enjoyable circumstances.

So, what to do? My suggestion is to do what Jesus did when He faced a circumstance that He didn't necessarily want to experience.

Jesus got alone and talked with His Father - He prayed.

Next time you sense the Lord is leading you to do something that you might not want to do, don't disobey - pray.

Remember, He loves you and knows what's best.

Today's Word is Matthew 26:39

"He went a little farther and fell on His face, and prayed, saying, "O My Father, if it is possible, let this cup pass from Me; nevertheless, not as I will, but as You will."

MARCH 9

DECEIVED

Deception comes in many forms but from only one source - the enemy.

The devil hates truth, and he has spent thousands of years trying to keep teenagers from seeing and experiencing what Jesus gave His life to provide for each one of us - true freedom.

I believe that the truth of the Gospel can be summed up in its totality in one word: LOVE.

If you find yourself confused or deceived today, you might want to take some time and receive His love - all over again.

When you are filled with the love of God, deception can't take up residence in your heart.

Remember, when you or me or anyone else is deceived, we are unable to see the truth, and it's the truth that sets us free.

Today's Word is John 8:32

"And you shall know the truth, and the truth shall make you free."

MARCH 10

HE'LL SHOW YOU

Every single journey you will ever go on will begin with your taking the first step or driving the first mile or maybe flying the first mile. There's always a beginning.

When the seemingly unknown is involved, taking that first step can be a real step of faith.

Many years ago, there was a guy named Abram who was instructed to leave his home and go to a land that God would show him. Now, to me, that's faith. Start out on a trip and have absolutely no idea what your destination is - can you imagine?

But Abram trusted the voice of God and followed His leading. It's absolutely no different today. Want to go on a faith journey with the Lord? Listen for His voice of instruction and then take a step of faith.

Remember, you must start where you are to get to where He wants you to be.

Today's Word is Genesis 12:1

"Now the Lord had said to Abram: "Get out of your country, from your family and from your father's house, to a land that I will show you."

MARCH 11

CORRECTION

If you've ever been grounded, paddled, or maybe had your cell phone taken away for a period of time, you know what it feels like to be corrected.

Growing up, when my mom or dad corrected me, they'd almost always say, "This is going to hurt me more than it hurts you." To which I'd usually think, "Well, if it's going to hurt you, why do it?"

It wasn't until much later in life that I more completely understood this process - correction is part of life's journey.

God loves you so much, He will not allow foolishness to hang out in your life - whom He loves, He corrects.

Next time you do something that causes correction to come your way, it might be helpful to remember that you really can't grow without some correction along the way.

Today's Word is Job 5:17

"Behold, happy is the man whom God corrects; therefore, do not despise the chastening of the Almighty."

MARCH 12

WILDERNESS EXPERIENCE

Ever had a time in your life when you felt all alone? Maybe you're in one of those times right now.

Even Jesus, when He lived on the earth, had a wilderness experience.

The Word teaches us that the Spirit led Jesus into the wilderness. After 40 days, however, He came out of the wilderness in the power of the Spirit.

What's the point? If you're going to be led into a wilderness experience, and we all are; no matter how alone you might feel during the process, know that Jesus is with you. And because He's with you, you can receive the lesson (the power) that was yours to learn from that experience.

Today's Word is Luke 4:1 & Luke 4:14

"When Jesus was in the wilderness for 40 days, He was led there by the Spirit. When He came out, He came out in the power of the Spirit."

"Then Jesus returned in the power of the Spirit to Galilee, and news of Him went out through all the surrounding region."

MARCH 13

CONNECTING

Almost every day that I speak in a school, students ask me how they can discover their destiny.

I follow their question with a question for them to consider: "Have you prayed about it?"

After many years of walking with God, I've learned the value of taking time to talk with Him.

Prayer is more than just me doing all the talking. Two thirds of my prayer time is listening.

Why two-thirds? God gave me two ears and one mouth, so I really try to listen more than I talk.

Want to get an answer to a question or situation in your life? I'd encourage you to pray.

Remember, prayer is what connects us to God's assignment for our lives.

Today's Word is Colossians 4:2

"Continue earnestly in prayer, being vigilant in it with thanksgiving;"

MARCH 14

DON'T DELAY

The timing of God is perfect, always has been, always will be.

I oftentimes share with teenagers that delay can lead to denial. When prompted to do or say something, do it - don't delay.

Picture this: God sitting on His throne with a master to do list. On this list is every assignment He has for everyone on the planet. Next to these assignments are His timelines.

Our job is to be so closely tuned into the Spirit of God that when He speaks, we hear; when we hear, we immediately obey. Why is our hearing and obeying so important? God uses us to accomplish His will in the earth.

Your obedience can be used to make the difference in the lives of others.

Here's something to consider: when it comes to helping someone else and you've been prompted to do so, don't put off until tomorrow that which you can do today.

Today's Word is Proverbs 3:27

"Do not withhold good from those to whom it is due, when it is in the power of your hand to do so."

MARCH 15

USE YOUR MOUTH

When God created the earth, He did so with His Words. Words are the most powerful force in the earth.

As a Believer, we're taught to speak the Word in faith; and as we do, we'll see results.

On the road I meet a lot of teenagers who are facing mountains in their lives. Maybe it's a mountain of relationship, perhaps one of insecurity; could be a mountain called addiction. Whatever the mountain, the Word teaches us how to overcome that which is an obstacle, a deterrent in our lives: speak to it.

The Bible never says we must physically go out, roll up our sleeves, and start digging to move a mountain. Instead, we're taught to speak to the mountains, and the faith-filled Words we speak will get the job done.

Next time you find yourself facing a mountain in your life, use your mouth.

Today's Word is Mark 11:23

"For assuredly, I say to you, whoever says to this mountain, 'Be removed and be cast into the sea,' and does not doubt in his heart, but believes that those things he says will be done, he will have whatever he says."

MARCH 16

BELIEVING

Thousands of years ago, some religious leaders asked Jesus how they could work the works of God.

When I read His response, I found myself looking at my life and our ministry.

Jesus' response was simple - to work the works of God, we must believe in Him whom He sent.

In order to believe in whom He sent, seems to me that we first must know whom He sent. In the book of John, we see that the Word became flesh and dwelt among us. God sent the Word, and it became flesh.

So, to believe in whom He sent is to believe the Word.

Want to know how to work the works of God? Believe the Word.

Today's Word is John 6:29

"Jesus answered and said to them, "This is the work of God, that you believe in Him whom He sent."

MARCH 17

WHO'S THAT KNOCKING

Teenagers often ask me about what they describe as a knocking they feel in their heart.

This knocking, as I understand it, is the Spirit of God doing what He does.

I share with audiences that the Holy Spirit is a Gentleman. He goes where He's invited. He leads but doesn't push. He's always available, but He never makes you or me choose Him.

God loves us so much that we have the freedom to choose what we will do with His prompting.

Next time you sense a knocking deep down in your heart, that's not something you ate. In fact, it's not a something at all; it's a Someone.

Remember, the Spirit of God will knock on the door of your heart, but He won't knock your door down.

Today's Word is Revelation 3:20

"Behold, I stand at the door and knock. If anyone hears My voice and opens the door, I will come in to him and dine with him, and he with Me."

MARCH 18

BEING

Are you one of those teenagers who have spent a lot of your life doing versus being?

I meet a lot of great young people on the road, and many of them are spending their teenage years doing rather than investing these same years in just being.

There's a major difference between doing and being.

When God created us, He did so as human BEINGS not as human DOINGS.

I'm convinced more today than ever before that He just wants us to be with Him, to hang out and experience His goodness.

Our lives were never meant to be all about what we've done. Instead, I really believe our lives are the sum total of who we've been in Him.

Nothing wrong with being productive and getting things done - just consider not letting what you do define who you are.

Remember, it's not up to us to do; it's up to us to be.

Today's Word is Colossians 3:3

"For you died, and your life is hidden with Christ in God."

MARCH 19

IT IS WELL

Ever been promised something that you could hardly wait to receive? If so, do you remember the expectation building as you got closer to having whatever it was that was promised to you in your life?

Thousands of years ago there was a lady known only as the Shunammite woman. Because of a seed that she and her husband had sown into the life of a Prophet of God, their harvest was the promise of her giving birth to a son.

God was true to His Word, and, sure enough, the Shunammite woman and her husband had a son. One day as this boy grew, he was out working in the field with his dad. The boy became very sick, and the Bible says that he died.

Instead of agreeing with her circumstances, the Shunammite woman held on to God and believed Him for a miracle. You see, her son was her harvest - the manifestation of God's promise to her – and she was not going to give up.

When her husband saw that she was in a hurry to get to the Prophet of God, her husband asked her why she was going to see God's Prophet. Her only response was, "It is well."

In reality, it wasn't well at all. Her son was dead, but she had a promise and knew the power of believing. After the Prophet got to the little boy and after he obeyed what he was led to do, the boy came back to life.

Next time you go thru something that causes you to shake in your boots, don't agree with circumstances that come against the Word of God. Instead, look up to Heaven, stand on the promises of God, and declare like the Shunammite woman did, "IT IS WELL."

Today's Word is 2 Kings 4:23

"So he said, "Why are you going to him today? It is neither the New Moon nor the Sabbath." And she said, "It is well."

MARCH 20

SAND

What do you think God thinks about all day, every day? The answer might surprise you.

I believe God thinks about YOU.

Ever considered just how much He loves you? Think of it this way. Let's say that you have someone in your life whom you really love. Because you love that person, you think about him or her.

Now, try to imagine God, the creator of the universe, loving you. Can you even begin to wrap your mind around just how many thoughts He has concerning you, your life, and your future? One thing He never thinks about, however, is your past. God is always moving forward.

Next time you go to the beach or perhaps see a picture or video of a sandy beach, I'd encourage you to take a minute and look at all that sand in that one spot on that one beach.

Now, consider all the sand that exists in the earth today and take that thought one level deeper: consider each grain of sand and imagine that each granular of sand is a thought God has about you.

Getting the picture? He really is thinking about YOU.

Today's Word is Psalms 139:17-18

"How precious also are Your thoughts to me, O God! How great is the sum of them! If I should count them, they would be more in number than the sand; when I awake, I am still with You."

MARCH 21

SURRENDER

No matter where you may travel and despite language barriers and cultural differences, there remains a universal sign of surrender: hands lifted in the air.

If you've ever watched a war movie or a police show on TV and see someone with his or her hands lifted high, that's the sign that a person is surrendering, giving up.

That sign is no different with the Lord. At the end of our chapel services, I oftentimes invite students to raise their hands and repeat a prayer.

When we raise our hands to the Lord, we're really just admitting what He already knows - we can't go on like this anymore. We give up. We surrender to Someone much more powerful than ourselves.

The instant we give up control of our lives, He happily takes over. In the case of raising your hands to the Lord, you're not getting weaker, you're becoming stronger.

Next time you just can't seem to make heads or tails out of life, might be a good idea to stop what you're doing, raise your hands, and let the Lord know, "I give up - I'm yours to command, Sir. I trust you."

Raise your hands and begin to experience true freedom.

Today's Word is Psalms 28:2

"Hear the voice of my supplications when I cry to You, when I lift up my hands toward Your holy sanctuary."

MARCH 22

MASTER CRAFTSMAN

Since I was fifteen years old, I've enjoyed watches. For some people, it's cars; for others, it's clothes; but for me, it's a watch.

Through the years I've seen some cool watches. Some have been vintage while others have just been fun. But no matter the story behind a watch, one thing is for certain. Even though many watch brands are mass-produced, somewhere way back when there was a Watchmaker who created the original.

Now, let's change gears. Forget the watch. Think instead about your very life. Since the beginning of time, billions of people have been created, and yet every single person ever to take a breath of life was created as a true original.

You were created by a Master Craftsman who made you, uniquely you. God has never ever made a mistake, and He's sure not going to start making them with you.

So today, if you find yourself maybe questioning your value, I'd encourage you to take a minute and realize that right now, seated on His heavenly throne is the Master Craftsman, smiling at His original called YOU.

Today's Word is Psalms 139:14

"I will praise You, for I am fearfully and wonderfully made; marvelous are Your works, and that my soul knows very well."

MARCH 23

FINISH YOUR ASSIGNMENT

Sometimes when I'm hanging out and talking with students after an event, I'm led to ask them this question: How do you glorify God?

The responses I get vary dramatically, but most often students try to give me spiritual, religious answers.

And really, a spiritual answer isn't what I'm looking for at all.

The Bible very clearly shows us how to glorify God, and it does so by using the words of Jesus as our example.

Want of glorify God with your life? Do what Jesus did. Finish the assignment, the purpose; the calling God has given you to do.

Today's Word is John 17:4

"I have glorified You on the earth. I have finished the work which You have given Me to do."

MARCH 24

STOP WORRYING

Have you ever met someone who seemingly worried about anything and everything? No matter what the situation, this person somehow always sees the worst-case scenario. Maybe you know someone like this, or maybe you are this someone.

If so, may I give you something to consider? What possible good does it do for you or me or anyone else to sit around worrying about something that may or may not ever even happen?

Let's go a step further. What does the Bible call it when we're instructed to do or not do something, and we disobey what it says? That's right, it's called SIN.

You might be thinking, "Are you telling me that if I worry, I'm sinning?" No, I'm not telling you that; the BIBLE tells us that.

So, if the Lord doesn't want us to worry, what are we to do? Get into faith. How? By getting into the Word. Remember, faith activates God just as fear activates the devil.

Today, ask the Holy Spirit to be your Comforter; and as you ask, stop worrying and pray.

Today's Word is Luke 12:22

"Then He said to His disciples, "Therefore I say to you, do not worry about your life, what you will eat; nor about the body, what you will put on."

MARCH 25

HUMILITY

For years I looked for a definition of humility that most spoke to me. I was looking for this definition, because for many, many years, living a life of humility was something I knew I was supposed to do - I just didn't know how to do it.

During those years, being humble never came easy to me. You see, because I was sexually abused at the age of 15, I became terribly insecure on the inside yet horribly too secure on the outside - can you relate?

The opposite of humility is pride and for way too long, I was full of pride.

The longer this pride stayed in my heart, the more I wanted it to leave.

Then one day, while sitting in the office of a Christian counselor, I was given a definition of humility that spoke to the deepest chambers of my heart: humility is having no pretense. What is pretense? A fake appearance intended to deceive.

From that moment on, I wanted to know how to have no pretense in my life. As He always does, the Lord answered my faith by giving me an answer in the Word.

He led me over to 1 Peter 5, where I saw the answer to my question: the only person who ever gets the grace of God is the guy or girl who is humble.

Want to live a life of no pretense? Grace is the answer.

Today's Word is 1 Peter 5:5

"Likewise you younger people, submit yourselves to your elders. Yes, all of you be submissive to one another, and be clothed with humility, for 'God resists the proud, but gives grace to the humble."

MARCH 26

WHAT'S IN IT FOR ME

Got a scenario to run by you today. Think back to the most recent time you can remember when you saw, let's say, a two or three- year-old child at a mall or a restaurant who wasn't getting their way. The more they wanted their way but didn't get it, the louder and more out-of-control they became.

I've seen this same attitude play out among teenagers; but in the teen years, the attitude has grown from, "I want my way" to "What's in it for me?"

Maybe today you know all too well what I'm talking about. If so, I've got a solution for you to consider. Ask God to help you get your mind off yourself and focus instead on caring about the need and/or desire of someone else.

This is important to understand: I'm not at all suggesting that you and I are to become people-pleasers or even that we're supposed to always put the needs of others ahead of our lives. We're not. God is the One who meets our need, but He leads people to be part of the process.

Want to start a revolution? Value your relationships and see past just what's in them for you.

Today's Word is Philippians 2:3

"Let nothing be done through selfish ambition or conceit, but in lowliness of mind let each esteem others better than himself."

MARCH 27

LOYALTY

Want to know one of the topics teenagers seem to be most concerned about around the world? Wherever I've ministered, Australia, England, Moscow, South Africa, the Caymans; anywhere I've ever gone to speak, I've encountered people who are concerned about what their friends are saying about them when they're not around.

It has really surprised me just how many students open up and share the fear they've experienced concerning the area of loyalty.

Here's what I've learned about loyalty: it's measured by what you say about someone when they're not around.

As I sit and listen to teens tell me about things that have been said about them behind their backs, I see the pain come to the surface as they're sharing with me and am reminded of what the Word says: "Vengeance is Mine, says the Lord." Ours is not to try and get even.

I then get to share with these students that repaying evil for evil never works - two wrongs don't make a right.

Loyalty among friends is earned. Loyalty from God is a done deal. No matter what's going on in your life, if you think there is no one whom you can trust, no one who will remain loyal thru and thru, hang on - God is the real deal. You can trust Him; He's got your back.

Today's Word is 2 Chronicles 16:9

"For the eyes of the Lord run to and fro throughout the whole earth, to show Himself strong on behalf of those whose heart is loyal to Him..."

MARCH 28

HE'S ABLE

If you've been a Christian for any length of time, there's probably a pretty good chance that you've either read or heard 2 Corinthians 9:8. This verse talks about God making all grace abound toward you so that you'll have everything you'll need to fulfill the good work He's called you to do.

If you take the time to really dissect this scripture, I believe there's something else He's saying to each of us. It's a three-word phrase that should give us great confidence in the God we serve:

God is able.

Next time you're facing seemingly insurmountable circumstances, don't be moved by what you see; choose instead to set your sights on the One who has the grace for every situation you and I will ever encounter.

After all, He's able.

Today's Word is 2 Corinthians 9:8

"And God is able to make all grace abound toward you, that you, always having all sufficiency in all things, may have an abundance for every good work."

MARCH 29

SHUT THE DOOR

Ever noticed what happens when you make a quality decision to set aside some time to pray or get in the Word? For a long time in my life, almost without fail, every time I would begin to pray, distractions would come and try to steal my time with the Lord.

For teenagers, distractions come in all shapes and sizes: emails, phone calls, Facebook, Twitter, TikTok, television, well-meaning friends. Anything that can take your focus from prayer, the enemy will try to send your way.

Can anything be done about these distractions? You bet.

Open your Bible and read what Jesus tells us to do: go into your room and shut the door.

Shutting the door on all outside influences and distractions will allow you the opportunity to get with your Father - when you're with Him, life begins to make sense.

Today's Word is Matthew 6:6

"But you, when you pray, go into your room, and when you have shut your door, pray to your Father who is in the secret place; and your Father who sees in secret will reward you openly."

MARCH 30

MAKE US ONE

I often share with students that one of the most used weapons the enemy has unleashed in high schools is the weapon of division.

The enemy knows all too well what happens when people of like, precious faith bind together in love and declare what the Word of God says about a situation.

Show me a group of students who have chosen to walk in love and choose to stay spiritually connected, and I'll show you a group of young people who are en route to seeing miracle-working power unleashed into their lives.

Want to beat the weapon of division? Pray that you and your friends become one.

Today's Word is John 17:22

"And the glory which You gave Me I have given them, that they may be one just as We are one:"

MARCH 31

YOUR IDENTITY

Ever been told you look like your mom or dad? Most of us have.

Today let's go a little deeper than just looking like someone else. For a minute think about growing up in your home. If asked to do so, could you list ten things that you've been taught while living at home? Could you list five?

You see, it's one thing to look like someone else, but it's something entirely different to develop your identity from what you've learned from someone else, someone like your dad.

Sadly, I meet a lot of teenagers who seem to be aimlessly wandering through this season of their lives. When we meet, I usually am led to ask about their home life. More times than not, these students share with me that their dad either doesn't live with them; or if he does, he's at best an absentee father.

Many years ago, I heard someone say something that has really stuck with me: a lack of a father creates a lack of identity.

Today, if you're going thru life with no identity, I'd encourage you to believe God for a spiritual father to come into your life. These are men called by God to minister the Word into your life; and as they do, you'll begin to discover your true identity in Him.

Today's Word is 1 Corinthians 4:15

"For though you might have ten thousand instructors in Christ, yet you do not have many fathers; for in Christ Jesus I have begotten you through the gospel."

APRIL 1

GOD LOVES YOU AS MUCH AS HE LOVES JESUS

Want to hear something that might, at first, be tough to believe? Ok. Here goes - God loves you as much as He loves Jesus.

When I share that truth with students, many immediately have a very perplexed look on their faces. For most of them, this is the first time in their lives that they've heard someone tell them that God loves them as much as He loves His Son, Jesus.

In fact, there are even those who think I'm being sacrilegious when I share this truth with them, but I'm not.

The Bible tells us that God cannot lie; and so, if it's in the Word, I take it as truth.

You might be wondering how or even why God loves you so much. It has absolutely nothing to do with what you have done, are doing, or will do in the future. He loves you as much as He loves Jesus for one reason and one reason only: He is love.

If you're having a challenge believing and receiving the truth that God loves you as much as He loves Jesus, I'd encourage you to take a step of faith, read the below Scripture, say out loud that you receive His love, and then ask your Heavenly Father to invade your heart.

If you ask Him to show up, get ready. Love is on the way.

Today's Word is John 17:23

"I in them, and You in Me; that they may be made perfect in one, and that the world may know that You have sent Me, and have loved them as You have loved Me."

APRIL 2

HE CAN'T LIE

Growing up in the 1970's I would, from time to time, hear my grandfather, Pap, say about someone with whom he was doing business that their word was their bond.

It wasn't until years later that I more completely understood what Pap had been saying about these businesspeople: he could trust them, because whatever they said, they were committed to their word.

That's a terrific reputation to have.

More than a reputation, however, is if there could be someone in your life right now whose Word has never failed, ever. Someone upon whom you can base the entirety of your life - both this life and the life to come - on truth that simply never fails.

Maybe you're wondering how this is even possible. After all, we've all lied at some point in our lives. Well, that's almost true, but there is One who has never, ever lied. In fact, it's not just that He hasn't lied, it's that He can't lie.

Want to have a relationship with this person? He's available, right here, right now.

You can trust God, because when you think of it, it's His Word that's holding all of this together.

Today's Word is Titus 1:2

"in hope of eternal life which God, who cannot lie, promised before time began,"

APRIL 3

STATE OF CONFUSION

One of the primary tricks of the enemy is to try and get teenagers to doubt that they've heard from God.

He'll plant a seed of doubt in their hearts and then almost like clockwork, he'll again and again send thoughts into their minds, trying to get them to buy the lie that they didn't hear the Truth.

I meet a lot of teens who share with me that they've experienced this process and what it has produced in their lives: confusion.

Once we hit the "c" word, I'm quick to ask them where confusion comes from. Some students know the answer; others don't.

For those who don't know, I show them in the Word that confusion does not come from God. It always comes from the enemy.

God doesn't change. Hold on to what you hear from Him. He has such amazing plans for your life - why else would the enemy try so hard to steal the truth?

Got an assignment for you to consider. Next time you recognize the enemy trying to steal Truth from your heart and mind, stop everything and quote the below Scripture out loud. When you do, the truth you're speaking will turn the table on the enemy, and suddenly he'll be the one in a state of confusion.

Today's Word is 1 Corinthians 14:33

"For God is not the author of confusion but of peace, as in all the churches of the saints."

APRIL 4

CHARACTER

One of the most interesting experiences I have in many high schools is meeting students who come to me after an assembly and tell me about their reputation.

Sometime these students are proud of their rep, while many others tell me a little bit of the painful journey they've been on as they've tried to quieten the voices advancing the stories behind the reputation.

Here's a little secret I share with students: your reputation doesn't have to define you for life.

If you've made some bad choices, and we all have, do what the Bible teaches us to do: confess that you blew it, repent to the Lord, and then move on with His grace forever covering that sin.

Once you've moved on, it'll probably be helpful if you'll realize that who you are today is more important than what you did yesterday.

Know what the result is of moving past mistakes and choosing to not repeat the past? Character.

Character is the ability for you to follow through on a decision you've made to live for God long after the mood or atmosphere in which that decision was made has dissipated, diminished, or completely disappeared.

It really is true: reputations are made in a second, character is developed over a lifetime.

Today's Word is Romans 5:3-4

"And not only that, but we also glory in tribulations, knowing that tribulation produces perseverance; and perseverance, character; and character, hope."

APRIL 5

DON'T WAVER

When it comes to the promises of God that are plainly printed on the pages of your Bible, have you ever really considered how much work is required to not believe those promises?

Let's say that you're believing God for a gift for someone in your family, but you don't have a gift, nor do you have a job. So, where's the gift or the money to buy it going to come from?

When you or I begin considering all that could possibly come against something happening that we really want to see happen in our lives, this consideration takes a huge amount of work.

So, what can be done about this scenario? Here's a suggestion for you:

Find yourself a Scripture that promises God will supply your need; and instead of wavering and doubting that His Word is true, shut the door on that doubt and boldly remind God that His Word is on the line. You're believing Him to supply the gift or to supply the money. Either way, you're trusting Him and the Word to do what you cannot do.

If you'll stay in faith, follow His instructions, and continue to walk in love, watch your faith produce results.

It's been this way since the beginning of time; it really is our choice. When it comes to faith, we'll either believe or we'll waver. God has done His part - now it's up to us to do ours.

Today's Word is Romans 4:20

"He did not waver at the promise of God through unbelief, but was strengthened in faith, giving glory to God,"

APRIL 6

KEEP IT SIMPLE

Today, the Holy Spirit gave me the coolest instruction: keep it simple.

Several days ago, I was speaking at a Christian High School; and as I was talking with these students, I was led to ask how many of them had introduced someone to Jesus over the past 30 days; the last 60 days, and finally, the last year.

I was astonished at how few hands were raised in response to my question. Since that day, I've been thinking about those students and began wondering how many people have so overcomplicated the Gospel that it is no longer seen as Good News, but rather just a bunch of rules.

If someone asked you today when was the last time you led someone to the Lord, what would your answer be? Whatever the answer is, maybe it's time that all of us get back to the basics of the true Gospel; and as we do, let's keep it simple.

Today's Word is 1 Corinthians 15:3-4

"For I delivered to you first of all that which I also received: that Christ died for our sins according to the Scriptures, and that He was buried, and that He rose again the third day according to the Scriptures,"

APRIL 7

GET AWAY FROM THE EDGE

There's an old saying that goes something like this: hang out with turkeys and you'll become a turkey; hang out with eagles and you'll learn to fly high.

What does that saying mean to you today? Association matters.

I've met a lot of teenagers who've gotten into trouble, because they began hanging out with a crowd who chose to live on the edge. The thing about living on the edge is that it doesn't take much to cross over the edge; and when that happens, you're no longer on a sure foundation.

If you hang out with the group who drinks and parties all weekend, look out, you're on the edge. If you are constantly trying to fit it with those who are experimenting with their given drug of choice, look out, you're on the edge. If you're compromising your values to go out with the guy or girl who doesn't live by a Godly moral code, you guessed it - you're on the edge.

God loves everybody. He loves us enough to warn us when we're on the edge.

Pay attention to His warnings. Stay close to Him - His is the sure foundation.

Today's Word is 1 Corinthians 15:33

"Do not be deceived: "Evil company corrupts good habits."

APRIL 8

LET HIM PROMOTE YOU

In high schools all over America, I've watched students try and promote themselves; and without fail, each time I've seen this happen, it's come off wrong. It's not that these young people are bad kids; it's not that what they did or what they're promoting is not something to be celebrated; it comes off wrong for one simple reason:

We were never created to tell everybody how great we are. Be it in sports, academics, music, the arts, or whatever, God is always the One who does the promoting.

I've had teenagers share their heart with me who have wrongly believed that if they didn't promote themselves, they wouldn't be promoted. I in turn always share this simple truth with them: Promotion comes from God.

Next time you've done something that maybe you believe needs to be promoted, do what the Word says and watch God move on your behalf.

Our responsibility is to humble ourselves; God's responsibility is to exalt / promote us.

Today's Word is 1 Peter 5:6

"Therefore humble yourselves under the mighty hand of God, that He may exalt you in due time,"

APRIL 9

SAY WHAT HE SAYS, DO WHAT HE DOES

Ever wondered why Jesus said what He said? Ever considered why He went where He went?

If you take the time to look at His life as recorded in the four Gospels, you'll see the secret to His life and ministry; and when you see it, you'll suddenly realize it wasn't a secret at all.

Jesus, while living here on the earth, was Jesus, the Son of Man, not Jesus, the Son of God. Because He was here as a man, He showed us, by example, how to live a life pleasing to God.

It was the standard operating procedure of Jesus to only say what He heard His Father say and to only do that which He saw His Father do.

Well, you might ask, if He heard His Father say and saw His Father do, and Jesus was here as a man, how can I do this? You and I do it the same way He did it - get into the presence of God and pray.

Instead of just blowing through life with an agenda of your own, maybe it's time to hit the brakes, get with God, and follow the Leader. Say what He says, do what He does.

You'll be glad you did.

Today's Word is John 14:10

"Do you not believe that I am in the Father, and the Father in Me? The words that I speak to you I do not speak on My own authority; but the Father who dwells in Me does the works."

APRIL 10

THE WAY

I have no idea exactly how many students across America and in nations of the world have told me the following sentence, "No matter how hard I try, I just can't find God."

Maybe you, too, feel or have felt this way. If so, it's common, but today, I have some good news for you to think about: God isn't lost.

When a young person tells me they can't find God and I in turn share with them that He's not lost, these students usually stand there with a blank look on their faces. I then quickly offer them another option to consider - maybe instead of trying to find Him, perhaps they've discovered their need to have Him take up residence in their heart.

I believe that within every single person there is a void that nothing and no one will ever fill - no one, that is, except Jesus, as you invite Him to become Lord of your life.

If you have found yourself more and more searching for a void- filler, maybe today's your day to embrace the truth that Jesus is the way to the Father.

Today's Word is John 14:6

"Jesus said to him, "I am the way, the truth, and the life. No one comes to the Father except through Me."

APRIL 11

WALK IN THE LIGHT

Is there an area of your life that no one knows about? Is there something going on that causes you to live in continual fear that someone else may find out about? Living a life of secrets is a life of bondage.

Whatever we keep in darkness keeps us in bondage.

Living in the dark and living a life of bondage never was God's plan for us, never. But how do we get out?

We get out of darkness by exposing the light. The Word of God is referenced as the glorious light of the Gospel. This light is a radiating light that causes darkness to flee; and when darkness is on the run, bondage is right on its heels.

Want to be free and have no fear? Ask the Holy Spirit to shine His light in the crevasses of your heart and expose to you whatever might be in there that doesn't belong.

Once sin is exposed, deal with it. Then walk in the light.

Today's Word is Ephesians 5:8

"For you were once darkness, but now you are light in the Lord. Walk as children of light."

APRIL 12

SOMETHING TO EXPERIENCE

Sometime ago I heard a friend of mine say something that has really stuck with me:

You can experience a kiss or analyze it, but you can't do both at the same time.

The more I've thought about that sentence, the more I've been led to apply the truth of it to my relationship with the Lord.

Maybe today you, too, can take some time to see if this is an area in your life that needs some attention.

We can experience God, His Son, Jesus, and the Holy Spirit, or we can spend our time analyzing Him.

He really is my friend. I don't spend my time analyzing my friends; instead, I invest my time experiencing life with them.

Nothing wrong at all with having an analytical mind. When it comes to your relationship with God, however, my prayer for you is that you have a real, genuine friendship with Him - that's something to experience.

Today's Word is Exodus 33:11

"So the Lord spoke to Moses face to face, as a man speaks to his friend. And he would return to the camp, but his servant Joshua the son of Nun, a young man, did not depart from the tabernacle."

APRIL 13

BY MY SPIRIT

If you were to look at what's on the inside cover of my Bible, you'd see a typed message I wrote to myself many years ago. It's a message that serves as a constant reminder to me of the necessity of my reliance on God in my life. Here's what it says:

"If what I am attempting to do does not require God being fully involved, then I am thinking way too small."

I get to talk with a lot of teenagers who take time from their schedules to share with me some of their hopes, dreams, and plans. As I listen to them, I wonder how many of them are yielding to the will and direction of the Holy Spirit for their individual lives.

One of the most important lessons the Spirit of God taught me early on in this ministry is that it is totally impossible for me to accomplish a divine assignment with the energy of my flesh.

In other words, without God, it isn't going to happen the way He wants it to happen. And you know what? His way is always the best way.

Maybe today would be a terrific time for you to think about where your life is heading. As you do, I'd strongly encourage you to invite the Spirit of God to take control. You'll like the results.

Today's Word is Zechariah 4:6

"So he answered and said to me: 'This is the word of the Lord to Zerubbabel: Not by might nor by power, but by My Spirit,' Says the Lord of hosts."

APRIL 14

SHEPHERD

You were never meant to navigate life on your own. None of us were.

I meet a lot of teenagers on the road who seem to be loners and disconnected. Maybe today you're feeling disconnected or lonely, or maybe you just want a friend. If so, I've got something for you to consider.

The Bible teaches us that if the Lord is the Shepherd of your life, you shall not want.

You won't experience lack in relationships, in love, in direction, or even in resources - if you are submitted to Him and His will for your life.

Now understand, I'm not suggesting that just because you hang out with God, He's going to give you everything you think you might want. But what I am sharing with you is that as you submit yourself to His will for your life, He'll supply what you want because you'll only want what He wants you to have. Again, He knows best.

Want to get connected to the best friend you'll ever have? Make the decision to let Jesus be your Shepherd.

Today's Word is Psalms 23:1

"The Lord is my shepherd; I shall not want."

APRIL 15

HE'S MY SOURCE

One of the most significant lessons I've ever learned is to make God your source.

For many years I looked to people instead of to God. And I know from very personal experience that people will never be able to do that which God has reserved for Him and only Him to do.

Very simply, where we focus becomes our source. Look to people, and you'll eventually be disappointed. Look to God and you'll see the difference.

Certainly, God uses people in the earth to distribute His provisions, but ultimately, our choice of where we place our focus and trust will determine the type of life we live.

Today, if you find yourself counting on someone else to perhaps meet a need or to provide a friend, lift your head and put your focus on God - He's right there with you right now, wanting to be your source.

Today's Word is Philippians 4:19

"And my God shall supply all your need according to His riches in glory by Christ Jesus."

APRIL 16

LOOK UP

Ever wondered about how high above the earth Heaven really is? I have.

I spend quite a bit of time in an airplane, and many times as we're flying to or from an event, I'll be led to stop what I'm doing, look out my window, and just gaze up into the sky. This is something that never gets old to me.

Maybe it's because we're high up in the air or maybe because I can see how fast we're flying as we soar past clouds. Whatever the reason, each time that I stop and adjust my focus, my heart is drawn ever closer to the Lord.

I believe today, whether you're at school, at home, at the mall or in an airplane, if you'll take a minute and gaze up into the sky and do so with a thankful heart, you'll experience drawing closer to Him.

It's true that He's high above the earth; but if you're a Believer, He's also as close as your heart.

Look up.

Today's Word is Psalms 97:9

"For You, Lord, are most high above all the earth; You are exalted far above all gods."

APRIL 17

WEAPONS

Do you know what I see when I look out across audiences as I minister in schools? Sure, I see students, but more and more I'm seeing the makings of an army for God - young men and young ladies who are preparing to advance further and further into the Kingdom of God, because they trust their Leader.

If you know anything about God, hopefully you are realizing just how much He loves you. And because of this love, there's no way He would lead you into a battle without first equipping you with His weapons.

Next time you sense the enemy is lurking around and looking for a fight, get with God, arm yourself with His weaponry, and then follow your Leader into battle.

Want to know a secret? If you are armed with His weapons and only say what you hear Him say, and only do what you see Him do, you'll soon see you're already on the winning side.

Remember, before you go to battle, get your weapons.

Today's Word is 2 Corinthians 10:4

"For the weapons of our warfare are not carnal but mighty in God for pulling down strongholds,"

APRIL 18

WIN SOULS

The Bible tells us that above everything else we are to get in life, first and foremost, we are to get wisdom. To me that's a heavy statement.

Ever wondered why wisdom is the principal thing? I have and so, in my wondering, I went on a search.

Here's an example of what I've learned: if someone takes you fishing and catches some fish for you, you'll eat that day. If, however, someone takes you fishing and gives you the wisdom to learn how to fish for yourself, you can eat for a lifetime.

I then began to wonder what would make us wise in the eyes of God. I found the answer to that question in the Word.

The Bible clearly tells us that he who wins souls is wise. Pretty clear, isn't it?

So today, if you find yourself desiring to be known as a wise young man or young lady, I'd suggest you get busy doing the very thing that God says makes you wise: win souls to Him.

Today's Word is Proverbs 11:30

"The fruit of the righteous is a tree of life, and he who wins souls is wise."

APRIL 19

WE HAVE AN ADVERSARY

Here's some news that I share with teenagers and many times this news comes as a surprise to them: we have an adversary, and he has a mission.

Sure, it would be wonderful to go thru life and never encounter any opposition, but we're assured in the Word that we'll have some challenging times in this life. Here's some good news, though - the challenging times don't last forever.

When it comes to our adversary, here's some truth to plant deep in the soil of your heart. He's walking around like a roaring lion, not as a roaring lion; he's seeking whom he may devour, not whom he will devour.

You see, the devil is your enemy, but he's an already defeated foe. Jesus made a public spectacle out of him, and today the enemy is constantly trying to get you to buy any lie that he's selling. Don't do it.

Be vigilant to know the truth, to declare the truth, and to receive the truth of the Word. As you do, that defeated foe won't waste much of his time trying to bring challenging times into your life. Instead, he'll slip away looking for someone else whom he may devour.

Today's Word is 1 Peter 5:8

"Be sober, be vigilant; because your adversary the devil walks about like a roaring lion, seeking whom he may devour."

APRIL 20

A RESURRECTED LIFE

All over the world during this season of the year, churches are filling up with people. For many, going to church this week will be the first time they've been to church in about a year; and, sadly, unless something happens in their hearts, it might be another year before they come back to church.

Going to church, though, really isn't the issue. Think about it. Cars go to the church every week, but none of those cars are going to Heaven.

Easter Sunday, known to many as Resurrection Sunday, should be so much more than our going to a church building, hearing some music that makes us feel something, hearing a message, and then going to lunch with family and maybe some extended family.

No, Resurrection Sunday is about one thing, one Person - Jesus Christ.

This time of the year is the time the church sets aside to celebrate the moment when Jesus, through the resurrection power of God, defeated the devil, made a public spectacle out of him, and split hell wide open. When He did, He left with the keys to death, hell, and the grave in His hands.

Know why Jesus died and was resurrected? Very simply, He did it for you. He did it for you because He loves you.

Today is a great day to receive His love. When you do, you'll be resurrected from death to life.

Today's Word is Revelation 1:18

"I am He who lives, and was dead, and behold, I am alive forevermore. Amen. And I have the keys of Hades and of Death."

APRIL 21

RENEW YOUR MIND

No one controls the thoughts you think. God doesn't, the devil doesn't; only you control what passes through your mind.

Sure, the enemy targets thoughts of evil at your mind, and thoughts that are full of love and peace come from God. But, at the end of every message sent your way, you control what you let pass through the gates of your mind. Think about that. You've got a lot of responsibility.

In His Word God shows us a simple process that anyone can employ in his or her life, a process that'll guard your mind from the thoughts of the enemy: renew your mind.

To renew something is to restore or replenish. What's that got to do with you and the thoughts that you allow into your mind? As you renew (restore & replenish) your mind with the Word of God, there won't be room in your mind for thoughts from the enemy.

Why do you think he fights teenagers so hard from getting into the Word? The enemy realizes that once the Word is in you, his tactics have no choice but to stay outside of you.

Want to win the war of thoughts? Renew your mind with the Word.

Today's Word is Romans 12:2

"And do not be conformed to this world, but be transformed by the renewing of your mind, that you may prove what is that good and acceptable and perfect will of God."

APRIL 22

JOY vs HAPPINESS

One of the first questions I often ask students is, "Are you happy?" Almost 100% of the time, they respond with the seemingly obligatory, "Yes." To which I respond, "OK, why are you happy?"

This series of questions and answers typically leads us on a path of recognizing the difference between happiness and joy. And man, there is a difference.

As I have learned, happiness is an emotion that can change as often as the weather, while joy is a fruit of the Spirit (see Galatians 5:22).

You see, joy isn't dependent upon how I feel or even what's going on in life. Joy is strength.

When teenagers realize that joy is so much more than many of us ever really realized, they begin to understand more completely why having joy in their lives is so vitally important to God and to them.

I encounter a lot of teens that are going thru some truly difficult times. Being happy in and of itself won't necessarily get anybody through those times. Having joy, however, propels us forward, being strengthened in our inner-man to face the day with confidence that we have His strength.

Today's Word is Nehemiah 8:10

"Then he said to them, "Go your way, eat the fat, drink the sweet, and send portions to those for whom nothing is prepared; for this day is holy to our Lord. Do not sorrow, for the joy of the Lord is your strength."

APRIL 23

ANXIOUSNESS

Do you know the definition of anxious? If not, here it is:

To be anxious is to be full of mental distress or uneasiness because of fear of danger or misfortune; greatly worried.

Any of that definition sound too familiar to you in your life?

Can anxiety leave your life? Absolutely, but it won't leave until you obey the instructions.

First, let's get honest. When the Bible instructs us not to do something and we do it anyway, very simply that's called sin. Well, as you'll see in a minute, the Bible instructs us to be anxious for nothing. If God doesn't want us to be anxious, then He obviously didn't give anxiety to us. So where does it come from?

Go back up to the definition I shared with you - anxiety is to be full of fear. The Word tells us that God did not give us a spirit of fear; so, if God didn't give it, it came from the enemy.

If anxiety is in your life, you can do something about it right here, right now: pray with a thankful heart, and watch God show up in your life and drive anxiety far from you.

I believe nothing draws the Spirit of God closer to us or faster to us than our coming to God with a heart full of thanks.

Want to get rid of anxiety? Talk with God about getting rid of fear, and you'll see the difference.

Today's Word is Philippians 4:6

"Be anxious for nothing, but in everything by prayer and supplication, with thanksgiving, let your requests be made known to God;

APRIL 24

BELIEVE & SAY

"If you are a Christian, how'd you get saved?" is a question I ask teenagers across the country.

The responses to this question vary but oftentimes, teens tell me that they're a Christian because they go to church. Wrong answer. When church is the answer, my response is, "My car goes to church, but it isn't going to Heaven."

When a person, young or old, becomes a Christian, the process is always the same: belief and confession are the two steps we take to move from us from eternity in hell to eternity in Heaven.

When we believe in our heart and then say with our mouth, we're operating in faith. Getting saved is so very important; but it's not the end, it's a brand-new beginning.

Today, if you find yourself wanting, maybe even needing, to see something take place in your life, it's time to find a Scripture that takes care of that need and employ God's way of doing business: believe in your heart and say with your mouth.

Today's Word is Romans 10:9

"that if you confess with your mouth the Lord Jesus and believe in your heart that God has raised Him from the dead, you will be saved."

APRIL 25

BE KIND

Kindness is more than just smiling and waving at someone. It's more than a casual phone call or text. A major part of being kind is having a tender heart and forgiving people for pain or harm that they've caused in your life.

When we sow the seed of kindness, we can be assured that somewhere up ahead the harvest of kindness is en route into our lives.

Over in the New Testament of the Bible, the fruit of the Spirit is clearly laid out for us. This fruit is, I believe, the template by which we are to live our day-to-day lives. Guess what? About halfway down the list of fruit, kindness is present and accounted for.

Next time someone hurts you or says something ugly to or about you, consider it as an opportunity you're being presented with to grow in faith. Instead of immediately wanting to get even, it might prove to be a better choice to go to one of the branches of the fruit of the Spirit and inject kindness into that situation. As you do, watch your life grow deeper and stronger in the Spirit of God.

Today's Word is Ephesians 4:32

"And be kind to one another, tenderhearted, forgiving one another, even as God in Christ forgave you."

APRIL 26

FOR THIS PURPOSE

Ever spend time wondering why you're here? For most of my teenage years, I wondered not only why I was here but also spent much of my time trying to figure out on my own what was I supposed to do now that I was here. Relate?

Without hesitation of contradiction, I can assure you that when God gave you your life to live, He did so on purpose and with purpose. When I discovered my purpose, the reason He gave me life, suddenly life began to make sense.

As it relates to your purpose, your God-ordained purpose, it's not yours or mine to decide; it's ours to discover.

While Jesus was here on the earth, He clearly knew His purpose - He told His disciples the very reason He had been sent to fulfill His earthly ministry.

Today might be a terrific day for you to hang out with the Lord and ask Him about your mission on planet earth. Want to be fulfilled in life? Discover your purpose.

Today's Word is Luke 4:43

"but He said to them, "I must preach the kingdom of God to the other cities also, because for this purpose I have been sent."

APRIL 27

CULTURE SHOCK

What would happen if people from another culture suddenly showed up in your life and for 30 days, they watched everything you did and listened to every word you said. What would these people have discovered over those 30 days about your life, your words, your beliefs, and your associations?

As they watched and listened, would they see a Believer or a doubter, a hard worker or laziness, kindness, or a jerk, disciplined or complacent?

It's one thing to say all the right things and go to all the right places; it's entirely something altogether different, however, to actually be the person many people want others to believe they are.

The more time you and I invest with the Lord by being in the Word and just hanging out with Him, the more we become like Him. The more we are like Him, the more opportunities He gives us to do what He did while He was here. In fact, He promised that we could do even greater works than He did.

Might be a good idea to be mindful that as you progress through life, people are looking to see your qualifications. As they look, what will they see?

Today's Word is Acts 4:13

"Now when they saw the boldness of Peter and John, and perceived that they were uneducated and untrained men, they marveled. And they realized that they had been with Jesus."

APRIL 28

KEEP ON DREAMING

In the Bible we're introduced to a young man who is a dreamer. He dreamed big and maybe more than he should have, he shared his dreams with his family.

There's a great lesson we can learn from the dreams of Joseph and how his dad and his brothers received those dreams. Not everybody is going to be quite as excited as you are about the discovery of your calling, your latest revelation from the Lord, or your dreams for the future. That's ok, God's excited.

The life of Joseph took some interesting turns; and as it did, Joseph was thrown into a pit (by his brothers); he was sold into slavery (by his brothers); he was thrown into prison (false accusations); and through Divine intervention, within a matter of minutes, Joseph went from the prison to the palace where he became the number two guy in the entire government.

When a famine hit the country, Joseph's brothers came to buy food, and it just so happened that Joseph oversaw the food distribution. Can you imagine how Joseph felt when he was able to provide for his family the food and shelter they needed?

You see, throughout his life, no matter where life took him, Joseph made the choice to not become bitter but to instead become better.

What does the life of Joseph have to do with you today? Dream your dream and irrespective of who's with you or maybe even against you, keep on dreaming. One day, that dream, if it's from the Lord, may very well be used for the good of others.

Today's Word is Romans 8:28

"And we know that all things work together for good to those who love God, to those who are the called according to His purpose."

APRIL 29

FIRST THINGS FIRST

Ever wondered why the first thing we see that God created was light. Why not a mountain or a tiger or a waterfall? Why light?

Years ago, I wondered about this and so I took my question to The Lord: "Why is light the first thing we see that You created?" To my surprise, just as quickly as my question left my lips, I immediately heard the Lord ask me a question: "What does light do?" To which I responded, "I asked You first."

As I thought about the question I had heard in my heart, I came up with two answers relating to the function of light: light dispels darkness and light enables vision.

I was then reminded of what the Word of God says about vision - without vision, people perish.

Could it be, right here, right now, that Genesis 1:3 is very much speaking to you and me? I believe so, and here's what I believe that verse is saying: VISION BE.

The very first thing we see God that created was light. For you and me, I really believe that the light is equivalent to vision. So, might be a good idea to spend some time with the Creator of vision and ask Him about the vision He has for your life.

Today's Word is Genesis 1:3

"Then God said, "Let there be light; and there was light."

APRIL 30

WHAT'S IN A NAME

Names have meaning. Sometime when you have a few extra minutes to spare and if you don't already know it, might be kind of fun to explore the meaning of your name.

Why do names matter? One reason is the association a name has to an activity or even a life's work. For example, if I say ***Michael Jordan***, you probably will think basketball. If I say ***Bill Gates***, I'd imagine you'd think of Microsoft. What about people in the Bible? If I say ***Mary***, I'd imagine that the mother of Jesus would come to mind. And ***Zacchaeus*** probably brings the image to mind of a short guy climbing a sycamore tree.

Today, if someone says your name, what do you think is the first thing that comes to their mind?

Having a godly name (what your known for) is something worth working for and preserving.

The Bible is very clear about the value of your name. Maybe it's a good time to reflect on what your name might mean to others.

Today's Word is Proverbs 22:1

"A good name is to be chosen rather than great riches, loving favor rather than silver and gold."

MAY 1

GOOD IS THE ENEMY OF BEST

Settling for just good enough can become a way of life. If so, compromising for good enough when best is attainable will oftentimes lead to disappointment, discouragement, and possibly even depression. Why is this?

It could be because we were never created to just do enough to get by. We were created for excellence - in every area of our day-to- day living. Notice that I said excellence, not perfection. There's a big difference between these two words.

I've read the Bible from Genesis to Revelation and within those 66 books, nowhere have I ever found where God required perfection from any of us. Excellence, however, is attainable.

I'm not at all suggesting that you go out there and run over people to be the best in every aspect of life, but I am suggesting that you should do your part and then trust the Lord to anoint you to be the best you that you can be. After all, you're the only you that has ever been or ever will be.

As I have taken time to understand the difference between good enough and excellence, here's what I've learned: good is the enemy of best.

Today's Word is Daniel 6:3

"Then this Daniel distinguished himself above the governors and satraps, because an excellent spirit was in him; and the king gave thought to setting him over the whole realm."

MAY 2

DOORS

Next time you're in the mall, look at some of the public signs posted throughout the shopping areas. As you do, you'll probably see at least one of the following messages:

DO NOT ENTER. EXIT. ENTRANCE. IN CASE OF EMERGENCY.

Each of these signs will be posted on or near a door.

Doors are entryways or exits, and they either open something or close something off.

With God it's no different. He opens doors and He likewise closes doors. The wise young person, in my estimation, is the one who recognizes a door opening or closing and responds accordingly.

Remember, when God opens a door for you and when He closes a door for you, irrespective of your understanding, He does so knowing what's best for you.

Today's Word is Revelation 3:7

"And to the angel of the church in Philadelphia write, 'These things says He who is holy, He who is true, He who has the key of David, He who opens and no one shuts, and shuts and no one opens'"

MAY 3

QUIET YOUR ENEMY

Next time you sense the enemy is on the attack in your world, want to freak him out? Begin to praise God for your breakthrough, your deliverance, from whatever the enemy is trying to release into and on your life. The devil will be so perplexed as to why he's the one freaking out and you're not.

Praise is a weapon. There's something very powerful about you raising your voice in praise and worship, declaring the goodness of God during a challenging time. Now be sure you're hearing what I'm saying: we're not thanking God for the enemy and his plans; we're instead praising our way through these times.

The enemy understands more than most people the power of praise. The revelation of what praise is and does is why he hates it so much.

One of the most powerful lessons I've ever learned and likewise ever shared with students is that when we praise, our praise to the Lord shuts the mouth of the devil.

Want to quiet your enemy? Make some noise.

Today's Word is Psalms 8:2

"Out of the mouth of babes and nursing infants You have ordained strength, because of Your enemies, that You may silence the enemy and the avenger."

MAY 4

FOXES

I meet a lot of teenagers who share with me that they really don't do anything too bad. They experiment here a little and there a little, but overall, they say they're good kids.

When I meet someone who believes that the little sin in his or her life really doesn't matter, I'm quick to share with them that in life, more times than not, it's the little sin in their life that they wrongly think no one will ever know about that becomes the very sin that will cause them the most challenge.

When you take time to get honest, here's the truth: sin is sin, and sin has consequences.

Today, if you are counted among those who wrongly believe that the little sins really won't matter that much in the long run, it might be a good idea to remember this: sin is sin, and if left undealt with, little sins often lead to a life of sin that we never imagined possible.

Keep your eyes on the foxes - those are the ones who spoil life's journey.

Today's Word is Song of Songs 2:15

"Catch us the foxes, the little foxes that spoil the vines, for our vines have tender grapes."

MAY 5

DIFFUSING ANGER

Let's say, for sake of example that you find yourself in a heated argument with somebody at school. This argument can either escalate or it can be dissolved. How you respond to what's going on will ultimately determine in large part how it will play out.

How's that possible? According to the Bible, how you and I answer a situation and whether our words are kind or harsh, become the deciding factors in diffusing angry encounters.

Soft, kind words are the language of love. Next time you find yourself slipping down a slippery slope toward an escalating argument, remember that you get to decide how it ends up for you.

Choose wisely.

Today's Word is Proverbs 15:1

"A soft answer turns away wrath, but a harsh word stirs up anger."

MAY 6

IT ONLY TAKES A SPARK

My wife, Lori, and I went on a three-day trip where we could get away and pray, rest, and plan. Our journey led us to a rustic and secluded cabin in the mountains of Tennessee.

On one of those three nights, we used a charcoal grill. I poured the charcoal into the grill and lit the fire. Within seconds, the spark that was used to light one of the charcoal briquettes had spread to every briquette inside that grill. Suddenly, we had a roaring fire.

As I stood there looking at what one single spark had produced, I thought about the students I get to see on the road. Each of you have within you a spark of the fire of God. When ignited, your spark will contact others and suddenly, your part of a major spiritual force for the use of God.

Maybe today, it's time for your life to be lit on fire for Jesus. As it is, your spark will ignite others and that, my friend, is where the power of agreement is a force to be reckoned with.

Remember, it only takes a spark to get a fire going.

Today's Word is Amos 3:3

"Can two walk together, unless they are agreed?"

MAY 7

DON'T QUIT

I see teenagers from all walks of life that share with me that they're ready to quit. Not just quit a sports activity or stop being part of a theatrical cast but ready to quit on life.

When I meet young people who feel like giving up, I encourage them to press in and endure until the breakthrough. It's when we press in that we come face-to-face with endurance.

What is endurance? Since the Bible says that we have need of it, might be a good idea to know what it is.

Endurance is the ability or strength to continue or last, especially despite fatigue, stress, or other adverse conditions.

If you find yourself in a fight to keep on keeping on for the Lord, ask Him to give you endurance; and when you receive it, make the choice to blow off quitting and choose instead to do the will of God.

Today's Word is Hebrews 10:36

"For you have need of endurance, so that after you have done the will of God, you may receive the promise:"

MAY 8

COMPROMISE

One of the messages I believe the Lord has commissioned me to share with students is that what we compromise to gain, we will eventually lose.

Here's what I mean -

If you find yourself having to compromise your moral values to stay in a dating relationship, you can be assured that what you compromise in that relationship you'll also lose in the relationship.

If you find yourself compromising your personal ethics (let's say, cheating on a test) to make the grade, you'll soon see that in that compromise, you'll lose when it comes to your base of knowledge of that subject in school.

If you find yourself compromising with God such as just playing church, you'll soon see what you'll be losing if you're talking the talk but not walking the walk.

Compromise is always the enemy's counterfeit to God's best.

Living a righteous life for God is a seed. Living a life of compromise is also a seed. Seeds produce after their own kind.

Want some advice from someone who's been there? Go ahead and do things God's way the first time, every time. With compromise out of your life, you'll be thankful for what the seed in your life is producing.

Today's Word is Genesis 1:11

"Then God said, "Let the earth bring forth grass, the herb that yields seed, and the fruit tree that yields fruit according to its kind, whose seed is in itself, on the earth"; and it was so."

MAY 9

SEEK FIRST

Seek first - those two words seem self-explanatory, don't they? They take on even greater importance when we realize that it was Jesus, the Head of the Church, who gave us this instruction.

Seek what first? The Kingdom of God and His righteousness. What in the name of everything that's good does that sentence even mean?

The kingdom of God is defined in the Bible as righteousness, peace, and joy in the Holy Spirit. Righteousness is God's way of doing and being right. Peace is God's aggressive weapon of warfare. And joy is the strength of His people.

So today, to seek first is to have the kingdom of God on the inside of you and to live your life accordingly.

Want the things that God has for you to come flowing into your life? Begin right now by seeking first His righteousness, peace, and joy.

Today's Word is Matthew 6:33

"But seek first the kingdom of God and His righteousness, and all these things shall be added to you."

MAY 10

RECORDERS & PROCESSORS

Some time ago someone said to me that ***teenagers are excellent recorders but not yet the greatest of processors***. When I heard that sentence, it really hit home.

Think about it. Teens are constantly capturing information, but have you ever stopped and wondered how much of this info is being processed? Beyond that, how much of this information that is ***going into the hearts and minds of young people is going in the way it was intended?***

Truth is truth, but truth minus grace can sound harsh.

You see, I can say the ***right*** thing in the ***wrong*** tone, and my message will be completely missed and/or misinterpreted. It comes back to an issue of our heart.

Today, whether you're recording information, processing it, or delivering it, might be a really good idea to consider the heart behind the message.

Today's Word is Proverbs 4:23

"Keep your heart with all diligence, for out of it spring the issues of life."

MAY 11

YOU WOULDN'T BE HERE

This is a very special time of the year. It's a time we get to celebrate our mom.

I remind students throughout the year, but especially during the Mother's Day season, that without their mom, they'd not be here. That revelation causes them to pause and think, and it's usually followed with them smiling.

I know that moms are important to the Lord because while hanging on the cross, close to taking His last breath, Jesus looked down and saw the pain and suffering his mom was enduring. He immediately then looked to John and said, "Behold your mother!"

Jesus made sure His mom was being cared for.

Whether it's your birth mom, your stepmom, or your spiritual mom, I'd encourage you to follow the example Jesus set: make sure your mom knows you love her.

After all, without mom, you wouldn't be here.

Today's Word is John 19:27

"Then He said to the disciple, "Behold your mother!" And from that hour that disciple took her to his own home."

MAY 12

REAL CHANGE

When you realize that you're in the wrong place or maybe you discover that there needs to be some real change in your life, what causes that change to occur? Is it peer pressure? Parental guidance? Spiritual influence? Guilt? Shame? Conviction? Condemnation?

I've learned from talking with so many teenagers after our events that more times than not, people don't necessarily change because they see the light. They change because they feel the heat.

Our feeling the pressure or heat of the moment will usually not be the lasting change God is looking for. Experiencing true change, the God-kind of change, comes from the heart.

When we realize that He wants us to change and that change is for our good, our heart is what we need to follow.

Want to have more than a momentary glimpse of what could be? Take time to listen to the guidance of the Holy Spirit as He leads you into and through real change - change that comes from being in the Word.

Today's Word is Deuteronomy 5:29

"Oh, that they had such a heart in them that they would fear Me and always keep all My commandments, that it might be well with them and with their children forever!"

MAY 13

AMAZING GRACE

Grace has been defined as God's unmerited favor. If you ask teenagers in just about any public or private high school what unmerited favor means, you'll get a number of answers.

My spiritual father shared a definition with me that he received from the Lord after years of praying about the word grace and its meaning: "Grace is My treating you as if sin had never occurred." Now that's something to shout about.

I meet many young people who tell me that they don't deserve the grace of God. Well, of course we don't deserve it. That's why it's a gift.

Until you and I have a true understanding of God's grace, it seems that when we need Him the most, our mind will lie to us and tell us that we deserve Him the least.

Grace isn't something we deserve or can earn. Grace is a gift. Why don't you take a minute and thank God for His amazing grace.

Today's Word is Ephesians 1:7

"In Him we have redemption through His blood, the forgiveness of sins, according to the riches of His grace."

MAY 14

UNCHANGEABLE

Some things in this life are unchangeable: there's 24 hours in a day; there's 7 days in a week; 12 months in a year; oil and water don't mix; and there's no right way to do the wrong thing - all are examples of unchangeable in life.

Want to get truly frustrated? Want to fail miserably? Try to change an unchangeable.

Here's an unchangeable that I'm often led to share with students: God loves you and no matter what you ever do, that'll never change. You see, God is love, and no matter how good we are or how seemingly bad, we can't do anything to make God love us anymore than He already does, and we can't do anything so bad to make Him love us any less.

He is love, and that my friend is unchangeable.

Today's Word is Malachi 3:6

"For I am the Lord, I do not change;"

MAY 15

THE HEART OF A FATHER

One of the greatest needs I see on the road as I listen to teenagers share their hearts with me is their need for a father in their lives. Many of these students have dads, but they don't necessarily have fathers. Is there a difference? Yes.

Remember that a dad may give you what you want but a father gives you what you need. I believe this is why God is known as our Father - He promised to meet all of our need.

If you're growing up in a home without a father or if your relationship with him is perhaps strained, believe God to show Himself to you as your Father. At the same time, love your earthly dad and talk with him about your hopes and dreams. Take time to pray for him; and as you do, watch your Heavenly Father influence your earthly father.

Don't be surprised how your heart turns to him, and your father's heart turns to you - prayer creates change.

Today's Word is Malachi 4:6

"And he will turn the hearts of the fathers to the children, and the hearts of the children to their fathers, ..."

MAY 16

ENCOURAGEMENT

Years ago, when I first began speaking in high schools, I invited my grandparents to go with me on one of my trips. Back then, it was just the Lord and me and my high-mileage Honda Accord.

I remember packing all our luggage in the car and off the three of us went to a series of high school assemblies in Hilton Head, South Carolina.

The assembly that my grandparents went with me to was being held at Hilton Head High School; and on that Friday morning there were about eight hundred students in the gymnasium where I was speaking.

Nothing out of the ordinary happened that day. I just followed my heart and said what I heard.

When it was over, Pean, my grandmother, pulled me aside and asked me to sit down. I did and she asked me a question: "Dean, do you know what you are?" She then answered her question for me: "You're an Encourager with a capital E."

Her words shot past my ears and went straight into my heart. What a compliment she had given me. And coming from Pean made it even more special.

Encouragement is a true gift from God. Maybe there's someone in your life right now who could use an encouraging word. Could be that the Holy Spirit is going to use you to brighten the day of someone else as my grandmother did for me.

If you look at the word encouragement, you'll see that there's a word inside it: courage. Today, my prayer for you is that you'll have the courage to be an encouragement to someone else.

Today's Word is Ezra 1:6

"And all those who were around them encouraged them with articles of silver and gold, with goods and livestock, and with precious things, besides all that was willingly offered."

MAY 17

THE ULTIMATE ROLE MODEL

Is there someone in your life that you admire, I mean that you really look up to and try to be like? That you pattern your life after? Is this person an athlete? Maybe an artist or actor? Could be that someone in your family is your role model?

What characteristics do you look for in a role model? Many teenagers have shared that what they look for, what they want to become someone who is wealthy, popular, and has influence on others. To me, there's nothing wrong with any of these characteristics if we have an established, biblically- based moral compass and a depth of relationship with the Ultimate Role Model.

To me, Jesus is our example. What He did on the earth is what we are to do while on the earth. He oftentimes drew away by Himself to pray and fellowship with His Father. While with His Father, Jesus received direction, timing, and revelation. His own analysis of His life on the earth was: "I only do what I see My Father doing and I only say what I hear My Father saying."

Patterning your life after Jesus makes life make sense.

Want a role model that will never let you down, that'll never leave you all alone, and Who will show you the true meaning of life? He's right there with you right now.

Today's Word is Ephesians 5:1

"Therefore be imitators of God as dear children."

MAY 18

HE KNOWS YOUR HEART

You know the old saying, you can fool some of the people all the time and all the people some of the time? That's probably close to being accurate but not so with God.

Your heart, my heart, everyone's heart, is what the Lord searches. He understands us better than we understand ourselves. When He's looking at what's in your heart, what's He seeing?

There's no reason to try and con God. He knows what's in our hearts and minds, and He knows what our intentions are.

Today, take God at His Word. Give Him your heart. Seek Him and you'll find Him.

Today's Word is 1 Chronicles 28:9

"As for you, my son Solomon, know the God of your father, and serve Him with a loyal heart and with a willing mind; for the Lord searches all hearts and understands all the intent of the thoughts. If you seek Him, He will be found by you; but if you forsake Him, He will cast you off forever."

MAY 19

CHECK YOUR LOVE WALK

For every violation of love there is a deposit of fear. The first time I heard that truth, I had to stop and meditate on what had just been said to me.

For every violation of love ... literally, every time I did something that violated the commandment of love, fear was deposited into my life. How's that possible?

Well, the Bible teaches us that perfected love casts out fear. So, love that's been perfected in your life and in mine literally casts out fear and the torment that comes with fear. That same fear, however, can creep back into our lives if we choose to walk away from the love walk, we're commanded to live.

Jesus gave us two primary commandments: Love God and love others. Today, if you're dealing with fear, you might want to check your love walk.

Today's Word is Matthew 22:37-39

"Jesus said to him, You shall love the Lord your God with all your heart, with all your soul, and with all your mind. This is the first and great commandment. And the second is like it: You shall love your neighbor as yourself."

MAY 20

HE'S THE WAY

Some years ago, I was in a meeting with a Christian Counselor, and he and I were talking about each of our relationships with the Lord. As I listened to him talk with such passion about Jesus, I began to feel like there was something missing in my life. (Ever felt that way yourself?)

The more he talked, the more intently I listened.

This Counselor then said something to me that has stayed with me all these years: "Jesus is the way to the Father." When I heard that sentence, I wanted to see it in the Bible and so I began to search.

My search took me over to the book of John where we see that Jesus declares about himself that He is the way, the truth, and the life. The more I looked at the beginning of that verse, the more clearly I saw what I believe the Lord was wanting me to see: Jesus (who is the Word) is the way to the Father.

When the Word became flesh, He did so for our benefit. One of those benefits is to show us the way to our Heavenly Father.

Want to be led right to the Father? Open your Bible and listen to the Word who became flesh for you and me.

Today's Word is John 1:14

"And the Word became flesh and dwelt among us, and we beheld His glory, the glory as of the only begotten of the Father, full of grace and truth."

MAY 21

TODAY, NOT TOMORROW

At some point during my time with students at a chapel or an assembly, I always ask them two questions:

1. What is potential?
2. Where is the most unused potential anywhere in the world?

The first answer is usually answered with, potential is the ability to become or do.

The second question is a bit tougher. (As of the writing of this book, only 94 people around the world have answered this question correctly and of these 94, 72 of these people have been in prison when they answered correctly.)

The answer to question # 2 is a cemetery. Think about it. Every book that was never written is perhaps today buried; every song that was never recorded is perhaps buried; every dream that was never realized and/or fulfilled is likewise perhaps buried.

The only time it's too late for you and me to fulfill our God-given potential is when we're no longer alive. Remember, the Bible tells us that tomorrow is not promised to anyone.

Don't put off until tomorrow that which you can do today.

Today's Word is Proverbs 3:28

"Do not say to your neighbor, 'Go, and come back, and tomorrow I will give it,' when you have it with you."

MAY 22

HE IS

One of the most important truths the Lord has given me to share with students is the value of each of us taking time to look and listen.

In fact, if you look at people from every country in the world, you'll see that irrespective of cultural differences, language barriers, and even varying spiritual beliefs, people are created the same the world over: two eyes, two ears and one mouth.

Point: When God created us, He did so with the purpose of each of us listening and looking twice as much as we talk.

Maybe you're wondering how we can hear from or see a God who lives in a place called Heaven when we live in a place called earth. I did, too, for a while but then one day I saw the answer.

The Bible tells us that if we want to receive anything from the Lord, we must first believe that He exists. If you'll take time to get into His Word, and once there, listen for His voice speaking to you through the pages of your Bible, you'll begin to hear His voice. If you'll take time to look at life through the eyes of the Spirit, you'll see evidence of a loving God all around you.

Want to see and hear from God? Begin by believing that He is.

Today's Word is Hebrews 11:6

"But without faith it is impossible to please Him, for he who comes to God must believe that He is, and that He is a rewarder of those who diligently seek Him."

MAY 23

WHERE ARE YOU WALKING?

On any given day, do you find yourself more in the Spirit or in the flesh? There is a difference.

Where this question is concerned, you might find it of interest to see what the Bible has to say and, what it doesn't say.

The Bible does not say that if you and I do not fulfill the lust of the flesh, then we will walk in the Spirit. It says that if you and I walk in the Spirit, we will not fulfill the lust of the flesh. Walking in the Spirit is the key.

What does it mean to walk in the Spirit? In plain talk, we walk in the Spirit as we live a life surrendered to the will of God. His will, not ours.

If you find yourself more in the flesh than in the Spirit, you can experience a course correction. Submit to God, hear His voice, and then obey what you hear.

Remember, God is a Spirit - purpose today to walk with Him.

Today's Word is Galatians 5:16

"I say then: Walk in the Spirit, and you shall not fulfill the lust of the flesh."

MAY 24

PURSUIT

Several years ago, I flew to South Australia where I was ministering in a number of high schools over the course of four days.

At one of those assemblies, a very successful Christian businessman was in attendance. After the event, this gentleman and I had a dinner meeting where I asked him question after question.

At one point during our time together, I asked him why he had agreed to spend so much time with me that day. His two-word response is one that I have never forgotten. He said, "You pursued."

He then went on to explain to me that pursuit proves desire.

What do you find yourself pursuing in your life? Is it a mentor, a relationship, money, things?

What are you desiring and how much pursuit are you giving to this desire?

It's no different with God. He loves being pursued.

Great thing about our pursuit of God - when we seek Him, we'll find Him.

Today's Word is Jeremiah 29:13

"And you will seek Me and find Me, when you search for Me with all your heart."

MAY 25

REVEALED SECRETS

Did you know that for thousands of years God has been revealing secrets to His children? That might sound a little bizarre, but it's the truth.

You might be going through something right now and you may have tried your very best to figure out what to do or maybe what to say, but there's just something missing. It might be a piece of news or information that you really need to make a scenario in life make sense.

Well, if you've tried it your way and you still don't have the answer, maybe it's time to go to God and ask Him to reveal to you what you need, when you need it.

God has a long history of showing up with the answer. Go ahead. Take a step of faith. Ask God to reveal the secret.

Today's Word is Daniel 2:28

"But there is a God in heaven who reveals secrets, and He has made known to King Nebuchadnezzar what will be in the latter days. Your dream, and the visions of your head upon your bed, were these:"

MAY 26

REJOICE

Want to hear a commandment from the Bible that, if you're not really growing in God, could be a challenge to obey?

The Bible tells us to rejoice in the Lord always. Now, think about what that really means. We are commanded to rejoice always, irrespective of what's going on in us or around us. Whether we're having a great day or a day when we wish we had just stayed in bed - no matter what, we're commanded to rejoice.

How's that possible? The short answer is choosing to do so by faith. You might be thinking, "That's impossible. You don't know what I'm going thru - there's no way I can rejoice in the Lord." Yes, you can. The Bible says to do it, and we wouldn't be instructed to do something if we weren't equipped by Him to do it.

Remember that faith, in its simplest form, is our believing and trusting the Word of God.

Want to freak the devil out and cause him to walk around confused? Rejoice in the Lord, always.

Today's Word is Philippians 4:4

"Rejoice in the Lord always. Again I will say, rejoice!"

MAY 27

NOT FOR IT, IN IT

There's a verse in the Bible that many young people have had a challenge to fully understand. In this verse, Christians are taught that it is the will of God for us to give thanks in everything.

The more I have looked at this scripture, the more one word in it has become the key to my better understanding of what the Lord is saying to us.

The word is "in". The Bible does not say, "for" everything give thanks; no, it says "in" everything, give thanks. See the difference?

Not everything that happens in our lives is from God. Therefore, if it's not from Him, I'm certainly not going to thank Him for it. We should, however, have a thankful heart in the process of whatever we're going through.

I know from very personal experience that a thankful heart will draw God into the equation.

Next time you find yourself in a less than desirable situation, give God thanks; not for it but thank Him for being with you in it.

Today's Word is 1 Thessalonians 5:18

"In everything give thanks; for this is the will of God in Christ Jesus for you."

MAY 28

COMFORT

The Holy Spirit is a real person. He's 1/3 of the Godhead. Lots of people have lots of ideas about who He is and where He is, but what does the Bible say?

The Word tells us that right now, God, the Father, is seated on His throne in Heaven. It also tells us that Jesus, the Son of God, is seated at the right hand of the Father, talking to Him about you and me. So, where's the Holy Spirit? Jesus tells us where He is.

If you remember, just before Jesus went to Heaven, He told His disciples that He was going where they could not yet go, but, after He went, He would send a "Comforter".

The Holy Spirit is in the earth today - He's in Believers, leading us to the will of the Father.

My relationship with the Holy Spirit is something I cherish. Every single day He leads me, directs me, and comforts me; He shows me where I missed the mark and always leads me back into fellowship with the Lord. He'll do the same for anyone who invites Him into their heart.

Remember, the Holy Spirit is a gentleman. He goes where He's invited.

Need some comfort today? Get to know the Holy Spirit - He is the Comforter.

Today's Word is John 16:7

"Nevertheless I tell you the truth. It is to your advantage that I go away; for if I do not go away, the Helper will not come to you; but if I depart, I will send Him to you."

MAY 29

A LANGUAGE ALL ITS OWN

I really enjoy aviation. There's something neat that happens when you are flying along above the clouds. To me I just feel closer to God.

Sometimes when we're flying, I put on a headset and listen as our pilot talks with the Air Traffic Controllers on the ground who are managing flights in the airspace that we're flying through.

A couple of days ago we were flying home, and I put on a headset. As I was listening, I heard the Lord speak up on the inside of me and this is what I heard: "Pay attention to what you're hearing - all of the pilots are speaking the same language."

And so, I listened and, sure enough, the pilots and the Air Traffic Controllers all were saying the same things - they were speaking the language of Aviators: "Climb to flight level ... Descend and maintain flight level ... Contact Atlanta Center on 121.7."

No matter the type or size of the aircraft, every pilot in the air knew and spoke the same language - knowing and speaking the language of aviation helps prevent disasters every single day.

It's no different with you and me. One of our primary responsibilities as a Christian is to know and speak the language of faith. To learn this language, we have the Instructor and the Book.

When you and someone with whom you are in agreement are speaking the same language, the language of faith, and you are doing so based on what the Word of God says, you can expect that agreement and faith talk to produce God's results in your life.

Today's Word is 1 Corinthians 1:10

"Now I plead with you, brethren, by the name of our Lord Jesus Christ, that you all speak the same thing, and that there be no divisions among you, but that you be perfectly joined together in the same mind and in the same judgment."

MAY 30

DON'T LOOK BACK

I meet many teenagers who come to me at the end of an event and want to talk about their past. They begin to rehearse what they've done wrong, then they usually want to talk about how they are worried about this or that.

I then typically ask them something along the lines of, "Are you still doing this?" And usually their answer is, "No". To which I respond, "So we're talking about something that's in the past?"

Once we've identified that what these students want to talk about is in the past and is no longer a part of their lives today, I give them a three-word piece of counsel: "Don't look back."

Have you ever really noticed that when you're in a car, there's a rear-view mirror and a couple of side-view mirrors, all of which are small by design? You also have a large piece of glass in front of you called a windshield. Those side view mirrors, and rearview mirrors are designed to let the driver catch a glimpse of what's behind them. The windshield, large and expansive however, is manufactured to give the driver a panoramic view of what's ahead.

It's no different in how you were created. God doesn't live in our past, so neither should we. Sure, it's fine to take a glance every-so-often in the rearview mirror of life, but of much more value, I believe, is our focusing on what's ahead.

Living in the past can be both dangerous and depressing. Keep your eyes fixed on God's vision ahead and watch as that vision become a reality.

Today's Word is Genesis 19:26

"But his wife looked back behind him, and she became a pillar of salt."

MAY 31

BEGINNING & END

What God begins, He finishes. He's not a part-time God. He's all in.

Whether it's you and I beginning a new attitude or maybe it's our beginning to forgive someone instead of figuring out a way to get even, He will direct us and show us how to complete it, if we let Him.

Ever wondered why you do things that are known as good works? What motivated you to be that kind person or what compelled you to write a note of encouragement? God is a good God; and when you've given His Spirit the leadership role in your life, guess what? Good works will become part of your spiritual DNA.

Trust God to finish what He begins. Remember, He's good, all the time.

Today's Word is Philippians 1:6

"being confident of this very thing, that He who has begun a good work in you will complete it until the day of Jesus Christ;"

JUNE 1

BUILD A WALL

Ever undertaken something so intense that by yourself it would have taken a terribly long, long time to complete? And then, somehow, someway, you finish this undertaking in a time so short that you were totally amazed? What happened?

The answer, in a word, is God.

What should have taken weeks maybe only took days. What should have taken days perhaps only took hours. God is the difference maker.

Thousands of years ago there was a guy named Nehemiah who was commissioned by the Lord to rebuild a wall. Back in Bible days, walls were a strategically big deal. When Nehemiah saw how bad of a condition the wall was in, he assembled workers, received Heaven's strategy, stood against the enemy, and trusted God. And in a supernatural short period of time (52 days), he fulfilled the mission, and the wall was rebuilt.

Next time you're facing a project or situation that looks almost insurmountable, remind yourself that God is no respecter of people. What He does for one, He can do for another.

God is still in the miracle-working business. If you need a miracle in your life, remind God that He helped Nehemiah build a wall, and He'll show up in your life as well.

Today's Word is Nehemiah 6:15-16

"So the wall was finished on the twenty- fifth day of Elul, in fifty- two days. And it happened, when all our enemies heard of it, and all the nations around us saw these things, that they were very disheartened in their own eyes; for they perceived that this work was done by our God."

JUNE 2

FROM HEARING TO KNOWING

There's a significant difference between hearing about something and experiencing something. That difference is what God oftentimes uses to help us grow and mature into the people He created and needs us to be for Him.

For example, it's one thing to hear about the thrill of bungee jumping. It's something entirely different, however, to experience free falling, tethered to a rope that leaves you hanging, suspended in air over a body of water. See the difference?

In your walk with the Lord, you can hear about all He does for others and hear about the love He has for you, or you can walk so closely with Him that it's your testimony others are hearing about.

When you and I go through a heavy situation, the process of being led by the Spirit of God through that situation can move us from hearing about God to seeing and knowing Him in a very personal, intimate way.

Today's Word is Job 42:5

"I have heard of You by the hearing of the ear, but now my eye sees You.

JUNE 3

YOUR TESTIMONY

Many times on the road I get to meet teenagers who say to me, "I've never really done anything too bad, so I don't really have a testimony to share with people."

When I meet a student who shares that sentence with me, I immediately begin talking with them about what a testimony really is. To me a testimony is you sharing part of your story with someone else. Who said your story must be full of pain and sorrow to help someone else? That's crazy.

Do you have any clue as to how many students are out there in this world who could benefit greatly from hearing a testimony that shows others that living a righteous life, which is enjoyable and not boring, is not only possible, but also attainable with God's help?

Now don't go beating yourself up if your testimony is one that says, "If you can imagine it, I tried it." Like me, take a minute and thank God for His mercy and grace.

Here's the point. Every single teenager today has a testimony. Good or bad, righteous or unrighteousness, here's the truth about each of our stories: the root word of testimony is test so, in many, many instances, before there's ever a testimony, there's first a test.

Today's Word is Luke 21:13

"But it will turn out for you as an occasion for testimony."

JUNE 4

RUN TO HIM, NOT FROM HIM

Want to know how much God knows you? He gives us an example of His intimate knowledge of you in His Word.

He knows so much about you that even the number of hairs on your head are numbered. Think about that - He knows the actual number of how many individual strands of hair are on billions of people around the world.

When I think about the fact that He knows each of us at such a deep and personal level, I then find myself wondering how well do I know Him?

Want to know your heavenly Father in a way that causes you to know that you know that you know He loves you with a love that can never be quenched. You might want to take some time today and hang out with Him.

Remember, since He knows how many strands of hair are on your head, He also knows all there is to know about you and what's going on in your life. Understanding this, I hope, will cause you to run to Him and not from Him.

Today's Word is Luke 12:7

"But the very hairs of your head are all numbered. Do not fear therefore; you are of more value than many sparrows."

JUNE 5

WHAT TO SAY, WHEN TO SAY IT

For decades now, there comes a point when I minister in a school that I notice the students have become terribly uncomfortable. Might surprise you what this moment is - silence.

Many, many times I'm led to stop talking and just stand in front of a room full of students. What's happening during that time? I've learned that in my silence, God is oftentimes speaking the loudest.

I don't ever want to come into a school and just talk. Everywhere we go, we go with the mission being, "Lord, use me today to say only what You want me to say and to do only what You want me to do."

Only the Spirit of God knows what each of us needs and when we need it. So, when speaking or ministering or recording or writing, I always ask the Holy Spirit to give me His words for that assignment. And you know what, He always does. My job is to listen, to hear, and to then obey.

Today, it's highly probable that God wants to use you to deliver a message to someone else. Want to know a secret I've learned to being used by Him more and more? Discipline yourself to hear from God and then let the Holy Spirit teach you what to say and when to say it.

He's talking. Are you listening?

Today's Word is Luke 12:12

"For the Holy Spirit will teach you in that very hour what you ought to say."

JUNE 6

KNOW WHAT THE WORD SAYS

Oftentimes I've heard people say, "Well, you know, the Lord gives and the Lord takes away." For a long time, when I heard that sentence, I'd get agitated. After a while I went to the Lord about it and as He always does, He directed me to the Word.

I was led over to the Book of Job; and as I read, I quickly learned that the Lord never said that it was He "who gives and takes away". You know who said that? Job said it.

We need to really know what the Word says, so that in turn we can live the life of faith that God intends us to live.

Next time someone says something to you, and they attribute what they're saying to Scripture; if you get agitated, don't get mad, get in the Word.

Find out for yourself what the Bible says, you'll be glad you did.

Today's Word is Job 1:21

"And he said: "Naked I came from my mother's womb, And naked shall I return there. The Lord gave, and the Lord has taken away; Blessed be the name of the Lord."

JUNE 7

THE HEDGE OF GOD

There's nothing quite like the hedge of protection that God promises and provides for His children - that's you and me.

When the enemy went to God and asked for permission to test Job, the devil quickly realized that the hedge around the life of Job was impenetrable. So, here's something for you to think about:

If Job couldn't bring the hedge down and God wouldn't bring that hedge down, but it did come down, who brought it down?

Job brought the hedge of protection down. How'd he do it? I believe that hedge came down for one reason and only one reason: FEAR.

You might remember what Job shared with his friends: "the very thing that I FEARED the most has come upon me."

Remember, fear activates the devil the same as faith activates God.

If you're a Believer, God has a hedge of protection around you; don't let fear bring that hedge down.

Today's Word is Job 1:10

"Have You not made a hedge around him, around his household, and around all that he has on every side? You have blessed the work of his hands, and his possessions have increased in the land."

JUNE 8

JESUS HASN'T MOVED

I meet many teenagers who share with me how they once were really tracking with God; but somewhere along the way, something happened that caused them to seemingly lose their passion to live for God. Maybe you, too, can relate.

Most of the time, not all the time, but a lot of the time, the loss of passion to live for God can be traced back to a person no longer doing what once was bringing them spiritual success.

Let's say that you used to wake up every morning and read your Bible and pray; and then one day, you didn't. That one day turned into one week and then you woke up one morning and realized you hadn't invested any time to speak of with the Lord in four months.

Maybe you feel dry and crusty on the inside. What happened? You stopped doing what had brought you into a deep, close relationship with Jesus.

Now, here's the good news. Jesus hasn't moved. He's still right there, right now, with you and extending an invitation for you and me to pick up where we left off.

Simply put: finish what you start.

Today's Word is Galatians 3:3

"Are you so foolish? Having begun in the Spirit, are you now being made perfect by the flesh?"

JUNE 9

WHOM ARE YOU TRUSTING?

If you and I put our trust in people to provide for us and allow our confidence to be in our ability to make something happen versus trusting God and His Word to supply what we need, the Bible tells us that we will not even see good when it comes our way.

I often share with teenagers that God will share His glory with no person. God is a jealous God, and He loves to be the One who blesses each of us. Part of you and I receiving His blessing, however, is our keeping our eyes on Him and off flesh.

Want to see big, spectacular things take place in your life? Trust God, don't rely on people, and stay on the Word.

Today's Word is Jeremiah 17:5-6

"Thus says the Lord: "Cursed is the man who trusts in man and makes flesh his strength, whose heart departs from the Lord. For he shall be like a shrub in the desert, and shall not see when good comes, but shall inhabit the parched places in the wilderness, in a salt land which is not inhabited."

JUNE 10

KNOW HIM ~ KNOW YOURSELF

Have you ever read the encounter that Jesus had with Peter when He asked Peter, "Who do you say that I am?"

Right before Jesus asked him that question, the disciples had told Him who the people thought He might be. Immediately, however, Jesus turned to Peter and asked him a question that, in and of itself, might have been a strange question to ask someone who traveled with you and with whom you lived.

Peter responded to the question of Jesus by telling Him that He was the Christ (the anointed One), the Son of the living God. Right after Peter told Jesus who He was, the very next words out of the mouth of the Lord were His telling Peter who he was.

What's the point? Once you know who He is, you can then discover who you are. Once you know who you are in Him, you then will be led to discover the revelation He has for you and your life.

Know Him and get to know yourself.

Today's Word is Matthew 16:15-18

"He said to them, "But who do you say that I am?" Simon Peter answered and said, "You are the Christ, the Son of the living God." Jesus answered and said to him, "Blessed are you, Simon Bar- Jonah, for flesh and blood has not revealed this to you, but My Father who is in heaven. And I also say to you that you are Peter, and on this rock I will build My church, and the gates of Hades shall not prevail against it."

JUNE 11

I'M NOT ASHAMED

For years I encountered teenagers in schools who seemed to be ashamed of their faith, their relationship with God. Then, several years ago, something happened. I began to meet students who were taking bold stands of faith, completely unashamed of Whose they are and the Word that they believed and shared.

What's the difference? Shame could not take up residence in the heart of a teen that was full of the love and Word of God.

The devil is known for being the agent of shame. But that's not who God is. No matter what you or I have done, God has never been, nor will He ever be ashamed of us. Remember, He's love.

You may find yourself feeling ashamed or possibly embarrassed when your friends discover your walk with God. Can I share something with you? If you're a Believer, that sinking, embarrassing feeling doesn't have the right to stay in your heart and life.

Today, I'd encourage you to blow off any feelings of being ashamed and instead, take time to discover the power that is the gospel.

Today's Word is Romans 1:16

"For I am not ashamed of the gospel of Christ, for it is the power of God to salvation for everyone who believes, for the Jew first and also for the Greek."

JUNE 12

TRUST HIM

I really think one of the toughest aspects teenagers face in day- to-day life is their ability and willingness to trust: to trust parents, to trust other teenagers, but maybe most of all, to trust God.

I've had many conversations with young people who've asked me, "How can I trust a Heavenly Father I've never seen when my earthly father is not someone I trust at all?"

That's a fair question. My answer may sound way too simplistic, but it's the truth:

Don't judge a perfect God by an imperfect person.

If there was only one thing I knew about God, it would be that He is worthy to be trusted. He only has good in mind for you and me.

Can I offer you a suggestion? Let your guard down and allow God and His Word entrance into your heart.

Trust me, you can trust HIM.

Today's Word is Job 13:15

"Though He slay me, yet will I trust Him. Even so, I will defend my own ways before Him."

JUNE 13

CAUSE

Thousands of years ago there was a teenager who was responsible for taking care of some family sheep while his brothers were off in a battle with a Giant named Goliath. You probably know that the name of that teenage shepherd boy was David.

If you take the time to study the life of David, you'll probably see multiple aspects of his testimony that caused him to become the man he ultimately was. Sure, he had moral failure. He was responsible for a murder and lost a child because of it. But you know what? He's the only guy in the Bible that is referenced as having a heart after God.

How do we, during life and all that comprise our lives, live in a way that the Lord says about us that we have also displayed in our day-to-day living a heart after God?

I believe that one of the secrets that David learned early on is the principle of living life on purpose, with a cause.

Today, it might prove to be beneficial for your long-term effectiveness as a Christian for you to seek after, identify, and then pursue with dogged diligence the cause God has assigned for your life.

Today's Word is 1 Samuel 17:29

"And David said, "What have I done now? Is there not a cause?"

JUNE 14

TALK TO IT

Have you ever found yourself in a situation that you can't seem to do anything about it except talk? Maybe for hours or even days, you talk and talk and talk about the situation: how it happened, why it happened, what's going to happen.

If you've done that, you probably have also realized that nothing too terribly positive has come from your talking about the situation. In fact, if you look closely, the situation might have even become more serious. Why is that?

Our words are creative forces. Talking about a situation will not necessarily change that situation. If, however, we stop talking about something and choose instead to believe God for His Word pertaining to that situation and begin to start speaking the Word to it, that situation will have no choice but to line up with what the Word of God says.

If you find yourself in a negative situation today, might be helpful to get out your Bible, talk with the Lord, stop talking about it, and choose instead to talk to it.

As you do and you do so in faith, watch what happens.

Today's Word is Mark 11:23

"For assuredly, I say to you, whoever says to this mountain, 'Be removed and be cast into the sea,' and does not doubt in his heart, but believes that those things he says will be done, he will have whatever he says."

JUNE 15

DADS

Teenagers often share with me that they wish their dads were more involved with their lives. To which I usually ask them, "How much of your life do you invite your dad to be involved in? That question oftentimes stings the air.

It's at that point that we talk about how they see the role of their dad in their lives. And today, that's a question I'd like for you to consider in your own life: what's the role of your dad?

Is he your spiritual hero? Do you look to him solely as your bank? How about your car dealer? Is he your cheerleader, or is he your motivation?

You see, how you look to your earthly father will play a large role in how you look to your Heavenly Father. And conversely, in many, many instances, how you receive from your earthly dad will have a direct effect on your initial ability to receive from God.

As a dad, there are certainly times I have failed our kids. But you know what? I've learned to be quick to share with Will, Ellie and Meg that even though I missed the mark as their dad, God, their Heavenly Father, never, ever misses the mark.

During this time of the year today might be a good day to let your dad know, whether he's your birth dad, stepdad or spiritual dad, just how thankful you are to call him your dad.

Consider this, if you're a wise child, your dad is delighting in you.

Today's Word is Proverbs 23:24

"The father of the righteous will greatly rejoice, and he who begets a wise child will delight in him."

JUNE 16

THE RIDE OF A LIFETIME

When I first realized I was called into full-time ministry, it really freaked me out. I wasn't at all sure what I was going to do in ministry, much less how was I ever going to be able to get married and support a family working for a God that no one had ever seen.

But you know what happened? The more I yielded my will to fit into His will for my life, I began to see Him open doors and become my total supply.

I went from "Why me?" to "Send me." When I did, the entirety of my life changed.

Maybe today you, too, know what it's like to be wrestling with answering a call and launching out into something known as Christian ministry. If so, may I give you some advice that might save you years of frustration? Go ahead and say "Yes" to God and His calling. Trust Him to open and shut doors. He will.

If you're called and are wrestling with saying yes to that call, the sooner you move from why me to send me, the sooner His joy will take up residence in your heart.

Since the day I asked Him to send me, I haven't stopped going. It's truly the ride of a lifetime.

Today's Word is Isaiah 6:8

"Also I heard the voice of the Lord, saying: "Whom shall I send, and who will go for Us?" Then I said, "Here am I! Send me."

JUNE 17

MEDICINE

When you invest your life into meeting and speaking with teenagers, guess what happens? You typically meet and speak with teenagers. That's the day- to-day function of our ministry - my traveling to schools, meeting teenagers, and then talking with them about their lives and the value of them including the Word of God in everyday life.

As I've been speaking with teens now for literally decades, I've met and continue to meet teenagers who have heavy hearts - young people who have gone thru some terribly challenging times; and as they've come thru those seasons in their lives, they seem to really need surgery on the spiritual side of their heart.

I don't mean an actual surgery. What I'm referencing is the medicine and healing that the Word of God brings when taken on a regular basis.

Perhaps today you know all too well the pain of past hurt. Maybe you find yourself weighted down with depression or oppression. If so, I've got a prescription for you to take at least once per day.

The Bible tells us that you having a merry heart does you good. The word merry means causing joy and happiness. So, your prescription today that will go to work on the inside to heal what is hurting and causing you pain is: read your Bible, speak the Word, and actually believe what you're reading and speaking is working on your behalf today.

Today's Word is Proverbs 17:22

"A merry heart does good, like medicine, but a broken spirit dries the bones."

JUNE 18

I WANT IT MY WAY

Have you ever been in a mall or maybe a grocery store and found that you're at the right place at the right time to see a child have a meltdown when he or she did not get their way? If the child is used to getting their way, what you might see is that child throwing an absolute fit until one of two things happens: 1) the child wins and gets what they want or 2) the parent wins and the child conforms to the boundary being established by the parent.

It's no different with some teenage Christians that I've met. Sometimes teenagers want their way so badly that they throw a fit, thinking that their fit is going to change the will of God.

In the Bible there's a guy named Naaman, who was used to getting what he wanted, when he wanted it. He had a deadly disease called leprosy and when the Prophet of God told him God's plan for his healing, Naaman became very angry - all because he had a certain way he thought God should and would heal him.

You know, God has a way of accomplishing His will in and through our lives. Our responsibility is to submit to His will, knowing that He really does know what we need, when we need it.

Next time you're tempted to throw a fit, you might be better off to put down your will and let the Lord know that you don't have to have your way. When this happens, you're growing up spiritually.

Today's Word is 2 Kings 5:10-11

"And Elisha sent a messenger to him, saying, "Go and wash in the Jordan seven times, and your flesh shall be restored to you, and you shall be clean." But Naaman became furious, and went away and said, "Indeed, I said to myself, 'He will surely come out to me, and stand and call on the name of the Lord his God, and wave his hand over the place, and heal the leprosy."

JUNE 19

THE WAY OUT

I encounter many teenagers who share with me after one of our events that they live life from one temptation to another. For some, its drugs, for others its sex; thousands have told me that they're tempted with suicidal thoughts, and many are tempted to cheat in school, but one of the largest temptations that teenagers take time to tell me they're dealing with is the temptation of pornography.

Temptation never ever comes from God. A loving God will never tempt you with evil desires - it's just not who He is. So, it's simple to understand where temptation comes from: the devil.

Anything God created for you and me to enjoy, the devil has tried to twist and pervert into something dirty and shameful. Maybe today you know all too well what dirty and shame feel like. If so, I've got more good news for you.

God has a way of leading us out of and away from the temptations that the enemy points in our direction. Our job is to be tuned into the frequency of Heaven, hear from God, and then obey what He leads us to say and do.

Fighting temptations on your own? Probably not working out too well. You might want to turn to God and ask Him to honor His Word in your life. If you'll follow His leading, He'll show you the way out.

Today's Word is 2 Peter 2:9

"then the Lord knows how to deliver the godly out of temptations and to reserve the unjust under punishment for the day of judgment,"

JUNE 20

IT'S NOT YOUR BODY

One day not too long ago I was having a conversation with my spiritual father, and our talk turned to the subject of my health. We discussed my eating habits on the road and my lack of routine daily exercise.

What had begun as a casual conversation quickly morphed into an intense moment of my being taught a very important lesson that I'm going to share with you right now.

Your body is not your own. It was bought with a significant price - the very blood of Jesus.

We actually have the responsibility of stewarding (taking care of and responsibility for) what we put into our bodies, how we exercise our bodies, and even how much rest we give our bodies.

Take it from someone who's already been through this process: choose to not defile your body by feeding it junk, refusing to exercise, and blowing off getting rest. Choose, instead, to honor what the Word of God says about your body - if you do, you'll start seeing the results of your obedience almost immediately.

Here's a lesson I've learned: If I take care of my body, my body will take care of me.

Today's Word is Daniel 1:8

"But Daniel purposed in his heart that he would not defile himself with the portion of the king's delicacies, nor with the wine which he drank; therefore he requested of the chief of the eunuchs that he might not defile himself."

JUNE 21

COVERED FROM HEAD TO TOE

Did you know that God has supplied you with an armor that will protect you from every assignment the devil ever launches in your direction?

This armor literally covers you from head to toe, but it's your responsibility to put it on ... everyday.

Because the devil knows his time is short, he's trying his best to take out a generation of teenagers, but you know what? If you put on the whole armor of God and take the time to listen to what God's Spirit has to say to you and then obey what you've heard, the devil will not succeed in taking you out. He can't - the Word is way more powerful than anything in the arsenal of the devil.

So today, it might be a really good idea for you to re-acquaint yourself with your weapons of warfare. Remember, we're in a battle, but we're on the winning side.

Next time you sense an assignment from the devil trying to creep into your life, don't freak out. Just make sure you've got all your armor on.

Today's Word is Ephesians 6:11

"Put on the whole armor of God, that you may be able to stand against the wiles of the devil."

JUNE 22

EMBRACE WISDOM

Did you know that if you live your life with wisdom being your guide, people will be drawn to not only what you have but also to what you know.

According to the Bible, wisdom is visible.

Thousands of years ago there was a Queen who had heard about a King named Solomon. What she had heard so intrigued her that she traveled a great distance just to see what people were talking about.

When the Queen of Sheba saw with her own eyes what the Spirit of wisdom had produced in the life of Solomon, she became so overwhelmed that the Bible says, "there was no more spirit in her."

It takes a lot to impress royalty. What must this Queen have seen to take her breath away? I believe she saw the blessing of the Lord in operation in the life and lifestyle of King Solomon.

Today, God is still the same for you and me. If we ask for wisdom, He'll give it to us.

Want to make the world stand still and take notice of what the Lord is doing through you and for you? Embrace wisdom and watch God be God.

Today's Word is 1 Kings 10:4-5

"And when the queen of Sheba had seen all the wisdom of Solomon, the house that he had built, the food on his table, the seating of his servants, the service of his waiters and their apparel, his cupbearers, and his entryway by which he went up to the house of the Lord, there was no more spirit in her."

JUNE 23

WHY WORSHIP

Worship to me is our outward expression to God of what's happening on the inside of our heart - for who He is and for what He's done and is doing in our lives.

Worship isn't something we just do; true worship is part of who we are.

Throughout the Bible we see examples of the power of worship. When we worship God, we're choosing to put our focus on the solution, not the challenge. We're choosing to change the atmosphere from maybe one of oppression to one of the peace that passes understanding.

Maybe today you're going through something heavy. If so, I'd encourage you to search for some worship music that ministers to your heart as you listen to it. Turn up the volume and stay in the presence of the living God.

As you worship the Lord, whatever you're going through will begin to diminish, and the presence of God will be on the increase.

Remember, worship isn't just something we do; worship is who we become.

Today's Word is 1 Chronicles 16:29

"Give to the Lord the glory due His name; bring an offering, and come before Him. Oh, worship the Lord in the beauty of holiness!"

JUNE 24

THE SHIELD

Do you ever feel like you just need a shield from all the junk the devil is throwing in your direction? Sometimes it might feel like he's ganging up on you and in those times it's difficult to tell up from down - sound familiar?

Is there a way out of the junk? Is there a way to be rid of the constant barrage of attacks from the enemy? Short answer is yes.

Throughout these daily devotions I hope you're seeing that the Word is the key. It's the key to joy, to peace, to provision, and yes, the Word coming out of your mouth in faith is also the key to your protection from the attacks of the enemy.

God's Word is proven. You and I can count on the integrity of the Word of God. It will do what it says it will do. Our job is to trust it, to confess it, and to walk in love.

Not only is the Word of God proven, it's also a shield to anyone and everyone who trusts in Him.

So, want to be protected from the attacks of the enemy? Get behind the shield of the Word and trust God. He's got you covered.

Today's Word is 2 Samuel 22:31

"As for God, His way is perfect; the word of the Lord is proven; He is a shield to all who trust in Him."

JUNE 25

WORDS TO SHARE

One of the neatest stories I've discovered in the Bible is the story of Samuel when he was a young person living in the temple and working for the Priest.

Samuel was literally growing up in church; and as he was, he saw a lot - some good, some not so good. Maybe you can relate.

As Samuel grew, the Bible tells us that the Lord was with him. The Lord would give Samuel words to share with the people and you know what? Every word from the Lord that Samuel shared came true. You know why? Because he only said what he heard from the Lord. He didn't add to it, and he didn't take away from it.

There's really no difference today. If you want your words to carry power and want to be used by the Lord in the lives of others, stay close to Him. Hear His voice; and when He's given you something to say, say exactly what you hear.

When you do, your words, like Samuels, will not fall to the ground.

Today's Word is 1 Samuel 3:19

"So Samuel grew, and the Lord was with him and let none of his words fall to the ground."

JUNE 26

GET BUSY

Did you know that Jesus has commissioned you to do a work for Him?

Me? Work for Jesus? No way.

Yes way.

He's got something for you to do, and you know what? You're the only one who can do it in the specific way He's called you to do it. Now, to me, that's pretty cool.

When Jesus was alive on the earth, He went into the world with His message of hope. Shortly before He left planet earth and went back to Heaven, He was talking with His Father and said, "You sent me into the world, I also have sent them into the world."

Jesus sent His disciples into the world. Guess what? Today, if you're a Believer, you're as called as those original disciples were called.

So, what now? Make yourself available to be a witness to those who are still in the world. Live the life He's called you to live, obey His promptings, and then let the Lord of Heaven step in and snatch people out of the world and position them in His Kingdom.

You've got a job to do. Get busy.

Today's Word is John 17:18

"As You sent Me into the world, I also have sent them into the world."

JUNE 27

WHAT'LL YOU BE DOING?

I meet a lot of teenagers who seem to be great young people, but I've found that many of them either aren't taking Jesus very seriously or they think they have the rest of their lives to live for God. And so, for this season known as the teenage years, they've chosen to live according to their will and desire versus His.

If I've just described you, you might want to pay close attention to what's said next.

There was a day when a group of people watched as Jesus, by the power of God on and in His life, suddenly ascended from the earth into the heavenly realm. The Bible teaches us that there's coming a day when this same Jesus is going to descend from the heavenly realm and come back to earth to get His children.

Now here's the part I don't want you to miss: Only God and no one else, not even Jesus Himself, knows the date and time of His return.

Could be today; perhaps tomorrow, or maybe a hundred years from now. We just don't know. What we do know, however, is that you and I are one day closer to our end of time. And so, that being said, my suggestion to you is that you choose to live each day with eternity in your heart and mind. As you do, some of your choices might begin to look different.

Don't live in fear; live instead with expectancy. He's coming back - on this you can be assured, and it will be suddenly.

Question is, when He does come back, what will He find you doing?

Today's Word is Acts 1:11

"who also said, "Men of Galilee, why do you stand gazing up into heaven? This same Jesus, who was taken up from you into heaven, will so come in like manner as you saw Him go into heaven."

JUNE 28

DON'T CLOSE THE BOOK

Living for God really takes on a different dimension when you begin to receive revelation straight from the heart of God.

A lot of teenagers wrongly believe that God no longer speaks; and even if He did, He wouldn't talk with them. That's simply not true. He most certainly still speaks, and He'll speak to you, too.

It's our responsibility, though, to have ears that hear.

What do you think God wants to talk with you about? I can assure you that whatever He says to you, He says it from His Word.

You see, I don't believe that there's going to be any new inspiration - His Word is a completed body of work. I do believe, however, that there's an unlimited supply of new revelation.

What is revelation? It's the Holy Spirit talking to you and showing you something that you've never seen.

Want to really get tracking with the Lord? Believe Him to open the pages of His Word to you in a way that causes you to experience revelation after revelation. As this happens, you will not want to close the Book.

Today's Word is Galatians 1:12

"For I neither received it from man, nor was I taught it, but it came through the revelation of Jesus Christ."

JUNE 29

THE TRAP OF PRIDE

Don't fall into the trap that I've seen so many teenagers fall into. It's the trap of pride.

Maybe you're a great looking teenager and being at the top of the popularity chain is your life. Could be that you're an athlete among athletes. Maybe you're a musician who's light years ahead of your peers. Or perhaps your intellect has you in college prep classes, putting you on the fast track into higher education.

Whatever it is that might seemingly set you apart from others, do yourself a tremendous favor at a comparatively young age - do not let the pride of your heart deceive you.

Today, it might be a good idea to take a minute and examine your heart. Are you thankful, grateful, and appreciative for the life God allows you to live? Or has your heart hardened? Don't ever assume that pride won't try to sink its teeth into you.

You know what I learned about pride and seeing God take it out of my life? Choosing to have a humble spirit, a thankful heart to the Lord, and a genuine desire to not be noticed caused pride to be taken away.

If you've got pride and you want it out of your life, begin the process by talking to Jesus. He's right there, right now, listening to what you have to say.

Today's Word is Obadiah 1:3-4

"The pride of your heart has deceived you, you who dwell in the clefts of the rock, whose habitation is high; you who say in your heart, 'Who will bring me down to the ground? ' though you ascend as high as the eagle, and though you set your nest among the stars, from there I will bring you down," says the Lord."

JUNE 30

NO MORE STUMBLING

Maybe you're one of those teenagers whom I've met along the way who have told me, "No matter how much I try, I just can't seem to stay out of trouble." If so, let's look at how you cannot only stay out of trouble, but also, no longer even desire the things that have historically landed you in hot water.

There's a way to not stumble. It's not a way; it's a Person. The Bible tells us that there is One who is able to keep you from stumbling. Now that's good news for sure!

This One is described as wise and is One who has glory, majesty, dominion, and power that lasts forever and ever.

You already know. I'm talking about Jesus.

So, want to stop stumbling into sin and one bad choice after another? Want your sin-based desires to change into desires that please God?

Ask Jesus to keep you from stumbling, and then ask Him to change your desires.

He's ready; are you?

Today's Word is Jude 1:24-25

"Now to Him who is able to keep you from stumbling, and to present you faultless before the presence of His glory with exceeding joy, to God our Savior, Who alone is wise, be glory and majesty, dominion and power, both now and forever. Amen."

JULY 1

RAISE YOUR ROD

Imagine you've been selected by God to lead six million people out of bondage and take them into a land of their very own.

As you are leading these people, they begin to murmur and talk under their breath - and they're talking about YOU. They are complaining, they're tired, frustrated, and now they're even saying they were better off as prisoners than they are now, even as they're heading to their promised land.

Now, to make matters even more interesting, you've led these six million people up to a sea, and the entire army of the enemy is chasing you and closing in. What do you do?

Well, this isn't just a story; it really happened. Thousands of years ago a Leader names Moses found himself exactly in the position I've just described for you.

You know what Moses did? He heard the instruction of God and no matter how seemingly silly it might have sounded, Moses obeyed.

The instruction? Raise your rod.

When Moses raised his rod, the Lord caused the sea to go back. What happened next was a miracle. Six million people followed Moses across that sea on dry ground. As soon as the enemy soldiers tried to do so, the sea wall collapsed and not one enemy soldier survived.

If today you find yourself being chased by the enemy, I'd suggest that you might want to get alone with God and quiet the noise. Ask Him what to do.

Once you've heard what to do, do it. Remember, He's already done His part.

Today's Word is Exodus 14:21

"Then Moses stretched out his hand over the sea; and the Lord caused the sea to go back by a strong east wind all that night, and made the sea into dry land, and the waters were divided."

JULY 2

WHAT MAKES YOU CRY

There's an old, old saying that says, Real men don't cry.

I hope you don't believe that crying is a sign of weakness. Much to the contrary, there have been so many times in my life that when I let myself cry, I became stronger.

In the book of Nehemiah, we see where Nehemiah had asked about some people who had survived captivity - he had a genuine interest in their well-being. What he heard from those who were bringing him the news caused Nehemiah to weep. He cried.

But you know what? His tears of sorrow ignited something within him and, as such, part of his calling was then revealed. What brought him tears would eventually bring him into his assignment.

Maybe today you should consider spending some time all by yourself. Think about the world and all that's going on. If, as you're thinking, something comes across the canvass of your heart that maybe sparks a tear or two to flow down your cheek, please pay attention. You might have just cried your way into a portion of your calling.

Today's Word is Nehemiah 1:4

"So it was, when I heard these words that I sat down and wept, and mourned for many days; I was fasting and praying before the God of heaven."

JULY 3

CHRIST IN YOU

To me, one of the neatest mysteries ever revealed to a born-again Believer is the mystery of Christ in you, the Hope of glory.

Ever heard that verse? Ever considered what it means?

Well, to begin with, Christ is not the last name of Jesus. Translated, Christ is the anointed One and His anointing. Well, what's the anointing? The anointing is the yoke-destroying, burden-removing power of God. Well, what does that mean?

In simple terms, the anointing is the power of God that comes through Jesus.

Think about that for a minute. Where does the Bible reveal the anointing is? If you're a Believer, the anointing is inside you. I believe the anointing causes us to have hope.

So today, consider that as a Believer, you have residing within you at this very moment the yoke-destroying, burden-removing power of God.

My Lord, with that kind of power at your disposal for good, can you now understand more completely why the Bible teaches us that nothing is impossible to those who believe.

Believe me - the anointing is the difference.

Today's Word is Colossians 1:27

"To them God willed to make known what are the riches of the glory of this mystery among the Gentiles: which is Christ in you, the hope of glory."

JULY 4

FREEDOM ISN'T FREE

All over America today teenagers are joining with family and friends, celebrating America's independence and freedom.

Whether you're at picnics or parades, lake parties or the beach, whether you're eating barbecue or hamburgers; all across this nation, there's a celebration.

But I'm often led to ask students if they really understand what the celebration of July 4th is all about. Sure, we're celebrating our independence, but I also encourage young people to simultaneously celebrate our dependence on God and on His Word.

America is a nation birthed out of a desire to freely worship God. My prayer for this generation on this day is that we never, ever forget why America was born and the price paid for our freedom.

During all of the celebrating today, might be a really good idea to take a minute and thank God for freedom. Then, I'd make it a point to identify a Veteran and thank him or her for the price they have paid for our freedom.

After all, freedom isn't free.

Today's Word is John 8:36

"Therefore if the Son makes you free, you shall be free indeed."

JULY 5

AN EVIL HEART OF UNBELIEF

What's the enemy of faith? Unbelief.

Did you know that in the book of Hebrews, we are warned not to have an unbelieving heart? We are. It's right there in black and white.

In fact, the writer of Hebrews goes a step further and says, "lest there be in any of you an evil heart of belief ..."

Now to me that verse just got serious on an altogether different level of serious.

There's no evil in God; evil is an attribute of the devil. There's no unbelief in God; unbelief is also of the devil. God is all about love and faith.

If you were to take a moment and give yourself a heart check, would you find faith or unbelief growing in the soil of your heart?

If you like what you see, that's great. If, however, you don't like what you see when you look at what's growing in your heart, then now's a terrific time to do something about it.

Beware of an evil heart of unbelief. Choose instead, a heart of faith and as your faith grows, watch unbelief disappear from your heart.

Today's Word is Hebrews 3:12

"Beware, brethren, lest there be in any of you an evil heart of unbelief in departing from the living God;"

JULY 6

FINISH THE RACE

Ever heard the statement, life is a marathon, not a sprint? It's true. As a teenager, how do you approach your life? Do you approach day-to-day life with an attitude of a marathon or that of a sprint? There is a difference.

If you're a runner, you might have trained for a marathon; and if so, I'd imagine that training for a marathon is totally different than training to run a sprint.

Both types of races require discipline, exercise, and nutrition; but one of these races is over very quickly while the other is more of a long-term undertaking.

In life, sure we have seasons that are more like a sprint, but more times than not, our life is a mirror-image of a marathon.

Sometimes it might seem like all we're doing is fighting the good fight of faith and then there are times when we find ourselves in a season of rest. And still there are other times when life might make little if any sense at all. Point is, we just keep going.

Whether it's a sprint or a marathon, finishing your race is what God is watching.

Fight the good fight, finish your race, and keep the faith.

Today's Word is 2 Timothy 4:7

"I have fought the good fight, I have finished the race, I have kept the faith."

JULY 7

THE LORD OF GRACE

The Bible teaches us that if we will confess our sins to God, He's faithful and just to not only forgive us from where we missed it, but He also cleanses us from all the unrighteousness that comes along with sin.

When it comes to getting free from sin, I share with teenagers that it sure seems to me that we have the easy part of that process. We come to God and confess to Him something He already knows we've done or not done - in other words, our missing the mark is not a surprise to Him.

As we acknowledge our sin, He does the forgiving and the cleansing. That's a pretty cool deal.

Today, if you see that you have sin in your life, it does no good whatsoever to try and hide from God. Remember, He already knows all that's going on.

Don't be afraid. Trust Him. Take Him at His Word - genuinely confess your sin and watch the Lord of grace go to work on cleaning out the junk in your heart.

Today's Word is 1 John 1:9

"If we confess our sins, He is faithful and just to forgive us our sins and to cleanse us from all unrighteousness."

JULY 8

FITTING IN

I see a lot of teenagers in public and Christian schools who are seemingly doing their best to imitate the evil that's in the world. Whether it's in dress, in music, or in web browsing, sometimes it's difficult to differentiate between Christian teens and young people who wouldn't necessarily know God from Adam. Why is this?

As I've shared with you in these devotionals, usually after our events, I get to talk with students; and as I do, they share some of their stories with me. It's in these moments of listening to teens that I'm again and again reminded of why so many young people are imitating the world...

They want to fit in and belong.

Want to belong to something that'll fit you for the rest of this life and the life to come? Want to know and experience what it's really like to be a part? If you do, I've got a suggestion for you to consider:

Hang out with people who love God. I didn't say who love religion. I said who love God. The teenagers in my life who are having the most fun and who are really enjoying this season of their lives are those teens who have a core group of Christian friends. They are all living for God and helping each other pass on imitating evil.

We all miss it. But when we do, it's sure encouraging to know that God still loves us, our true friends are still with us, and we can start fresh, all over again.

Today's Word is 3 John 1:11

"Beloved, do not imitate what is evil, but what is good. He who does good is of God, but he who does evil has not seen God."

JULY 9

THE NOW SOCIETY

Are you a patient person or do you want what you want when you want it? If we're honest, at some point in all our lives, patience probably wasn't what we were best known for.

Human nature is to get all you can, can all you get, and then sit on the can. That, however, is not the character of God.

For the most part, today's teens have grown up in a "now" society. Drive-thru restaurants, ATMs, microwave ovens, instant gratification versus delayed gratification - sound vaguely familiar? It's our society.

But in the Word of God, He clearly shows us that there is another way. He puts it like this: precept upon precept, line upon line, here a little, there a little. What's that mean?

To me, He's saying to pace yourself and learn as you go; enjoy the moments of life and recognize beauty along the journey.

Sure, we could be pedal-to-the-metal 24/7, but we sure would miss a lot that I'm quite sure He wants us to experience.

Next time you have the choice between now and maybe a few minutes from now, you might want to choose a few minutes from now - who knows, maybe in those few, precious minutes, you'll hear from God, or see a sight, or experience a moment. Give it a chance; you might be surprised.

Today's Word is Isaiah 28:13

"But the word of the Lord was to them, "Precept upon precept, precept upon precept, line upon line, line upon line, here a little, there a little,"

JULY 10

EXPERIENCING & DOING

As a teenage young man or young lady, do you know that God spoke about you and what you'd be doing as a young person in His Word? He did.

In the Bible, the Spirit of God spoke through a guy named Joel, and here's the paraphrased version of what was said:

I'm going to pour out My Spirit on everybody; and when I do, your sons and daughters will prophesy, and they'll see visions of what's to come.

How cool is that? You know what's even more cool than reading those words in the Bible? Meeting teenagers who are experiencing and doing exactly what The Spirit of God said to Joel they'd be doing.

Almost without fail, each week, somewhere on the road, a teenager comes to me and shares with me what they're experiencing. As they share their experience with me, I immediately know that what they are saying is coming straight out of the book of Joel in the Bible.

Remember, God is no respecter of persons. Get your Bible out. Take some time with the Lord. If you really want to experience what others your age are already experiencing, give the Word of God top priority in your life - before long you too may very well find yourself living right out of the book of Joel.

Today's Word is Joel 2:28

"And it shall come to pass afterward that I will pour out My Spirit on all flesh; your sons and your daughters shall prophesy, your old men shall dream dreams, your young men shall see visions."

JULY 11

IF GOD SAYS SPEAK, DON'T STRIKE

When God gives us an instruction, He really has no intention for us to deviate from the way He tells us to say or do something.

I've learned from experience that I'm much better off to simply obey. I don't always understand the why or the how, but I'm learning that my having a full understanding of a situation isn't really the point.

The point really is all about my obedience.

When Moses was leading the Children of Israel from Egypt to their Promised Land, at a point along their journey, they ran out of water. Moses went to God, received specific instruction as to what he was to do, and he obeyed what he'd heard. The result? God supernaturally supplied water from a rock.

Sometime later on during this same journey, the people were once again without water. They complained and murmured and this time, Moses got angry. In fact, he became so angry that he took matters into his own hands and struck a rock - water was still supplied but, in his anger, and disobedience, Moses missed out on ever stepping foot into his Promised Land.

Don't miss out on what God has planned for you. Don't let emotions control your life. Take it from me; obeying God will result in a blessed life even if you don't understand all of what's going on.

Look no further than the life of Moses: if God says speak, don't strike.

Today's Word is Numbers 20:10-12

"And Moses and Aaron gathered the assembly together before the rock; and he said to them, "Hear now, you rebels! Must we bring water for you out of this rock?" Then Moses lifted his hand and struck the rock twice with his rod; and water came out abundantly, and the congregation and their animals drank. Then the Lord spoke to Moses and Aaron, "Because you did not believe Me, to hallow Me in the eyes of the children of Israel, therefore you shall not bring this assembly into the land which I have given them."

JULY 12

IT'S WORTH THE WAIT

One of my favorite experiences in the Bible comes from a guy who had a dream of owning a mountain. He chose not to complain or grumble when faced with literal giants and he never, ever let go of his dream.

At forty years old, Caleb was one of the twelve spies who were sent to spy out the land that was to become their land. Caleb and Joshua were the only two spies who saw past the obstacles they were facing and chose instead to stay in faith, wholly trusting God.

Some forty-five years later, Caleb was still hanging on to his dream. Know what happened? He got his mountain!

Maybe today you too have a dream; a vision of something the Lord wants to do with and through your life. If so, I'd encourage you to do what Caleb did: stay in faith, speak words of faith, and never, ever let go of what God has shown you is yours.

You really don't have to look past the life of Caleb to realize that when your dream is from God, it's worth the wait.

Today's Word is Joshua 14:10-12

"And now, behold, the Lord has kept me alive, as He said, these forty- five years, ever since the Lord spoke this word to Moses while Israel wandered in the wilderness; and now, here I am this day, eighty- five years old. As yet I am as strong this day as on the day that Moses sent me; just as my strength was then, so now is my strength for war, both for going out and for coming in. Now therefore, give me this mountain of which the Lord spoke in that day; for you heard in that day how the Anakim were there, and that the cities were great and fortified. It may be that the Lord will be with me, and I shall be able to drive them out as the Lord said."

JULY 13

YOU'RE GONNA SERVE SOMEBODY

Whom we serve determines the life we live.

That's a straightforward sentence, isn't it; but it's true. What's it mean to you?

If you serve a thief, he'll steal from you. If you serve Love and you're a giver, you'll be blessed.

The choice of whom we serve is 100% ours. God loves us so much that He has given us freedom - in every area of our lives.

Serving a thief is just another way of serving the devil. Serving Love is just another way of serving God.

Today, it might be helpful to be mindful that the enemy's constant assignment on your life is to steal, kill, and destroy. On the other hand, the constant plan of God for your life is to love you, to bless you, and to give you abundant life.

It's your choice: whom are you going to serve?

Today's Word is Joshua 24:15

"And if it seems evil to you to serve the Lord, choose for yourselves this day whom you will serve, whether the gods which your fathers served that were on the other side of the River, or the gods of the Amorites, in whose land you dwell. But as for me and my house, we will serve the Lord."

JULY 14

24/7/365

Can you think of anything in your life that never changes? Can you name one person in your life that is as consistent as the day is long, 24/7/365?

The only thing in my life that never changes isn't a thing; it's a Who.

Jesus never changes. He's the same today as He was thousands of years ago, and you know what? He'll still be the same a million years from now. How's that possible? It's who He is.

I've learned that no matter how much I love my wife, there are still times when I do something that lets her down and even disappoints her. For that matter, sometimes I do or say things that make her angry. Doesn't mean I don't love her; just means that I'm human.

Not so with Jesus. No matter what's going on in our lives or in our world, Jesus proves every day that His consistency is something in which we can place 100% confidence.

Maybe you have a real issue placing trust and confidence in someone else. If so, I've got something for you to consider. Get more into the Word and get to know Jesus. As you do, your trust in who He is will begin to increase. As it does, you, too, will know that Jesus is the same, 24/7/365.

Today's Word is Hebrews 13:8

"Jesus Christ is the same yesterday, today, and forever."

JULY 15

A WATCH OVER MY MOUTH

When you are with teenagers as much as I get to be, you discover in short order that one of the greatest mistakes young people make has a lot to do with the words they speak. Words that are spoken in many instances without any thought to what's getting ready to be said or how those words might affect someone else.

A long time ago someone coined this phrase: Ready. Aim. Fire.

What I'm seeing among teens is a little different take on that phrase: Ready. Fire. Aim.

See the difference? That readjustment of two words isn't really a big deal on a paper, but, switching those two words - aim and fire - makes all the difference.

Really, it's a seemingly small adjustment but, remember, small keys open big doors.

One of the messages the Lord has me sharing with students is that every day before you get out of bed, consider doing what King David did in his life. Ask the Lord to put a watch over your mouth so that you only say what He wants/needs you to say. As you do this, He'll answer your prayer.

Today's Word is Psalms 141:3

"Set a guard, O Lord, over my mouth; keep watch over the door of my lips."

JULY 16

BE A REFRESHER

More often than not, there's a sentence that I'm prompted to share during an assembly or chapel program at schools which causes teenagers to really laugh. That sentence goes something like this:

"When your teachers see you walking down the hall on a Monday morning, they're probably thinking either, 'Oh, thank the Lord they're here today' or, 'Oh dear Lord, they're here today.'" As I'm sure you can tell, there's a significant and noticeable difference between those two thoughts.

The Bible talks about the effect you and your love for others can have on and in the lives of people in your world.

Maybe today you could take a minute and consider what happens when you show up in the lives of your friends. If you'll be willing to be used by God, I promise you He'll show you a way to be a refreshing gentle breeze to someone who may very well need a little extra attention or love.

Go ahead. Be available. Take a step of faith and ask the Lord to let you be used to bring some joy or hope into the life of someone who needs a little extra love today. If you ask, He'll answer.

Today's Word is Philemon 1:7

"For we have great joy and consolation in your love, because the hearts of the saints have been refreshed by you, brother."

JULY 17

JESUS HEARS EVERY WORD

Did you know that Jesus is always listening to what you and I are saying? Every single word. Know why? Because part of the responsibility He has is to ensure that if we are speaking His Word, He's going to bring that Word to pass.

You might want to take a few seconds and go back and re-read the previous paragraph one more time and let those words really sink in.

The Word of God explains to us that Jesus is the High Priest of our confession. The word confession is referring to our saying the same thing that the Word says about a situation that's in our life. Simply put in today's language, when we say what the Word says, and we do so in faith; as our High Priest, Jesus is ensuring that His Word coming out of our mouth in faith will get the job done.

So here are a couple of thoughts to consider as it relates to our daily conversations: 1) Jesus hears everything we say and 2) when we speak the Word in faith, it's His responsibility to accomplish that Word in and through our lives.

Pretty cool to think and know that our big Brother is the High Priest of the words we speak from the Word of God.

Today's Word is Hebrews 3:1

"Therefore, holy brethren, partakers of the heavenly calling, consider the Apostle and High Priest of our confession, Christ Jesus,"

JULY 18

HE'S PATIENT

I've been told that there are 7,700 promises in the Word of God. Think about that: 7,700 promises that await you and me. How do we get them?

Well, first you must know what the Word says. Then, study and discover for yourself what your part is in receiving a particular promise. And finally, once you see the promise in the Word and you're doing what you've seen in the Word to do in order to receive that promise, what's left? Be patient, keep walking in love, and continuously thank God that that promise is on its way to your life.

Give God some time to work; and as you do, patience will be working in you in a way that only patience can.

7,700 promises ... We're not waiting on God; He's waiting on us. Thankfully, He's a patient God!

Today's Word is Hebrews 6:15

"And so, after he had patiently endured, he obtained the promise."

JULY 19

GOD WANTS TO ASTONISH YOU

I'm fully convinced that until we are truly tracking with the Lord, God always says more than we hear; He always gives us more than we receive; and He always leads more than we follow.

In fact, I believe God takes a lot of pleasure in astonishing us. And His astonishing us isn't a big deal when you think about it. Who is man that God is even mindful of us?

There was a day when a group of professional fishermen had been fishing all night and had caught absolutely nothing. Jesus was in one of their boats and was using it as a stage. So many people were pressing to get so close to Him that He had to literally be out on the water to minister to those who were on land.

Remember, Jesus doesn't owe any man anything. So, because of the seed the fishermen sowed in letting Jesus use one of their boats as a stage, Jesus instructed that fisherman to drop his fishing nets in the water.

The fisherman (Peter) did so; and when he obeyed, he and his fishing partners were astonished. So many fish jumped into the net that it began to break.

Want to be astonished by the Lord? Begin by sowing seed and obeying His instructions.

Today's Word is Luke 5:9

"For he and all who were with him were astonished at the catch of fish which they had taken;"

JULY 20

OBEDIENCE & TIMING

For a long time now, God has had me looking at the life of Jesus. What He did and when He did it.

Think about it: We see Jesus arrive on His birthdate and then we neither see nor hear anything from him for twelve years. At twelve, we see Him in church, teaching the teachers the Word of God. Then, eighteen years pass until John the Baptist sees Him and baptizes Him in the Jordan River.

As I've spent time with the Lord on His life, He's taught me a lot. One of the lessons I'm learning has to do with God's timing. Another is the obedience of a Son. But one of the coolest lessons He's teaching me has to do with when Jesus began His earthly ministry.

If you read the Word, you'll see that when John baptized Jesus, immediately following that act, the Holy Spirit, in the form of a dove, descended from Heaven and the voice of God thundered across the earth, declaring how pleased God was with His Son. The very next verse tells us that then, and only then, after He received the Holy Spirit and waited for the blessing of His Father, Jesus began His ministry.

Today, whatever you're called to do, I'd encourage you to follow the life and example of Jesus: be filled with His Spirit, allow God to set you up, and then, fulfill your destiny. It worked for Jesus, and it'll work for you, too.

Today's Word is Luke 3:22-23

"And the Holy Spirit descended in bodily form like a dove upon Him, and a voice came from heaven which said, "You are My beloved Son; in You I am well pleased." Now Jesus Himself began His ministry at about thirty years of age, being (as was supposed) the son of Joseph, the son of Heli,"

JULY 21

THE HINGE OF LOVE

There's a verse in the Bible that I really enjoy ministering to students. It says, "Yet in all these things we are more than conquerors through Him who loved us."

If you're in the Word of God for any length of time, that verse is a familiar one. But sometimes I think we become so familiar with a scripture that we may miss some of its meaning.

Maybe we should take a closer look at the verse I shared above. It says:

In all these things, we are more than conquerors. Do you know who causes us to be more than a conqueror? And if you know who and you realize what more than a conqueror is, do you know why?

Here's my take on this verse. In everything we go through, it's Jesus (the Word) who causes us to be more than a conqueror if we allow Him to work through us. But here's where it gets interesting to me - everything Jesus has ever done, is today doing, or will tomorrow do for us, He does so because HE LOVES US.

Everything hinges on love.

Today's Word is Romans 8:37

"Yet in all these things we are more than conquerors through Him who loved us."

JULY 22

THE HEREAFTER

Through the years, many teenagers have asked me about the hereafter. They ask about Heaven and hell, God, and the devil. They truly wonder if there really is life beyond the life we live on planet earth.

My response is always the same: everyone, even a self-proclaimed atheist, bases his or her life on a system of belief or non-belief. For me, my belief system is 100% Bible-based. I believe the Word of God.

If you read and believe what the Word says, you'll know without any hesitation of contradiction that God is real, He's love, and there's a real place He's prepared for you and me known as Heaven.

Getting to spend the rest of your life with Him in Heaven is His will. But He'll never superimpose His will on anyone. He'll lead, He'll guide, and He'll show you the way to Himself. But, at the end of the day, we must choose what we believe, whom we believe, and where we will spend eternity.

If you've got questions about the hereafter, He's got answers. Just read what His Word says.

Today's Word is Proverbs 23:18

"For surely there is a hereafter, and your hope will not be cut off.

JULY 23

YOU'RE THE ONE

Many years ago, King David saw someone he wanted, and he did what he wanted to get her. He didn't really take into consideration how his decision would affect other people but focused instead on his desire and getting his way.

When the Prophet of God was sent to David and told him about someone who had taken much from someone who had little, David became furious. Then the Prophet said something that brought David into a reality check. He told the King that he was the man who had much and had taken from a man who had little.

Suddenly, the gravity of what David had done hit home.

Selfish desires lead to selfish decisions. Selfish decisions lead to painful results. Maybe you can relate to David's mindset - wanting what you want when you want it. If so, before you do something you'll later regret, it might be a good idea to get with God, have a heart check, and ask Him to change some of your desires.

God always looks at our heart. We should, too.

Today's Word is 2 Samuel 12:7-8

"Then Nathan said to David, "You are the man! Thus says the Lord God of Israel: 'I anointed you king over Israel, and I delivered you from the hand of Saul. I gave you your master's house and your master's wives into your keeping, and gave you the house of Israel and Judah. And if that had been too little, I also would have given you much more!

JULY 24

IT'S ALL ABOUT JESUS

Want some more good news today? The Bible says we're blessed because our transgression is forgiven, and our sin is covered. Think about that. Our transgression is forgiven, and our sin is covered - go a little deeper: forgiven by whom and covered by what?

When we sin, we transgress the will of God. Getting us back in right relationship with God is why Jesus came, died, and rose again - all for you and me.

You probably already knew or maybe you guessed it. When we sin, it's Jesus who forgives our transgression, and it's the blood of Jesus that covers our sin.

It's all about Jesus.

Today's Word is Psalms 32:1

"Blessed is he whose transgression is forgiven, whose sin is covered.

JULY 25

THE B I B L E

I was recently on the road and saw a sign on a billboard that really caught my attention. Printed on this billboard were the words THE BIBLE. Below the word Bible we're five more words:

Basic Instructions Before Leaving Earth

When I saw that little message, I was immediately led to think about the simplicity of the message of the Gospel: God loves us so much that He gave us His very best. Jesus loves us so much He died for you and me. The Holy Spirit loves us so much that He's the One who sticks closer to us than even a brother. To me, the Bible, in one word, is all about love.

Once we have received and are sowing love, then the Word really comes alive. When I think back over the five words printed on that billboard, I'm reminded of what the Bible really can be for anyone who chooses to ascribe to its principles and directives: an instruction book on how God wants us to live while here on the earth.

Remember, God loves you. He wants what's best for you. Trust Him. Open the B I B L E today and ask the Holy Spirit to give you your Basic Instructions Before Leaving Earth.

Today's Word is Psalms 119:105

"Your word is a lamp to my feet and a light to my path."

JULY 26

BE CONSISTENT

I often am led to share with teenagers the value of being consistent.

When we're consistent, we are constantly adhering to the same principles. Now to me, that sure sounds like the character of God. Among all that He is, God is surely consistent.

Here's an example of consistency:

The Bible teaches us that if we cast our bread, we'll find it after many days. What does that mean to you?

To me, the Lord is showing us that if we'll do our part and be consistent in casting our bread (sowing our seed) upon the waters (where He shows us to sow), then after many days (a time span) we can be assured that we will find (reap) our harvest.

Sowing seed goes so far beyond finances, but it certainly includes the financial realm. Today, think about consistency or maybe the lack of consistency in your life; and as you do, maybe a take a minute and contrast your level of consistency with that of your being a consistent sower.

When you are or when you become a consistent doer of the Word, guess what happens? You also become a consistent recipient of what the Word of God promises you can have.

Recommit to being consistent - it's who God is.

Today's Word is Ecclesiastes 11:1

"Cast your bread upon the waters, for you will find it after many days."

JULY 27

IT'S AN HONOR THING

One of the surest ways any of us will ever get the attention of Heaven is to simply obey what the Word of God instructs us to do. One of those instructions has to do with honoring those who are in positions of authority over us.

King David is an excellent example of someone who knew the value of obeying God and honoring people in his life. Even after all that David had gone through with King Saul, David honored him.

Many would probably think that there would have been no reason for David to honor King Saul, especially after he tried to kill him with a spear. But David had tapped into something else at work in his life - he knew the value God places on honor.

When King Saul died and was buried by a group of men from a place called Jabesh Gilead, David sent word to these men and pronounced a blessing on their lives - all because they honored Saul and buried him with respect.

Maybe today there's some people in your life that God wants you to honor. Don't delay. Make the decision to give honor where honor is due.

Today's Word is 2 Samuel 2:5-6

"So David sent messengers to the men of Jabesh Gilead, and said to them, "You are blessed of the Lord, for you have shown this kindness to your lord, to Saul, and have buried him. And now may the Lord show kindness and truth to you. I also will repay you this kindness, because you have done this thing."

JULY 28

FRIEND OR ENEMY

Here's a question that's really a no-brainer. Do you want to be a friend or enemy of God?

Hopefully, your answer comes down on the side of friend.

Did you know, however, that the Bible shows us how to become an enemy of God? It does. The Bible reveals that anyone who wants to be a friend of the world makes himself an enemy of God.

Does that mean that you and I cannot be friends with people who, maybe at this point in their lives, are not living for God? No, I don't think so. We're commissioned to be the light in an otherwise dark world. I believe the Scripture is saying that anyone who lives in the world and by the standards of the world versus living for God with the Word of God as the standard does so at the absolute risk of becoming an enemy of God.

Today, it might be a prudent decision to look at your life and the lifestyle you're living. As you take this look, are you a friend or enemy of God?

Today's Word is James 4:4

"Adulterers and adulteresses! Do you not know that friendship with the world is enmity with God? Whoever therefore wants to be a friend of the world makes himself an enemy of God."

JULY 29

AUTHORITY

Ever noticed how different voices in your life carry different levels of authority?

For example, if a friend tells you to do something you don't necessarily want to do, you probably will choose not to do it. But if your mom or dad tells you to do the same thing, my guess is, no matter how much you might not want to do it, you'll obey what they told you to do out of respect for their authority in your life as your parents.

What's the point? The more respect you have for someone who's in authority in your life, the more authority that person's voice will be in your life.

The Word of God has a voice. The more time you invest with the Word, the more you'll recognize the voice speaking to you from the Word. If you give the Word first place in your life, you'll recognize the authority you have as a Believer.

Take time today to submit to what the Word says, acknowledge the authority that comes from the Word. As you do, use your authority to speak the Word and get the results from the Word.

Today's Word is Luke 7:8

"For I also am a man placed under authority, having soldiers under me. And I say to one, 'Go,' and he goes; and to another, 'Come,' and he comes; and to my servant, 'Do this,' and he does it."

JULY 30

TRUST YOUR FATHER

One of the saddest encounters I have on the road is when I meet students after one of our events who begin to share with me what it's like for them to be afraid. It may be fear of being hurt emotionally; afraid of someone who's already hurt them, hurting them again, or afraid to tell someone what has already happened in their young lives.

What do you do when you're afraid? I can share with you what the Word of God tells us to do - trust God.

That sounds simple, doesn't it? And the closer you live with and for God, the easier it is to trust Him. But trusting God requires you and me doing our part. Here's an example:

When our kids were very small, I'd ask them to jump in the swimming pool. They'd be standing on the edge, afraid, and shaking their head no. I noticed after a while, however, that once they trusted me enough to take one step off the edge of the pool, no matter how afraid they were, they'd jump into the water, and I'd catch them.

The more they trusted me to catch them as they jumped in the water, the less afraid they were. Before too long, what had once caused them to be so afraid no longer affected them at all. Why? They trusted their father.

No difference right here, right now. If you're afraid of anything or anyone, trust your Father and watch that fear go away.

Today's Word is Psalms 56:3

"Whenever I am afraid, I will trust in You."

JULY 31

WRITE IT DOWN

More times than I can imagine, I've encouraged people to write down on paper the vision God has given or is giving them for their individual lives.

Why write it down, they ask? I then have the joy of sharing with them that God is the original Visionary. He set the example of writing down vision - the Bible is the first book ever written and from cover to cover, His vision for His children is seen throughout its entirety.

If you read Genesis 1:27 & 28, you'll see that He created you in His image. Since He wrote down on paper His vision and did so very plainly, you plainly writing down on paper His vision for your life makes total sense.

Here's a little nugget I share with students relating to writing down their respective vision on paper:

Nothing in your life will ever become dynamic until it first becomes specific - write down the specifics of your God-given vision.

Today's Word is Habakkuk 2:2

"Then the Lord answered me and said: "Write the vision and make it plain on tablets, that he may run who reads it."

AUGUST 1

IT'S A PROMISE

After decades of speaking in high schools where I've met, spoken with, and listened to so many students, I've seen that one of the main traps the enemy sets for teenagers is the trap of impatience.

So many students are in a hurry to grow up. They talk with me about wanting to get out of school, get out of their home, and move forward with living their dream and vision. I really understand where they're coming from - I was the same way when I was their age.

As students share these thoughts with me, I try to encourage them to be patient; to not rush the process. If what they are pursuing is truly God's vision for their life, that vision will come to pass, even if it takes some time to come to fruition. It's a promise in the Word of God.

Tired of being frustrated by the enemy? Ask God to give you the gift of patience. When you're patient, you'll freak out the devil.

One cautionary note, however, when you ask God for patience, He'll most probably allow you to be in a position that requires your faith to be exercised in the arena of having it.

Remember, if you do your part and do it in faith, based on the Word of God, His vision for your life will surely come - it's a promise.

Today's Word is Habakkuk 2:3

"For the vision is yet for an appointed time; but at the end it will speak, and it will not lie. Though it tarries, wait for it; because it will surely come, it will not tarry."

AUGUST 2

WALK IN TRUTH

A long time ago I heard someone say that God's greatest pain is to be doubted; His greatest joy is to be believed.

When I heard that statement, I began to think about what I could do as a Christian to bring joy to God. Ever thought about that yourself?

The more I considered my question, the more I was led to a particular verse in the Bible. It's way over in the New Testament in the Book of 3rd John. In this one verse I saw the answer to my question.

Want to bring joy to God in your own life? I'll share with you what He shared with me - walk in the truth of the Word.

When we know what the Word says and we conform our lives to its teachings, we'll be walking (living) in the truth of the Word.

Sounds simple, doesn't it? Well, in many regards, I think it is. I also believe it's an hourly decision.

Next time something happens that tries to take you out of peace and maybe even over into what I call the battle zone; instead of reacting, maybe you'll be better served if you ask the Holy Spirit to lead you into truth for that specific situation. As He does, make the quality decision to walk in that truth.

Today's Word is 3 John 1:4

"I have no greater joy than to hear that my children walk in truth."

AUGUST 3

FORGET IT & PRESS ON

The past is the past at last. Another way of saying that is yesterday ended last night.

I see too many young people who spend too much of their time worrying about the past.

The Bible tells us that worrying is a sin. Plain and simple. So, if God doesn't want us worrying; once we've repented, changed our actions, and learned our lesson, what are we supposed to do about our past?

The Bible tells us exactly what to do. Forget it and press on for those things that are ahead. Set goals and move toward them. Stretch for the calling God has for your life.

Next time you feel like worrying about your past, might be a much better idea to obey the Word:

Forget it and press on.

Today's Word is Philippians 3:13-14

"Brethren, I do not count myself to have apprehended; but one thing I do, forgetting those things which are behind and reaching forward to those things which are ahead, I press toward the goal for the prize of the upward call of God in Christ Jesus."

AUGUST 4

HE'S ALWAYS WITH YOU

Ever feel like you're walking through something so intense that it's seems almost unimaginable that death itself could be worse? If so, you know what it feels like to maybe to have hit rock bottom. How do you get through such a season - a season of warfare and assaults from the enemy?

You might want to begin by opening your Bible and reading out loud the words David wrote when he, too, experienced a season of pain and torment.

You see, David did not deny that he was going through a tough season; he just made a quality decision that he was going to get through it, not camp out in it.

One of the greatest lessons David teaches us in the Word is that irrespective of what you're walking through, even the very valley of the shadow of death, make the decision to refuse to fear. Remind yourself, remind God, and especially remind hell itself that you're not going through this season alone. God is right there with you, leading you, comforting you, every step of the way.

Today's Word is Psalms 23:4

"Yea, though I walk through the valley of the shadow of death, I will fear no evil; for You are with me; Your rod and Your staff, they comfort me."

AUGUST 5

WHAT'S YOUR MIND ON

Do you ever find yourself caught up in the world? Maybe you spend a lot of your time thinking about what you want to have, how you're going to get it, and what life here on earth is going to look like for you.

There's nothing wrong with planning for the future. I consistently am encouraging students to take time with God and dream. Here's where we can get off base, though: when we keep our minds on the here and now versus the true, lasting, eternal life God promises to us as born-again Believers.

The Bible is actually very clear on this subject. In the Word, God instructs us to set our minds on things above and not on things on the earth. In other words, don't get sucked into the trap of what you can get. Apply discipline to a life of focusing on Jesus and what He wants you to do with Him and for Him - both here on the earth and in the life to come.

Today's Word is Colossians 3:2

"Set your mind on things above, not on things on the earth."

AUGUST 6

YOU'RE A WITNESS

Did you know that one of our responsibilities as a Believer is to be a witness for the Lord all over the earth? We are. It's in the Book.

The word witness is defined as, "to bear witness to; testify to; to give or afford evidence of." So, what's that mean to you as a student?

Part of your calling wherever you are is to bear witness to, to testify of, and provide evidence of the reality of the Lord Jesus in your life.

Think about it. You may very well be the only person some of your friends see Jesus living in and through. No matter where the calling of God takes you on this journey we know as life, you are a witness every single day.

I sure take this as a serious responsibility; I hope you do too.

Today's Word is Acts 1:8

"But you shall receive power when the Holy Spirit has come upon you; and you shall be witnesses to Me in Jerusalem, and in all Judea and Samaria, and to the end of the earth."

AUGUST 7

CALL THOSE THINGS THAT BE NOT

One of the coolest things about God is His ability to create, to give life. Beyond these aspects of God, His Word has such power that when He speaks His Word, He can call those things that do not exist to become and exist. Now that's power!

Want to know something else that's powerful? When you have the Word of God in you, you, too, become a giver of life. You also can look at a situation, hear from God about that situation, declare the Word of God, and stand in faith. The result? Your declaring the Word of God in an uncompromised stand of faith will cause that Word to go to work to change that given situation.

You see, the Word of God is life-giving. He wants to trust all His children to handle His Word with great maturity. Before that can happen, however, we must believe His Word is true and His promises are for the here and now just as much as they were for those who lived thousands of years ago.

Want to get the attention of people who need more of God? Start calling those things that are not as though they already are and watch the Word produce the miracles.

Today's Word is Romans 4:17

"(as it is written, "I have made you a father of many nations") in the presence of Him whom he believed—God, who gives life to the dead and calls those things which do not exist as though they did;"

AUGUST 8

STOP CHOKING

Got a question for you. When it comes to believing God for something or someone, what's your choke point?

Let's say you're somewhere between the ages of 15 - 18 and let's say, for example, that you're really wanting your own car. Let's also say that you're a Believer and so you've been talking with God about this desire of your heart. Now what?

How do you move from desiring to believing to receiving? The process is known as faith, and each of us has a measure of it. It's what we do with our measure of faith that counts.

First, can you see yourself having your own car? Is it used or brand new; is it the color you want; does it have cloth seats, or the leather seats you really want? Does it have debt or is it debt-free?

As you answer these questions and do so honestly, your answers will reveal the choke point of your faith. What's that?

The choke point of faith is where we stagger at the promise of God as it relates to something we either want or no longer want in our lives. It's the point where we are not fully convinced that God will do what He said He'd do.

Don't beat yourself up if you discover that your faith isn't necessarily where it could be at this point. Choose, instead, to start from where you are. Get more into the Word, declare what the Word says over your life, and then get on the God-side of the faith equation. As you do, you'll stop choking and instead be fully persuaded that what He's promised, He's well able to perform.

Today's Word is Romans 4:21

"and being fully convinced that what He had promised He was also able to perform."

AUGUST 9

FROM HIM & HIM ALONE

A long, long time ago the Lord taught me a life lesson that's stuck with me all these years. It's something He led me to share with you today.

In the summer of 1996, I was speaking at a convention that had close to eight thousand people in the audience. The Lord really blessed my time on stage; and when it was over, there was a sustained length of applause from the people for what I had been led to share that day.

As I stood on that stage thanking the people for their response, deep down in my heart I heard this sentence ever so clearly: "The applause of man will never overpower My silence."

I walked off that stage with that sentence fresh on my heart. I went to my hotel room and talked with the Lord about what I had heard. As I did, I saw what He was saying to me. Don't ever measure your success in ministry based on the response of people. True, measured success in what any of us are called to do comes directly from God and from Him alone.

Whether you're speaking to eight thousand or delivering a meal to eight hungry people, don't be moved by how people respond or don't respond. Choose, instead, to receive your reward from God.

Today's Word is 1 Corinthians 4:5

"Therefore judge nothing before the time, until the Lord comes, who will both bring to light the hidden things of darkness and reveal the counsels of the hearts. Then each one's praise will come from God."

AUGUST 10

YOU CAN BE THE DIFFERENCE

Do you treat people differently?

Let's say two new students were to transfer to your school today. One of them is dressed in the latest fashion, he or she is driving a sports car, and the popular students in your school automatically surround this student.

Now let's say that the other student walks into your school and he isn't dressed in the latest fashions. He is dropped off at school in an older car, and no one goes up to greet him.

What's happened in these two scenarios? Very simply, partiality has been shown. And you know what? The Word of God instructs us to not do this.

When we show partiality, we are, in effect, judging. And if you've been around the Word at all for any length of time, you may very well know how God feels about our sitting in the seat of judgment. If you don't know, let's just say that it's not a seat He wants us to ever sit in.

Today, look around you. See anyone who seems to be left out for all the wrong reasons; someone who's been wrongly judged? You can help change that; God can use you to be part of the difference.

Start by being their friend.

Today's Word is James 2:2-4

"For if there should come into your assembly a man with gold rings, in fine apparel, and there should also come in a poor man in filthy clothes, and you pay attention to the one wearing the fine clothes and say to him, "You sit here in a good place," and say to the poor man, "You stand there," or, "Sit here at my footstool," have you not shown partiality among yourselves, and become judges with evil thoughts?"

AUGUST 11

FOR THE WHOLE WORLD

Can you imagine how much love Jesus has in His heart for you, me, and for every other person on the planet? How much love must He have that it motivated Him to not only pay the penalty of sin that you and I would commit, but also pay the price for every sin everyone who would ever breathe a breath of air would ever commit? That's love beyond any love anyone else has ever had; but after all, that's who He is: LOVE.

It's one thing to pay the price for you and your family or for my family and me. But to pay the price for everyone, everywhere - the whole world over? That's a lot to comprehend.

But that's exactly what Jesus has done. It's a completed work.

So how do we get in on this work of love? After all, we can't earn it, can't work for it; all we can do is receive by faith what He's already done.

Sounds almost too easy, doesn't it? Well, the Gospel is a simple message full of profound truth and wisdom. Our responsibility is to have a childlike faith and embrace the One who paid the price for you, for me, and for the whole world.

Today's Word is 1 John 2:2

"And He Himself is the propitiation for our sins, and not for ours only but also for the whole world."

AUGUST 12

HE NEVER FAILS

Were you aware that when you choose to live for God, you align yourself with the One who never fails? Imagine that you're on a heavenly team being coached by the all-time, most-winning Coach in the universe.

Why would anyone, anywhere willfully choose to not submit to what God, who never fails, instructs them to do? Well, in a word, it's called sin - our wanting our way, irrespective of what the will of God is for our life.

The opposite of sin is obedience. When we allow the Holy Spirit to lead our thinking, our actions, and our words, and we obey His promptings, we then position ourselves to be on the winning side.

Obedience isn't always the easiest path to take, but remember, our obedience keeps us in good standing with the One who never fails.

Today's Word is Zephaniah 3:5

"The Lord is righteous in her midst, He will do no unrighteousness. Every morning He brings His justice to light; He never fails, but the unjust knows no shame."

AUGUST 13

RESISTED BY GOD

One of the most quoted verses in the Bible asks a question: If God be for you, who can be against you? I was at a Ministers Conference where this verse was quoted, but the minister quoting this verse then asked a follow up question to the audience, a question that immediately had my full attention.

Here's what he said: "If God be for us, who can be against us. I wonder if the reverse is true. If God be against us, who can be for us?"

Hearing his question, someone sitting on the front row then said, "If that's the case, boy you're in trouble."

Ever thought about what would cause God, your Heavenly Father who loves you so very much to resist you, to be against you? Well, after hearing this ministers' question, I wanted to know what would cause God to ever be against me.

Didn't take long to find the answer to my question. The one thing that causes God to resist us, to be against any of us, is pride.

The opposite of pride is humility. While God is vehemently against pride and what pride produces, He gives more and more and more grace to the humble.

Want God resisting you? Be prideful. Want Him filling your life with His grace? Be humble.

Today's Word is James 4:6

"But He gives more grace. Therefore He says: "God resists the proud, but gives grace to the humble."

AUGUST 14

A TIME SUCH AS THIS

Teenagers all over the world are awakening to the truth that God put them in the earth for a time such as this.

Never before this generation has the technology existed that allows us to, with the push of a few buttons, communicate with people all over the globe in real time.

To give you an example of what I'm talking about, when I first began ministering to teens in high schools, the Internet was not universally used. At that point in time, one of the most far-reaching and technologically advanced tools the general public had was the fax machine. Today, I don't know anyone who even uses a fax machine.

So, since you're here at such a time as this, ever considered why? Why not in the Bible days, the pre-historic days, or during one of the World Wars? Why here? Why now?

Here's what I do know concerning your very existence: God has never made a mistake. His timing is perfect. You're alive now; because for whatever reason He has (and surely you must know that He does have a reason), He has need of your gifts and calling for a time such as this.

To me, that's exciting.

Today's Word is Esther 4:14

"For if you remain completely silent at this time, relief and deliverance will arise for the Jews from another place, but you and your father's house will perish. Yet who knows whether you have come to the kingdom for such a time as this?"

AUGUST 15

HE MAKES HOUSE CALLS

Years ago, during an unusually difficult season of my life, I came face-to-face with the harsh reality that I had a hard heart - the Bible refers to it as a heart of stone. A heart of stone is a heart that's emotionally and even spiritually shut down and is void of real emotions.

I didn't want to have a hard heart that was incapable of feeling; but irrespective of what I wanted, that's what I had. Maybe you can relate.

What caused me to have such a heart condition? I discovered that, for me, it was the result of years of my not dealing with my emotions. I share with audiences every week that if they do not deal with their emotions, their emotions will surely deal with them.

When the Lord took me to Ezekiel 36:26, He showed me the way out of my heart condition. I had to trust God and receive His love. When I began to confess that God had given me a new spirit and that He'd taken the heart of stone out of me and placed within me a heart of flesh, guess what happened? My heart softened, and I began to feel.

In what God has called me to do, I get to meet a lot of teenagers and their parents who, like I was, sure seem to need a heart transplant - spiritually speaking.

If that's you, I'd encourage you to go the Great Physician and let His Word perform spiritual heart surgery on you - He's available 24/7 and yes, He makes house calls.

Today's Word is Ezekiel 36:26

"I will give you a new heart and put a new spirit within you; I will take the heart of stone out of your flesh and give you a heart of flesh."

AUGUST 16

THE SAME SPIRIT OF FAITH

Faith-filled words produce results. The types of results your words are producing however rely solely upon what you put your faith in. Is your faith rooted in what others can do for you or even what you can do for yourself, or is your faith rooted in the promises found throughout the Word of God?

Concerning your faith, here's something you might find of interest and consider. If people can give you something, people can take that something from you. Not so with God. His motivation in honoring our faith in His Word is always for our good.

He loves us so much that He's given us the same spirit of faith that raised Jesus from the dead. What are you going to do with that power? My suggestion is that you do what the Bible says. Since you've got this same spirit of faith, exercise your faith, believe the Word of God, and take those words and speak them over your life and calling.

If you do, you'll like the results.

Today's Word is 2 Corinthians 4:13

"And since we have the same spirit of faith, according to what is written, "I believed and therefore I spoke," we also believe and therefore speak,"

AUGUST 17

CONVICTION

Ever been sick? Maybe it started out with you having chills one minute and you had a fever of 102 degrees only minutes later. Or maybe you ate lunch at school, and forty minutes later you were wishing you had not eaten that lunch.

Whatever symptoms you've experienced, those symptoms are your body's way of telling you that something's wrong.

It's no different with your Spirit, your conscience. When we get out of the will of God, we will experience the conviction of God.

Conviction is to your Spirit what pain is to your body.

Now please notice that I did not say we'd experience condemnation from God. That's not His style. But conviction, you bet.

Any of us who've ever been disciplined in love by a parent or guardian knows that the correct type of discipline lovingly leads us back into fellowship - right standing. It's the same with God. Whom He loves, He disciplines and oftentimes does so with and by the conviction of the Holy Spirit.

Today's Word is Hebrews 12:6

"For whom the Lord loves He chastens, and scourges every son whom He receives."

AUGUST 18

IN TUNE WITH HEAVEN

Let's say that this morning that you and your family are going to drive 300 miles from your home to the beach where you're going to meet up with some friends for a vacation.

As you leave your home and head out toward your destination, all of you are listening to a local radio station that's broadcasting something that has your attention. The further you navigate away from your hometown, however, you begin to lose the signal from that radio station and the further you drive, the less of the broadcast you hear. Then suddenly, you hear nothing. What happened?

The radio station is still broadcasting loud and clear, but you no longer hear what's being said. The radio station didn't move; you did.

It's not a bit different with your relationship with God. He's broadcasting, talking right now. The question is are you close enough to the signal to hear what's being broadcasted?

I meet teenagers every week that tell me that they used to hear God all the time; now they never hear Him. They then inevitably ask me why. I share with them what I just shared with you. God hasn't moved.

If today you're having a challenge hearing the voice of God in your life, might want to see how close or how far you are from Heaven's broadcasting signal.

If you discover that you've drifted further away than you even realized, here's the good news. God hasn't moved at all. Repent and ask Him to get you back in tune with the frequency of Heaven.

Today's Word is Isaiah 55:6

"Seek the Lord while He may be found, call upon Him while He is near."

AUGUST 19

STAY ON COURSE

Many years ago, I was sitting in the right seat (the co-pilot's seat) of a Cessna jet. The pilot is a dear friend of mine; and as we were flying along, he began to teach me about some of the instruments that were in the cockpit of that jet.

There was one instrument that really got my attention. In fact, the more I understood the function of that instrument, the more I realized just how important it was and is to each flight.

This instrument deals with navigation. It has within its design a place where a pilot can punch in coordinates that the plane then flies by. For example, let's say you were going to fly from Fort Worth, Texas, to a destination that was 300 miles due east of your present location. The pilot would punch in the coordinates 090, because exactly due east of your present location is 90 degrees.

But here's where it gets interesting. If the pilot mistakenly punched in 070 instead of 090 and flew along that heading for an hour and a half, that plane would miss its destination by a number of miles.

If you're going along and are on track with the Lord but get with the wrong crowd or begin compromising your values, you might not think it's a big deal. But guess what, if you keep flying off course and moving away from your moral compass, you're going to miss God.

Maybe you're thinking that what you're doing isn't that bad and nobody even knows and certainly no one is getting hurt. If that's your mindset, though, beware. It's the little things that we think no one knows about or that really don't mean that much which bring people down.

There's a solution: get with God, set your course, and fly the coordinates He gives you.

Today's Word is Song of Songs 2:15

"Catch us the foxes, the little foxes that spoil the vines,"

AUGUST 20

HURTING PEOPLE HURT PEOPLE

When I first began in ministry the Lord showed me that He wanted me to speak and minister in schools. And so that's what I do. About five years into our ministry, He showed me that in addition to our school outreach, He wanted me to be mindful to minister to students who were in Juvenile Detention Centers and at Teen Challenge Ministry Centers. And I do that as well.

I share that with you because when I began ministering in detention centers and Teen Challenge centers, I met some of the most honest teenagers I've ever met anywhere. For the most part, these young people aren't bad people at all; they're teenagers who've been hurt and maybe just didn't know what to do with the pain.

In fact, it was while ministering at a juvenile detention center that I got a revelation while talking with one of the students who was locked up, a revelation that totally changed how I minister today. The revelation? Hurting people hurt people.

Now that sentence is true whether you're a student, a prisoner, a pastor, a lawyer, a construction worker, or the President of a country.

If you're hurting and you've not taken that hurt to Jesus, odds are very strongly stacked against you that in and of yourself, you're hurting people in your life.

This can change. When we give Jesus the pain in our heart, He takes it and heals us. He then allows us to be available to help other people who are today going through what we have already come through.

Admit you're hurting. Give it to Jesus and watch the healing begin.

Today's Word is Luke 6:19

"And the whole multitude sought to touch Him, for power went out from Him and healed them all."

AUGUST 21

PAIN SEEKS PLEASURE

We all have a mission. Part of mine is sharing hope with people who've really blown it and really need to know that in Him, there's still hope.

In sharing our message of hope, I've met a lot of people who've opened up and shared their stories with me. One story that I'm hearing more and more these days has to do with the abuse of sex, drugs, and alcohol.

As I listen to these stories, and as those sharing their story with me let their guard down and just get brutally honest with themselves, here's what is oftentimes discovered. Pain seeks pleasure.

Maybe you can relate. Here's the truth: sin, for a season, sure seems fun. Otherwise, why would it be so enticing on so many levels? Of course it seems fun until ... the reality that the wages of sin is death kicks into operation.

But what leads any of us to seeking pleasure that comes from sin? I believe part of the answer is found in unresolved pain. Left undealt with, pain seeks pleasure to numb out from reality. This never, ever works.

What then does work? Glad you asked. Get real with Jesus. He already knows what's going on and always makes a way of escape from sin and from the temptation of sin.

Tired of pain leading you to pleasure that just doesn't last? Turn to Him and experience intimacy like none other.

Today's Word is 1 Corinthians 10:13

"No temptation has overtaken you except such as is common to man; but God is faithful, who will not allow you to be tempted beyond what you are able, but with the temptation will also make the way of escape, that you may be able to bear it."

AUGUST 22

LAUGHTER

What do you do when oppression or depression knocks on the door of your heart? Do you open the door and invite those visitors from hell into your life to set up residence, or do you take a stand of faith and resist the enemy? If you have opened the door, did you know that you don't have to?

For too long I opened the door and just let the enemy in. I hadn't yet learned how to stand on the Word in faith. But after a while, I went to the Lord about how to keep the enemy from depositing oppression and depression into my heart - you see, I had a responsibility in this process.

And so, when I asked, God answered. His answer came in three responses: first, He reminded me to speak the Word and so I did. God answers honest prayers.

The second instruction He gave me as it relates to being rid of oppression and depression was to - ready for this - LAUGH. What? You heard me. He instructed me to laugh.

The third instruction He gave me was to look at my wife. Lori really enjoys laughter. When she laughs, you can't help but smile. The more Lori laughs about a situation, the more joy she operates in.

The Lord then told me that laughter is a choice. He reminded me that in His Word, He plainly tells us that laughter is therapeutic like medicine. And so, in faith and in obedience, I began to laugh. As I did, I was also reminded that the Word says the joy of the Lord is the strength of His people.

The more I prayed the Word, the more I laughed, and the more I watched Lori, the more joy came into me, and the stronger I became.

Might be a good idea for you, too, to pray the Word and laugh on purpose. As you do, God will honor your obedience.

Today's Word is Proverbs 17:22

"A merry heart does good, like medicine, but a broken spirit dries the bones."

AUGUST 23

A SACRIFICE OF PRAISE

Want to get the attention of Heaven today? Offer God a sacrifice that costs you something.

I often am led to share with teenagers when they ask me about offerings that if what you are giving doesn't get your attention, it probably will not get God's attention, either.

Don't miss what I'm saying here. This isn't necessarily about an amount of money; much more importantly, it's about the attitude of our heart.

When King David had it in his heart to build an altar to God, the place where he was going to build that altar was offered to him as a gift. In his response to being given a place to build an altar, King David gave us a glimpse into his heart: he paid full price for the land, because he wasn't about to offer God something that cost him nothing.

Again, when it comes to giving, it's not all about the amount; it's much more a reflection of the heart.

Want to get God's attention in your giving? Offer Him something that is of value to you and cost you something personally. When you do, it's known as a sacrifice of praise.

Today's Word is 1 Chronicles 21:24

"Then King David said to Ornan, "No, but I will surely buy it for the full price, for I will not take what is yours for the Lord, nor offer burnt offerings with that which costs me nothing."

AUGUST 24

IT WAS MEANT FOR EVIL

Remember the story of Joseph in the book of Genesis. As a young man Joseph had some dreams, shared those dreams with his father and his brothers. His brothers became extremely jealous and ultimately sold Joseph into slavery.

Several years later, there was a famine in all the land. Leading up to this famine, God had promoted Joseph to the number two governmental position in all the land. In fact, Joseph oversaw the governmental food distribution plan.

One day Joseph's father sent his brothers to the place where the supply of food was being stored and literally right back into the life of their brother. Joseph's dreams did come true, but here's a takeaway lesson to consider: instead of being brutal, haughty, and revengeful, Joseph eventually revealed his identity to his brothers and the family was re-united.

What's the point today? Sometimes seemingly bad things might happen to you in your life. If so, instead of getting bitter, choose instead to get better.

After all, the Word teaches us that what the enemy meant for evil against you, God meant it for good. No matter what, trust God.

Today's Word is Genesis 50:20

"But as for you, you meant evil against me; but God meant it for good, in order to bring it about as it is this day, to save many people alive."

AUGUST 25

IT'S NOT AN AGE, IT'S A SEASON

One of the questions I'm asked quite often by students has to do with when's the right age to go into ministry.

Here's the response the Lord gave me to answer that question: There's no right age, but there is a right time.

You see, God knew from the foundation of time what He'd called you to do, when He'd called you to do it, and where He'd called you to do it. Our responsibility is to be so tuned into His presence and so obedient to this Heavenly call that when He opens the door, we're equipped to move into that season of our lives.

For some, their season is at mid-life; for others, it begins fresh out of school. And yes, for some, working in their calling begins at young, tender ages.

You really must look no further than the life of Jesus - He had such a relationship with His Father that at age twelve, He was in the Temple, teaching the Teachers.

Want another example? Look at the childhood ministry of Samuel - even as a child, he was full time in the Temple of God.

What's the right age to enter ministry? Remember, it's not an age, it's a season.

Today's Word is 1 Samuel 2:18

"But Samuel ministered before the Lord, even as a child, wearing a linen ephod."

AUGUST 26

WE'LL CARRY NOTHING OUT WITH US

Some time ago I saw a sign that said, "I've never seen a U-Haul truck loaded with all of your possessions following your coffin."

Make sense? I think the point is clear: when we leave this journey we know as life, none of our physical possessions are going with us.

So, if our earthly possessions aren't going to be part of our eternal life, what do you think is? Our eternal harvests from the seeds of faith we deposited into others while here on earth.

Want to really make a difference in this world for God? Focus on the eternal aspect of life.

That doesn't mean we aren't supposed to enjoy life and the blessings in life that He sends our way; we are. What I'm saying today is if we truly want to make a difference for eternity, then eternity must be our focus.

So, right here, right now, why don't you take a minute and ask the Holy Spirit to show you one thing you can do in the life of someone else that'll make a difference for eternity.

Remember, we entered life with nothing; when we leave, we're not carrying anything out with us.

Today's Word is 1 Timothy 6:7

"For we brought nothing into this world, and it is certain we can carry nothing out."

AUGUST 27

HE'LL DO HIS PART

When God sees that you're serious about fulfilling something He's put on your heart to get fulfilled for Him and His Kingdom, stand on the Word and stay in faith, then count on it, you're going to see results. And maybe sooner than you expect.

Here's an example of what I'm talking about.

I was at church one Sunday, and our Pastor was led to ask the entire congregation to write down names that the Lord put on our individual hearts. Now these weren't just any names; these were to be names of people who we were led to believe would have a serious encounter with the Lord Jesus Christ.

I prayed about who He wanted on my list, and, immediately, two people came to my heart. So, I wrote down their names and simply believed God that somehow, someway, He'd use me to connect with these two people in a way that when we did, He'd use me to minister to them.

Two hours later, my wife, Lori and one of our daughters and me went to a new place for lunch. I had never eaten there before. As we were walking to the front door of this Cafe, one of the people on my list walked right out and in front of me. I had not seen this person in ten years.

I said what I was led to say to him, and we went our ways. My job was to believe God, to sow the seed of the Word, and then to trust the Lord of the Harvest to do that which only He can do.

Maybe today you, too, have someone on your heart that you're believing God to touch. If you'll be available to do your part, you can be assured He'll do His.

Today's Word is Mark 9:23

"Jesus said to him," If you can believe, all things are possible to him who believes."

AUGUST 28

HE'S GOT THE ANSWER

One of the coolest aspects I've discovered of the character of God is His ability to make things happen that we, in and of ourselves, could never make happen.

Have you heard about the life of Moses? Know anything about his childhood? At the time he was born, Pharaoh put a law in place that every Hebrew male child that was born was to immediately be put to death.

When Moses was born, his mother put him in a basket and placed him in a river, hoping to keep him from being murdered. Each day, Moses' sister stood off to the side and watched out for her baby brother.

One day the daughter of Pharaoh came down to the river and discovered Moses in the basket on the water. For some reason, Pharaoh's daughter had compassion on him. Within only minutes of discovering Moses, the daughter of Pharaoh took him as her own and was led in her heart to find someone she could pay to take care of the baby.

Moses' sister spoke up and volunteered her mom to be the lady who could take care of Moses. Know what happened next? The daughter of Pharaoh hired the mom of Moses to be his caregiver. Only God.

Maybe today you're facing something that you have no idea how to handle. Trust that God already has it worked out. Don't sweat it.

I've learned that before I even knew there's a question, God has supplied the answer.

Today's Word is Exodus 2:8-9

"And Pharaoh's daughter said to her, "Go." So the maiden went and called the child's mother. Then Pharaoh's daughter said to her, "Take this child away and nurse him for me, and I will give you your wages." So the woman took the child and nursed him."

AUGUST 29

SUFFERING & OBEDIENCE

If you and I serve God for any length of time, there will be times on our journey when we will suffer. The Bible says that Jesus suffered as He was learning obedience, so you and I can be assured that since He suffered, we will as well.

But don't freak out. Learning obedience is to our advantage.

One of the neatest lessons I've learned in life is that no matter what happens to me, God uses it for my good...every time. Even if I don't immediately see the good, He ensures that it's at work for my benefit.

Could be that you're suffering right now. Don't resent the process you're in; embrace it, knowing that Jesus has promised to never leave or forsake you - He's right there with you.

Take it from someone who's been there: as uncomfortable as suffering is, embrace the process; because as you suffer, you're simultaneously learning something about obedience.

Today's Word is Hebrews 5:8

"though He was a Son, yet He learned obedience by the things which He suffered."

AUGUST 30

DON'T DECEIVE YOURSELF

One of the toughest lessons some of us ever learn in life is to not think we're all that great. And for some of us, discovering that we're not God's singular gift to the planet comes as a real shocker.

The Bible has something serious to say about this subject. It tells us that if we think we're something when outside of who we are in Christ, we're nothing, guess what? We deceive ourselves.

Want to live a life of total frustration and disappointment? Live a life where you're constantly deceiving yourself.

As I was growing up, my mom taught me a lesson that's stuck with me throughout my life. I haven't always lived by this lesson, but the truth contained within it hasn't changed: to thine own self be true.

What's that mean? When you look in the mirror, be truthful with the person staring back at you. Living a life of deception will wear you out.

From this day forward, I challenge you to make sure that you don't deceive yourself. Instead, be thankful for the part He gives you to fulfill in and for His Kingdom.

Today's Word is Galatians 6:3

"For if anyone thinks himself to be something, when he is nothing, he deceives himself."

AUGUST 31

HE'S WILLING

If you read Matthew, Mark, Luke, and John, you'll be reading the same basic accounts of the life and ministry of Jesus while He was on the earth, but you'll be reading about these accounts from four varying perspectives.

One of the accounts that is consistent throughout the four Gospels is that Jesus was then and is today willing to heal. It's part of who He is - our Healer.

While it's true that Jesus heals us because His Word declares that by His stripes we were healed, He also heals us because He loves us so much.

If today you're not feeling well or maybe you've been given a bad report from the doctor, do not deny the symptoms you're feeling or the facts you're hearing. Just deny those symptoms and facts the right to stay in your body.

Remember, He's willing.

Today's Word is Mark 1:41

"Then Jesus, moved with compassion, stretched out His hand and touched him, and said to him, "I am willing; be cleansed."

SEPTEMBER 1

FRIEND OF GOD

Do you believe you can be a friend of God? For that matter, do you believe God has or desires friends? If He does, is being God's friend even comprehensible to you?

The short answer to two of the three above questions is YES. Yes, you can be a friend of God and yes, God has and wants friends. The third question, however, is entirely up to you and how you see your relationship with your Heavenly Father.

Throughout these daily devotionals, my assignment is to remind you that God is accessible to you, that His Word is alive, and that His love for you is unfailing.

So, with the Lord assigning me to search His scriptures to confirm and publish all of the above to you, then surely you must know that He wants to be your friend. Remember, He's all about relationship.

Take Abraham for example. The Word tells us that his faith in God caused him to believe God. His believing put him in right standing with God. As such, he was then called the friend of God.

What moves God? Our faith in His Word. Today, I dare you to believe that God wants to be your friend, too. As you believe, you will experience right standing with Him and then look out; you will then be a friend of God.

Today's Word is James 2:23

"And the Scripture was fulfilled which says, "Abraham believed God, and it was accounted to him for righteousness." And he was called the friend of God."

SEPTEMBER 2

MOSES SAW HIS BACK

Do you ever go through times in your life when you just need to know that God is with you? Maybe you've hit a rocky patch in a relationship, maybe things are tough at home, could be that all your so-called friends have taken a break from being your friend, and you're doing life, seemingly all alone.

Thousands of years ago there was a leader named Moses who was apparently experiencing a time in his life when he just needed to know that not only was God still with him, but he also needed to experience God in a way that reassured him that he was anointed by God to lead His people. In today's language, Moses needed to know that God had his back.

If you read this account in the book of Exodus, you'll see that although no one has ever seen the face of God, Moses got to see the back of God. Now isn't that interesting? Moses needed to know that God had his back and as a sign of reassurance, God allowed Moses to see His back as He passed by him as he was hidden in some rocks.

Maybe today you also need to know or be reminded that God's got your back. He may not come down and let you see His back, but I promise you this, if you'll draw near to Him, He'll move Heaven and earth to draw near to you.

Today's Word is Exodus 33:20-23

"But He said, "You cannot see My face; for no man shall see Me, and live." And the Lord said, "Here is a place by Me, and you shall stand on the rock. So it shall be, while My glory passes by, that I will put you in the cleft of the rock, and will cover you with My hand while I pass by. Then I will take away My hand, and you shall see My back; but My face shall not be seen."

SEPTEMBER 3

WAIT ON GOD

Want to renew your strength? Want to mount up with wings as eagles? Want to run and not be weary or walk and not faint? You can. It's a promise in the Word.

But as is the case with every promise we have from the Lord, we have some responsibility in receiving the results of those promises in our everyday lives.

In this case our responsibility is to wait on the Lord. But, that word "wait" doesn't mean to just sit around and wait on God to show up. It means something entirely different. It paints the picture of a waiter at a five-star restaurant who is constantly attending to your needs, as you are a guest at his restaurant.

So, considering that illustration, what's God saying to you as a high school student as it relates to you waiting on Him? In other words, what can you do to be of service to the King of Kings?

Here's some actions to consider as you ponder waiting on the Lord: pray for others, lead a devotional, sow the seed of kindness in the life of somebody else. Say something nice to your teachers.

Do something that shows God that reflecting His character is your desire. As you do, you'll be waiting on Him and He'll be sure that your strength is renewed, that you mount up like eagles, that you run and aren't weary, and that you walk and don't faint.

Today's Word is Isaiah 40:31

"But those who wait on the Lord shall renew their strength; they shall mount up with wings like eagles, they shall run and not be weary, they shall walk and not faint."

SEPTEMBER 4

HUMBLE REPENTANCE

Every time I get to give an invitation for students to make a public demonstration of a private matter of the heart, I talk with them about the necessity of all of us repenting. Repenting isn't just being sorry for something we did or were caught doing. No, true repentance is when we acknowledge to a Holy God that we know we missed the mark; and with His help, we're changing.

I also share with students that sin angers God. Many young people are surprised by that revelation, but, it's in the Bible.

What I've learned that moves the heart of God on my behalf, however, is my coming to Him with humility, asking Him in faith to forgive me. Know what? He always does.

Maybe this type of relationship is foreign to you or maybe what you have with God is light-years ahead of where I am. Either way, humility and seeking forgiveness when we miss it always gets the attention of Heaven.

Today, if you know that you've missed the mark, humble yourself and have a heart-to-heart with Jesus.

Today's Word is Zephaniah 2:3

"Seek the Lord, all you meek of the earth, who have upheld His justice. Seek righteousness, seek humility. It may be that you will be hidden in the day of the Lord's anger."

SEPTEMBER 5

THE COMMANDMENT WE'VE HAD FROM THE BEGINNING

Almost without fail, after speaking at an assembly or chapel in a school, someone walks over with tears in his or her eyes and asks to talk. As we sit together on the edge of the stage or maybe in the chairs on the front row of the auditorium, this student usually breaks down and tears freely flow.

After they regain their composure, I ask them what's going on. And more times than not, the response is that someone has been really mean to this student. So mean that this teenager who seemingly has it all together on the outside is literally falling apart on the inside.

Today you may know how this feels.

Each time I have one of these encounters, I wonder about the person who said or did something cruel enough to cause that much pain.

You know, the Bible isn't a book of suggestions; it's the Book of commandments. And the number one commandment, the one that is the foundation of all others, is that we love.

Loving God and loving others as ourselves are His commandments to each and every one of us.

If in the future you're tempted to be ugly to someone else, I'm praying that the Holy Spirit will gently tug on your heart and remind you of the commandment we've had from the beginning: that we love one another.

Today's Word is 2 John 1:5

"And now I plead with you, lady, not as though I wrote a new commandment to you, but that which we have had from the beginning: that we love one another."

SEPTEMBER 6

STANDING BEFORE HIM

I've noticed that one of the subjects teenagers aren't always too terribly interested in hearing about is the end of time. Just to be blunt: I've met a lot of teens who are scared to discuss the end of time, as we know it.

Scared or not, that time is coming.

What'll happen? What are we going to experience? Well, if you take time to read the Word, God tells us what to expect when every one of us is standing before God in judgment.

Once I get teenagers to approach the subject and begin to talk about it, a lot of them believe that when it comes their time, they'll be judged on what they did while here on the earth.

That's not necessarily true. If we read the Word, here's what's going to take place. Our works will be judged according to not only what we did, but by what we were called to do.

This is why our ministry is so focused on helping students discover their God-given destiny.

Once we are born again, we become eternal beings, and we make the choice as to where we spend it. So, eternity isn't something to necessarily fear. Jesus gave His life so we could spend eternity with Him, and we invest our entire life getting ready for it.

Might be a good idea to spend some time today asking God what He wants you to do down here before you stand before Him up there.

Today's Word is Revelation 20:12

"And I saw the dead, small and great, standing before God, and books were opened. And another book was opened, which is the Book of Life. And the dead were judged according to their works, by the things which were written in the books."

SEPTEMBER 7

FAITHFULNESS PRODUCES PROMOTION

Don't ever, ever underestimate what God can and will do if you're available to be used in His Kingdom.

To this end, one of the greatest lessons I've learned from God is that He sure honors and blesses our faithfulness and obedience.

When you're faithful to obey His promptings, when you're faithful in your schoolwork, when you're faithful working where He's given you a job to do, count on it - your faithfulness positions you for promotion.

A long time ago there was a guy named Amos who was a sheep breeder. He wasn't yet in ministry and his family wasn't a ministry family; yet, as Amos was faithful to take care of those sheep, God recognized his faithfulness, spoke to him, and gave him an assignment for the Kingdom.

No different with you today. Be faithful where you are, take care of business. As you do, watch for God to tap you on the shoulder with an assignment with your name all over it.

Today's Word is Amos 7:14-15

Then Amos answered, and said to Amaziah: "I was no prophet, nor was I a son of a prophet, but I was a sheepbreeder and a tender of sycamore fruit. Then the Lord took me as I followed the flock, and the Lord said to me, 'Go, prophesy to My people Israel.'"

SEPTEMBER 8

THE BALL IS IN YOUR COURT

Did you know that the very first commandment in the Word of God that has a promise from God attached to it is for children to obey their parents and to honor their mom and dad?

Want to live a long life on earth and want things to go well for you as you're living life? If so, the Bible puts the ball squarely in your court.

Honor your parents by obeying them. When you do, God promises that you'll live long on the earth.

Sadly, I meet a lot of teenagers who seem to think that their parents are from another planet and that whatever wisdom they may have once had has long gone away. They think their parents are too old-fashioned and just don't get this generation.

You know what I've learned from talking with a great number of teenagers and their parents? Every generation of teens has had teenagers who thought their parents just didn't get them, and therefore, those teenagers didn't feel the need to obey their parents, much less honor them.

This must stop. When God gave you your mom and dad or your legal Guardians, He chose them specifically for you. He knows exactly what He's doing.

God has a lot for you to do. In fact, you fulfilling His calling on your life may very well take a lifetime to accomplish. He needs you around. So, want a long life? Start by doing your part: obey your parents, honor them, and watch God extend the very days of your life.

Today's Word is Ephesians 6:1-3

"Children, obey your parents in the Lord, for this is right. "Honor your father and mother," which is the first commandment with promise: "that it may be well with you and you may live long on the earth."

SEPTEMBER 9

GET GOING

Got something for you to look at and then consider. Look at the word GOD. See anything? I do.

Two-thirds of the name of God is GO. God wants us to go for Him.

One of the last instructions Jesus gave His disciples before returning to Heaven was for them to go and make disciples of all the nations. That instruction, thousands of years later, hasn't changed. (Remember that Jesus is the same yesterday, today, and tomorrow.)

He's still instructing us to go for the Father.

Whether you're called to go to college or whether you're called to go start a business. Whether you're called to go into the military or called to go be a homemaker. Whatever you're called to do, somewhere within that calling is the commandment to go.

Going for God doesn't necessarily mean geographically. It does, however, always have to do with being about your Fathers' business.

You've got something you're called to do. Want some friendly advice? Get going.

Today's Word is Matthew 28:19

"Go therefore and make disciples of all the nations, baptizing them in the name of the Father and of the Son and of the Holy Spirit,"

SEPTEMBER 10

GET SOME REST

At the time that I'm writing this devotional for teens, my wife, Lori, and I have three teenagers. The other day Lori and I were somewhere, and I mentioned that our oldest, Will, could seemingly just sit down on our couch; and if no one said anything for a few short minutes, he'd be asleep.

Lori then explained to me that next to infancy, teenagers need more rest now than at any other time in their lives. Hearing Lori share that with me caused me to think about a verse over in the book of Matthew.

In this verse, Jesus tells us to come to Him; and as we do, He'll give us rest.

Now that's a Word from God for every teenager who will ever read this book. Come to Jesus and He'll give you rest. But rest from what?

Rest from the burdens of life. Rest from the curse of toiling.

Consider taking some time today to just curl up in the arms of your Heavenly Father. Maybe turn on some worship music. Close your eyes; listen for His voice of instruction. As you do, unplug from the entrapments of the teenage life, and let the Giver of life give you rest.

Today's Word is Matthew 11:28

"Come to Me, all you who labor and are heavy laden, and I will give you rest."

SEPTEMBER 11

THE HEAT IS ON

If you've ever been to a vacation spot where people dress up and offer you a glimpse into how things were done centuries ago, you may have seen a boiling pot or a fiery furnace on display somewhere within that vacation location. And if you happened to get close to either, you could probably feel the heat.

The Bible talks with us about a refining pot and a furnace. It tells us that the refining pot is for silver and the furnace is for gold. The very next verse however tells us that God tests the heart.

That scripture really got my attention. Here's why. We might go through some times when it feels like the heat is on. If you can relate, then it might be a good idea to better understand why we go though some of what we go through.

In Proverbs God tells us exactly what's going on when the heat is on. The Lord is testing the quality of our heart. You see, silver is refined in the boiling pot. Gold is purified in the furnace of fire. Our hearts are no different. When we go through the fire, the condition of our heart is being examined.

No one that I know of necessarily enjoys these times of testing. But the people who I do know who are being used mightily by God are the ones who, when their heart is being tested, pass the test.

How about you? How's your heart test?

Today's Word is Proverbs 17:3

"The refining pot is for silver and the furnace for gold, but the Lord tests the hearts."

SEPTEMBER 12

THE GREATER ONE IS IN YOU

Overcoming the enemy is no big deal to God. In fact, He's already completed the work. The Bible tells us that Jesus made a public spectacle out of the devil - He drug him through the streets of hell and just embarrassed the devil on his own turf.

That same power that Jesus used to defeat the devil thousands of years ago is readily available to you right now. Sure, the devil walks around like a roaring lion, seeking whom he may devour, but here's a point I hope you don't ever forget: he is not a roaring lion and he's looking for who he may devour, not who he will devour.

If you're a Believer, the Greater One is living inside you right now. He's your protector. Call on Him; talk with Him. Listen for His voice of instruction.

Might be that today you're in an all-out war with devil. Maybe you're just not sure what to do. If that's you, open your Bible up to 1 John 4:4 and remind yourself, remind the Lord, but most of all, remind the devil that He who is in you (the Spirit of the Living God) is greater than he (the devil) who is in the world.

Today's Word is 1 John 4:4

"You are of God, little children, and have overcome them, because He who is in you is greater than he who is in the world."

SEPTEMBER 13

YOUR ANSWER IS ON THE WAY

Ever feel like when you're praying, either your prayer never made it past your bedroom ceiling; or if it did, somewhere between here and Heaven that prayer took a wrong turn and never even made it to the throne of God?

If you prayed from your heart and in accordance with the will of God, what happened? Let me give you an example from the Bible.

Many years ago, a guy named Daniel was praying about a very serious situation. He wasn't getting an answer to his prayers; and because of the seriousness of what Daniel was praying about, God sent an Angel to him to explain what was going on.

The Angel told Daniel that he had come to Daniel because of the words Daniel had prayed. In fact, the Angel explained that from the first day Daniel had prayed, he was on his way to Daniel with the answer. Along his way, however, the Angel of God encountered spiritual resistance - warfare.

The Angel then told Daniel that he had been in a spiritual war for twenty-one days. Because a breakthrough was needed, God sent a higher-ranking Angel named Michael to ensure that the answer to Daniel's prayer got to him.

If today you find your prayers are being hindered, don't automatically question your faith. Instead, stand on the Word of God, stay strong in faith, recognize that warfare is real, and choose to believe that your answer is on the way.

Today's Word is Daniel 10:12 - 13

"Then he said to me, "Do not fear, Daniel, for from the first day that you set your heart to understand, and to humble yourself before your God, your words were heard; and I have come because of your words. But the prince of the kingdom of Persia withstood me twenty-one days; and behold, Michael, one of the chief princes, came to help me, for I had been left alone there with the kings of Persia."

SEPTEMBER 14

PRIVILEGE & RESPONSIBILITY

The longer I'm a parent, the more I learn about the balance the Lord wants us to strike with our teenage children; the balance between privilege and responsibility.

If you're a teenager today, you probably have some privileges in your life; and if you're like most teens I meet on the road, you probably enjoy them. You may have your own car or have access to one of your parents' vehicles. Maybe you have a later curfew this year than the one you had last year.

Ever wondered beyond just asking your mom or dad for more of these privileges what you might do to earn more of what you want? That might be a radical thought to consider, but it's a good thought that I believe deserves your attention.

When our teens adhere to and obey our instructions, my wife and I entrust them with more privileges. If our children choose to disobey us, you guessed it: our trust diminishes, as does the privileges they enjoy.

It's no different for any of us, regardless of our age, with our Heavenly Father. The more He trusts us to obey His Word, the more privileges He sends our way. The less He can trust us, the fewer privileges show up in our lives.

Now don't miss this. His love for you and me never changes. What we receive from Him, however, is in direct proportion to what the Word of God teaches us in Luke 12:48: to whom much is given, much will be required.

Today's Word is Luke 12:48

"But he who did not know, yet committed things deserving of stripes, shall be beaten with few. For everyone to whom much is given, from him much will be required; and to whom much has been committed, of him they will ask the more."

SEPTEMBER 15

IT'S YOUR HERITAGE

The word HERITAGE is a word that I'd strongly encourage you to get to know. Webster's defines heritage as, "Something that comes or belongs to one by reason of birth; an inherited lot or portion."

Did you know that, as a Christian, you have a heritage promised to you by God Himself? You do.

Here's part of your heritage. No weapon formed against you will prosper, and any and every word spoken against you in judgment shall be condemned. That's huge! What a heritage from the Lord.

If you're going along in life and suddenly realize that the enemy has thrown an assignment against you, stop what you're doing, be mindful of your heritage, and then remind the devil of your heritage.

Quote Isaiah 54:17 out loud, and then get on with life. After all, being protected from the enemy is your heritage.

Today's Word is Isaiah 54:17

"No weapon formed against you shall prosper, and every tongue which rises against you in judgment you shall condemn. This is the heritage of the servants of the Lord, and their righteousness is from Me," says the Lord.

SEPTEMBER 16

WALKING IN THE LIGHT

One of the topics I most enjoy talking about with students is the subject of fellowship.

I enjoy this topic, because I've seen too many teenagers who live the life of a loner. Being by yourself all or most of the time was never the plan of God for any of us. Sure, we all need time to get away by ourselves to rest and hear from God. Apart from those times, however, I believe the Lord makes it clear throughout the Word that His will is for us to have fellowship with each other.

Maybe you're wondering with whom you should have fellowship. Great question. What does the Bible say? It says that if we walk in the light (the Gospel) as He is in the light, we have fellowship with one another.

So, to be obedient to the Lord, why don't you consider taking some time right now and believe God to put someone in your life with whom you can have fellowship? Someone who, like you, is walking in the light.

Today's Word is 1 John 1:7

"But if we walk in the light as He is in the light, we have fellowship with one another, and the blood of Jesus Christ His Son cleanses us from all sin."

SEPTEMBER 17

IT REALLY IS WHAT WE'RE CALLED TO DO

Next time I meet a teenager who shares with me that he or she doesn't really understand the love of God, I'm going to ask them to quote 1 John 3:16. Not John 3:16, but 1 John 3:16.

John 3:16 is probably the most memorized verse in the Bible; but do you know what 1 John 3:16 says and, more specifically, what it says relating to the love God has for us? Here's a clue.

There is absolutely, positively no unloved person on the earth today. Period.

When God asked Jesus to lay down His life for you, His motivation was love. When Jesus obeyed the Father and willingly died for you on a cross, His motivation was love. No matter where you are as you read this devotional, I need you to know that you are loved.

The assignment of the enemy is to isolate teens and make them feel unloved and all alone. Not so with God. He just wants you to know and experience His love; because as you do, guess what? You then are better equipped to go share this love with others.

Sharing the love of God with others ... It really is what we're called to do.

Today's Word is 1 John 3:16

"By this we know love, because He laid down His life for us..."

SEPTEMBER 18

BE STILL & KNOW

Early one morning I got a text from one of our kids.

In part of their text, they were sharing with me some of their thoughts on where they were this morning in their walk with the Lord. As I read their words, I sure heard their heart.

In fact, it's their words that gave birth to this devotional.

Ever been through a season where you just don't seem to be as connected to God as you once were? Ever been through a season where, at every turn and in every decision, it's unmistakable that God is right there with you, leading you every step of the way? What's the difference and what can you do about where you are?

Part of this difference is the busyness of our life. Someone told me a long time ago that if the enemy can't slow us down, he'll do his best to speed us up. Our job is to be ruled by the peace of God; and in that peace, follow His direction. Sometimes we allow ourselves to just get too busy.

Each of us goes through seasons. Some are more comfortable and enjoyable than others. But in those seasons when it just seems quiet, when you might even feel a little disjointed from God, I've got a suggestion for you to consider which comes directly from the Word:

Be still and know that He is God.

In my response to our child text that morning, I reminded them that no matter what we feel, God is ever-present with us. Our responsibility is to get in a position to really hear from Him.

Oftentimes our hearing from God first requires that we be still and know that He is.

Today's Word is Psalms 46:10

"Be still, and know that I am God; I will be exalted among the nations, I will be exalted in the earth!"

SEPTEMBER 19

TO DO HIS WILL

When Jesus came to the earth He did so with a specific purpose. He made it abundantly clear that His coming to earth was all about Him fulfilling the will of His Father.

As a young person alive on planet earth today, guess what? You're not here on your own authority. You're here because God sent you here. He sent you here because He has something He needs you to fulfill for Him; something that you and you alone are uniquely gifted and called to do by God Himself.

Know what? I meet a lot of adults who tell me of their private frustrations in the life they live. My first question in response to what they share with me is: "Are you doing what God called you to do?"

Want to put an end to frustration being an overwhelming force in your life as it relates to you fulfilling your calling? If so, learn the lesson early: you're here not to do your will but the will of your Heavenly Father who sent you.

Today's Word is John 6:38

"For I have come down from heaven, not to do My own will, but the will of Him who sent Me."

SEPTEMBER 20

HE NEVER FAILS

One of the greatest truths I believe God wants you to be mindful of every single day of your life is that regardless of what's going on in your life, God never fails.

Simply put, failure is not part of His DNA.

His lack of failure surely qualifies Him to lead your life. Many, many teenagers, however, come to me with bewildered looks on their faces, telling me of how something in their lives has gone terribly wrong. And often these teenagers ask me, "Where was God; why did He let me fail?"

I then can share with them and now with you that in our successes and in our defeats, God is with us every step of the way. Our being aware of His presence, however, has everything to do with the spiritual condition of our heart. If today you suffer great loss; if you're walking with the Lord, somehow, someway, He can turn that loss into something good in your life. Him doing so, however, has much to do with your faith in Him and in this truth - He never fails.

Today's Word is Zephaniah 3:5

"The Lord is righteous in her midst, He will do no unrighteousness. Every morning He brings His justice to light; He never fails, But the unjust knows no shame."

SEPTEMBER 21

GOD WAS WITH HIM

Want to be great in life? Want to do something for God that cannot be erased? Want your life to count? If so, get ready to see some keys to this happening.

In the Bible, the only guy throughout the Word of God who was identified as having a "heart after God" was King David. And if you know anything about his life, King David proved over and over that the human race was alive and well. At times, he really blew it.

What caused David to be great, however, is the same thing that will cause you to be great. David had a relationship with God, and David knew that unless the Lord was with him, he could and would never reach his potential for greatness.

Now think about it; since King David, the only guy in the Word to be known for his heart being after the heart of God, knew the value of having both a personal relationship with and a dependent relationship on God, shouldn't you and I follow that example?

If you want to see greatness in your life, you might consider having these two aspects present and accounted for. First, your relationship with the Lord being more than just a passing occurrence and second, your total reliance upon Jesus being with you 24/7- a truth upon which you can build a sure foundation.

David became great because God was with him. You can, too.

Today's Word is 2 Samuel 5:10

"So David went on and became great, and the Lord God of hosts was with him."

SEPTEMBER 22

THE LIFE YOU LIVE

What you give your attention to reflects where your heart is. If you focus on sports, that'll be reflected in competition on the field.

If you focus on dating someone, that'll be reflected in that relationship.

If you focus on earning money, that'll be reflected in your bank account.

And it's absolutely no different with the Lord. If you focus on Him and His will for your life, that'll be reflected in your heart and ultimately in the life you live.

How do you focus on the Lord? Purest way to do so is by being in the Word. In the book of Proverbs, we're instructed to give our attention to the Word of God, to turn our ears in the direction of the Word. We're even told to not let the Word of God depart from our eyes but to keep His words in our heart. The Bible tells us that it is life and health.

So, if you put your focus on the Word, guess what? That'll be reflected in the life you live.

Today's Word is Proverbs 4:20-23

"My son, give attention to my words; incline your ear to my sayings. Do not let them depart from your eyes; keep them in the midst of your heart; for they are life to those who find them, and health to all their flesh. Keep your heart with all diligence, for out of it spring the issues of life."

SEPTEMBER 23

HELP IS ON THE WAY

Sometimes we get off track; and if we stay off track, we begin to realize we're a long, long way from the will of God for our lives.

Maybe you know all too well what it feels like to get off track with God. Could be that you're off track right now.

If so, what can be done to get back on track? What can you do at this moment to help the process? As simple as this might sound, you can start by asking the Holy Spirit to turn you back to the plan and will of God. If you ask and do so in faith, He'll answer. Your job then will be to obey His instructions.

When you ask the Lord to turn you back, what you're saying is, "I need your help." He loves you so much that the instant you ask, you can be assured that help is on the way.

When the Lord helps a person get back on track, restoration takes place.

Tired of being off track and out of the will of God? Ask for His help and watch restoration take place in your life.

Today's Word is Lamentations 5:21

"Turn us back to You, O Lord, and we will be restored; renew our days as of old,"

SEPTEMBER 24

KNOWING

One of the most powerful words in the Bible is the word KNOW. Knowing is something altogether different than thinking and knowing is also different from believing. When you take the time to study faith, you might see varying stages of development your faith grows to and through.

As we hear more and more of the Word and then apply the Word we hear to our lives, our faith grows. As our faith grows, we move from thinking about a promise in the Word to believing that promise, and ultimately KNOWING that promise is ours.

When you know something, it's not easy for someone to talk you out of that knowledge.

Thousands of years ago there were two sisters named Martha and Mary, whose brother, named Lazarus, had died. This family was very close to Jesus. We know this because when Lazarus died, it's the only time in the Bible that records, "Jesus wept."

Several days after Lazarus had been buried, Martha approached the Lord and said, "Even now I KNOW that whatever You ask of God, God will give you."

Martha wanted her brother to come back from the dead. She had such confidence in Jesus that she boldly approached Him with her knowing of His power and of His relationship with His Father. She knew that her faith could and would bring Lazarus back to life. And you know what? It did.

What do you KNOW today? Wrap your faith around your request, knowing that Jesus will respond. Then believe God for your miracle.

Today's Word is John 11:21-22

"Now Martha said to Jesus, "Lord, if You had been here, my brother would not have died. But even now I know that whatever You ask of God, God will give You."

SEPTEMBER 25

HE WAS, HE IS & HE WILL ALWAYS BE

From the beginning of time and running throughout eternity God is the same.

He has no beginning and has no end; yet, He was, He is, and He always will be. How cool is that?

It's true. Our minds cannot grasp a God who has no beginning or end, but our Spirit sure can. Your Spirit is what connects you to God through Jesus.

Developing confidence in God comes in large part when you settle in your heart that God never changes and that His years have no end.

Knowing that God never changes and that He's never going away, what would you do for God right now if you knew you'd succeed in that endeavor? What would you pursue with unparalleled confidence if you really knew in your heart, your Spirit, that you'd accomplish that undertaking, because you'd be doing so with the knowledge that God isn't a God who changes?

Living life with that kind of confidence is what God wants for you and me. How do we get that confidence? Begin by knowing that He's the same, and His years will have no end.

Today's Word is Psalms 102:27

"But You are the same, and Your years will have no end."

SEPTEMBER 26

BEAR A BURDEN

When you go through a difficult season, sometimes it's a little easier to go through that situation when someone comes alongside you and walks with you through it.

When that someone comes along, in many instances, just their support for you will help lift the weight of whatever it is you're experiencing.

Why is this? What is it about someone coming alongside us when we are going through something that just his or her presence alone seems to make such a difference?

Maybe we feel stronger and less burdened when someone comes along because it's a scriptural mandate.

In the book of Galatians, we're commanded (yes, commanded) to bear one another's burdens. Our doing so positions us to have someone come alongside us when we need a friend to help us endure a tough time that we might be going through.

Remember, everything in the Kingdom of God is seedtime and harvest.

Begin today to plant the seed of being there for someone else. As you do, when you need someone to be there for you, you can confidently call on the Lord of the harvest to send you a friend who will help you bear a burden.

Today's Word is Galatians 6:2

"Bear one another's burdens, and so fulfill the law of Christ."

SEPTEMBER 27

FIRST PLACE

In Exodus 20 we are given the Ten Commandments by which God expects us to live life. Notice that He did not call them the "ten good ideas". Nope, He very specifically and purposefully named them the "Ten Commandments".

A "command" is a military term, and it's one that isn't too terribly difficult to understand. If you ever serve in the military and your Commanding Officer gives you a direct command, there will be no doubt in your heart about what that Officer said nor will there be any room for negotiation. He/She said it, and your part is to fulfill what was commanded to you.

It's the same with the Commandments of God.

The thing about God's Ten Commandments is this. He gave them to us being wholly motivated by His love for us. He knows what will keep us out of trouble and He knows the path He wants us to take that leads us to a life that's blessed with His blessing. That's why He gave us His commandments.

The very first of His Ten Commandments is that "we shall have no other gods before Him." Why is this? Is God insecure? Of course not. We are to have no other gods before Him because there is no other god like Him.

God is God, and in Him exists all of life. If we wrongfully and willfully exchange the One, true God for a god (lower case g) of this world, guess what happens? We get a counterfeit god with a counterfeit life.

God so wants to be first place in your life. Put Him there by obeying His commandments.

Today's Word is Exodus 20:3

"You shall have no other gods before Me."

SEPTEMBER 28

GIVERS & TAKERS

I wonder if someone has ever used you. Used in the sense of having been taken advantage of or taken for granted.

You may have poured your heart into the life of someone else and been there for that person over and over, but, somehow, what you've done for that person has never been reciprocated. What you have is a give and take relationship; you do all the giving while they do all the taking.

Doesn't seem too fair, does it? Might even anger you. What can you do?

Well, the Bible tells us exactly what to do. In the book of Matthew (in red letters) Jesus very plainly says to you and to me, "Love your enemies, bless those who curse you, do good to those who hate you, and pray for those who spitefully use you."

So, what are we to do? LOVE. BLESS. PRAY.

Those instructions make absolutely no sense to our natural way of thinking; but with God, He deals with our heart. So today as you're reading this, maybe someone has come or is coming to your heart; someone who has been a "taker" in your life. Instead of being hurt, angry, or maybe even retaliatory, choose God's method instead.

Love, bless, and pray. As you obey His instructions, your life will be blessed.

Today's Word is Matthew 5:44

"But I say to you, love your enemies, bless those who curse you, do good to those who hate you, and pray for those who spitefully use you and persecute you,"

SEPTEMBER 29

MY GRACE IS SUFFICIENT

I've met a lot of students who are living life with the attitude of, "I've got this." These young people have sadly bought the lie of the enemy that they are self-sufficient, that they really have no need for God, because their life is pretty good; and after all, they know what they're doing.

When I meet these teenagers, I'm often led to share more of my testimony with them. For way too long I also lived life with an attitude that I had it all together and really had no need for anyone, especially a God I could not see.

Then one day I came to the harsh reality that, "I didn't have this"; and when that moment happened, I really didn't know what to do or where to turn.

It was then that a scripture came to the forefront of my heart. It's a Word found in 2 Corinthians; and in it we're reminded that God's grace is sufficient; that His strength is made perfect in our weakness.

Maybe you know all too well what it feels like to wake up and realize that you really need Someone much greater than you to take the reigns of your life. Guess what? He's right there beside you right now, and His grace is available.

I believe with every fiber in my body that Grace is not a "thing" but is, instead, a person. Are you ready to experience true Grace and strength? Then turn to Jesus, to Grace Himself, and watch your life forever change.

Today's Word is 2 Corinthians 12:9

"And He said to me, "My grace is sufficient for you, for My strength is made perfect in weakness." Therefore most gladly I will rather boast in my infirmities, that the power of Christ may rest upon me."

SEPTEMBER 30

DO IT NOW

One of the lessons the Holy Spirit taught me when I first began our ministry is, "Don't put off until tomorrow what you can do today."

That lesson has stuck with me for decades; and it's a principle I'm reminded of on an almost daily basis.

For example, someone leaves me a voice mail and asks me to return their call. Maybe I've just gotten home from a trip and I'm tired and not very talkative, or maybe I just don't want to call them back right then. But in their voice mail, it was clear that they needed some information I could provide. It wasn't an emergency; they just had need for info.

Sure, I could wait until tomorrow and return his or her call when I was rested and ready to talk. But if I have that information now, why not go ahead and press through my flesh and do something for someone else?

Could be that you know all too well what I'm talking about. If so, I'd encourage you to do what the Bible says in the book of Proverbs; do it now.

You doing so is a seed that will produce a harvest.

Today's Word is Proverbs 3:28

"Do not say to your neighbor, "Go, and come back, and tomorrow I will give it," when you have it with you."

OCTOBER 1

A WILLING MIND

How many times have you really felt led in your heart to do something for the Lord, but you've not acted on that prompting because you just didn't think you had what it took to get the job done? Maybe you felt ill-equipped, maybe you thought you were too young, or perhaps you just didn't think you had the necessary qualifications at that moment to successfully accomplish what was in your heart to do for Him.

Here's something you might want to think about. If you're being led to do something for the Lord and you don't necessarily feel qualified to do what you're being led to do, don't you think God knew how you'd feel before He led you to do it? Of course He would. So, what do you do?

The Bible says that if there is first a willing mind, it is accepted according to what you have, not according to what you do not have. What's that statement got to do with you and your feeling unqualified to do something for Him?

God is looking for your willingness, not your qualifications.

Throughout the Word we see example after example of ordinary people being anointed by God to do the extraordinary for Him.

Next time you're led to do something that seems way beyond your ability, trust God and be willing.

Today's Word is 2 Corinthians 8:12

"For if there is first a willing mind, it is accepted according to what one has, and not according to what he does not have."

OCTOBER 2

SUCCESSFULLY ACCOMPLISH

In the Bible we're introduced to Solomon, who was known for his wisdom. In fact, the Bible talks specifically about the wisdom with which Solomon lived his life.

When he had the prompting and the desire to build a house for God's presence, Solomon set out to build something that had never been built. To do so, he would have to lean heavily on the Spirit of Wisdom to accomplish that undertaking.

One day I was reading about the building of the temple, and as I read, I came to a verse that really caught my attention. It was a word in a verse that got my full attention. The word was "successfully".

As I read this one verse over and over, I saw a Kingdom principle. Not only did Solomon accomplish all that came into his heart to make in the house of the Lord, he also SUCCESSFULLY accomplished all that came into his heart.

In this one verse and in that one word, the Holy Spirit taught me a lesson. When you're led by God to do something for Him, don't just accomplish it, follow the Spirit of Wisdom and go a step further; successfully accomplish it.

Today's Word is 2 Chronicles 7:11

"Thus Solomon finished the house of the Lord and the king's house; and Solomon successfully accomplished all that came into his heart to make in the house of the Lord and in his own house."

OCTOBER 3

NEVER FORSAKEN; THAT'S A PROMISE

Do you know that there are thousands of promises in the Word of God? No matter what you face and despite what the enemy tries to use against you, within these promises, God has already provided a way of escape for you and for me.

One of those promises that I find myself going back to time and time again has to do with the faithfulness of God. In Psalms 37 the writer reminds us that he's been young and was now old, yet, throughout all his years of life, he'd not one time seen the righteous (those people who are in right standing with God) forsaken, nor had he ever witnessed the descendants of the righteous begging for bread.

Maybe today you're a teenager or maybe you're the parent or the grandparent of teenagers. Wherever you are along the timeline of life, I believe the Lord wants to remind all of us that He'll never forsake our descendants or us.

What's our part in that equation? To remember it's in Him that we are to live our lives as the righteousness of God.

Beyond the promise we've talked about today, there's so many more additional promises in the Word waiting for you right now.

Today's Word is Psalms 37:25

"I have been young, and now am old; yet I have not seen the righteous forsaken, nor his descendants begging bread."

OCTOBER 4

TALK WITH GOD ABOUT YOUR MONEY

Many years ago my wife, Lori, and I began teaching our children about money. As a couple, Lori and I see money as a tool; and as such, tools are used in building and maintaining.

So, when our three children were very young, Lori and I set off on an adventure to teach Will, Ellie, and Meg what we had learned about money and stewardship; how to be led by God to use money to both build and maintain.

We gave each of our children four Mason jars and asked them to label, color, and design each of their four jars in whatever manner they chose. Each jar, however, had to have a label. The four labels were GOD, OTHERS, SAVE & TOY.

When our kids were given an allowance or they earned their own money, we showed them how to divide those funds into the four jars.

We taught our kids to first tithe. To then give an offering to others. Next, we taught them to put money up in savings. And, finally, after the first three priorities were met, we taught them to buy a toy.

Like every other aspect of God, He's very specific, even about money. Maybe today you feel the need to spend some time with the Lord to get some specific direction about your finances. Nothing is too small for God, and surely nothing is too big.

Talk with Him about money and how to manage it. His principles are clearly laid out in His Word.

Today's Word is Malachi 3:8

"Will a man rob God? Yet you have robbed Me! But you say, 'In what way have we robbed You?' In tithes and offerings."

OCTOBER 5

SAY WHAT HE TELLS YOU TO SAY

One of the most dangerous things any of us can ever do is tell someone what they want to hear when the Lord is clearly leading us to tell that person something they need to hear. Telling them what they want to hear is comfortable, but your obedience to the prompting of the Lord and telling them what they need to hear is oftentimes anything but comfortable.

It has surprised me how many times a teenager has wandered over to me after one of our events and asked to talk about something they had been led to share with one of their friends; but for whatever reason, they just couldn't seem to find the courage to say what they'd heard from the Lord. They felt convicted because they had not obeyed God.

Without fail, their disobedience was rooted in fear. They wondered, "What if what I tell them is wrong? What if I tell them, and they get mad at me?" "What if I obey God, and they tell all my friends that I've become a fanatic?"

What if, what if, what if - the badge of fear.

If God trusts you enough to prompt you to tell someone something from Him, it'll probably be a terrific idea if you in turn trust Him enough to obey His promptings.

Today's Word is Numbers 22:38

"And Balaam said to Balak, "Look, I have come to you! Now, have I any power at all to say anything? The word that God puts in my mouth, that I must speak."

OCTOBER 6

HE IS ABLE

Teenagers oftentimes share with me that that they just seem to repeatedly stumble in their walk with God. They tell me that they're walking along in life doing well and growing in faith, then, seemingly out of nowhere, a temptation comes in like a torpedo. Instead of them standing firm on the Word, they seem to stumble under the pressure of that temptation.

I'm usually led to then share with these students that, in and of ourselves, we're not equipped to stand and not stumble when the devil puts on the pressure. Our security and stability must instead be found in our being hidden in Christ, our living life by the direction of the Word of God.

Next time you feel yourself becoming spiritually weak in the knees and exposed to the attack of the enemy, don't freak out. Instead, run over to the book of Jude and declare out loud what the Word says about the God we serve; He is able to keep you from stumbling.

Today's Word is Jude 1:24

"Now to Him who is able to keep you from stumbling, and to present you faultless before the presence of His glory with exceeding joy,"

OCTOBER 7

LIKE A FLOOD

The Bible tells us that when the enemy comes in, like a flood, the Spirit of God will lift up a standard against him.

Please take note that the Bible doesn't say, "if the enemy comes in." No, it says, "When the enemy comes in."

As a student, you must have a sure foundation, one that is anchored in and by the Word of God. You can be assured that the enemy is looking for a way into your life. If you let him in and your spiritual foundation is weak, he'll come and he'll come with force.

While that might sound intense, if you're a Christian and stand on the Word, your resisting power will be so much greater than the assignment of the devil when he comes face-to-face with the standard that the Spirit of God lifts up against him.

God's standard is His Word.

Today's Word is Isaiah 59:19

"So shall they fear the name of the Lord from the west, and His glory from the rising of the sun; when the enemy comes in like a flood, the Spirit of the Lord will lift up a standard against him."

OCTOBER 8

FROM MILK TO MEAT

When you were a baby, you were fed with milk. That milk helped you to grow, and for a period of time, it was all your body needed. One day, though, a steady diet of milk no longer satisfied you. As your body grew, it required more nutrition.

It's no different with your spiritual growth. Everyone starts off in Christianity as a spiritual baby. God knows this about us and meets us where we are and begins to then lead us by His Word to where He wants us to be.

At first, you're fed the milk of the Word; the basics. Maybe you get fed at home or at church or perhaps Christian TV. As you grow and your Spirit is developing, however, you require more spiritual nutrition, more of the Word. But here's where the journey gets interesting. You acquiring that extra nutrition into your system is not God's responsibility. It's yours.

Can I just be blunt with you? I meet too many students who are spiritual babies. If that's you, please don't feel condemned; instead, maybe it's time to get a spiritual checkup and do something about your spiritual growth.

The Holy Spirit has much to teach you. Before He can do so, however, you've got to move from the milk of the Word to the meat of the Word.

Today's Word is 1 Corinthians 3:2-3

"I fed you with milk and not with solid food; for until now you were not able to receive it, and even now you are still not able; for you are still carnal. For where there are envy, strife, and divisions among you, are you not carnal and behaving like mere men?"

OCTOBER 9

BELIEVE YOUR FATHER

If you're a born-again Believer, your bloodline runs all the way back to a guy in the Bible named Abram, whose name was later changed to Abraham. Since Abraham is part of your family, I share with teens that it's vitally important for them to know who Abraham was and what he did that caused him to be such an integral part of God's plan for humanity, and why he was given a name no one else has ever had.

The name? Abraham is known as the "Father of Faith". Know why? Because he believed in the Lord, and as he did, God accounted his believing as righteousness. In other words, because Abraham stood strong in faith and believed the Word of the Lord, his believing put him in right standing with God.

Now think about this. Somewhere way back in your family tree is the Patriarch Abraham. He set an example for you and for me and for every other Believer, an example to believe God and to not be overwhelmed at whatever God promised Him.

As you consider the life of Abraham, please understand that even though he was strong in faith, he wasn't perfect. Just like you and me, he also missed God. And so, I encourage you to go a step further. Consider Jesus. He is our true example, as He believed God and was obedient every single time - obedient even to His death.

As a Christian we have quite a family tree and heritage. The giants of faith in your family and mine have at least one thing in common: they all believed God.

Want to be counted among the faithful, those full of faith? Follow the example of Abraham and Jesus. Believe your Father.

Today's Word is Genesis 15:6

"And he believed in the Lord, and He accounted it to him for righteousness."

OCTOBER 10

TIME TO FAST

In the years that I've been on the road ministering to students, there's one subject that when I mention it, most of the students in attendance routinely know very little about.

The subject? Fasting.

Yet, in the Word, Jesus, the General of the Church, very clearly speaks about fasting when He says, "When you fast ..." Notice that He doesn't put a choice with His declaration of you and me fasting. He simply and matter of factly says, "When you fast ..."

He goes on to instruct us that when we fast, we aren't supposed to let people know what we're doing; instead, we're to anoint our head, wash our face, and let our Father reward our obedience.

Obedience is why we fast. As we go without some food or maybe some soft drinks, or as we go through some time without our music or being on social media, we are purposefully setting aside time to distance ourselves from what we want so we can instead hear what He wants from us and for us.

I've never found fasting to be too terribly enjoyable. But every single time I've obeyed His leading to fast, I've seen breakthrough in my life, and He's surely rewarded my obedience.

Need a breakthrough in your life today? Might be that the Lord is gently tapping you on your shoulder and calling you to a time of fasting. Pray about it, talk about fasting with your mom and dad. If you're on medicine or you have a medical condition, consult your doctor before you fast.

Everyone everywhere can fast something. Ask the Lord about it. If you ask, I assure you that He'll answer.

Today's Word is Matthew 6:17-18

"But you, when you fast, anoint your head and wash your face, so that you do not appear to men to be fasting, but to your Father who is in the secret place; and your Father who sees in secret will reward you openly."

OCTOBER 11

WHAT'S IN A NAME

If you spend any time at all in the Word of God, you'll quickly realize that there are many names attributed to God the Father, God the Son, and God the Holy Spirit. Each name reveals yet another quality and characteristic of who God is.

God is an all-consuming fire. Jesus is the Messiah. The Holy Spirit is a still, small voice. There are so many differing names of God throughout the Word, yet each name has something to do with the life you live.

In the twelfth chapter of the book of Hebrews, we see two names of Jesus; names that, each time I see them, bring such confidence to my heart. Next to Jesus the Savior, these two names are the ones I most talk about with students. The names are Author and Finisher of our faith.

In other words, what Jesus authors, He finishes.

Our responsibility is to be so tuned into Him that when we see Him authoring, beginning something that is designed to grow our faith, we jump right into the process and begin to believe Him to finish that which He has begun.

Today's Word is Hebrews 12:2

"looking unto Jesus, the author and finisher of our faith, who for the joy that was set before Him endured the cross, despising the shame, and has sat down at the right hand of the throne of God."

OCTOBER 12

PRAISE YOUR WAY TO A NEW SEASON

Sometimes we go through a season where it seems like nothing is going our way. Friends disappear, opportunities go away, frustration sets in, and it's as if God is nowhere to be found.

To make matters even worse, the enemy comes lurking around in those seasons doing what he does. He tries to get you to buy a lie to convince you that God really doesn't love you.

What can you do to stop the enemy in his tracks? What can you do to help turn this season into a season of joy? You can begin by opening your mouth and praising the Lord.

The Bible reminds us that the Lord is greatly to be praised. In fact, He's worthy to be praised.

To me, praise is the highest form of faith we can exercise.

When we praise the Lord, we do so not necessarily for what we're going through. We instead praise Him that He's getting us through it.

Want to see seasons change in your life? Begin declaring out loud that the Lord is great and greatly to be praised.

Today's Word is Psalms 48:1

"Great is the Lord, and greatly to be praised in the city of our God, in His holy mountain."

OCTOBER 13

HE'S WATCHING

Many times, when I minister at a Christian high school chapel program, that school will receive an offering for a missions project that they've connected with, usually just before it's my time to speak.

I watch as some students sow their seed, and I watch as many do not. For the longest time I wondered about this. Why some gave, and many did not. And so, I began to dig a little.

Know what I discovered? Students really didn't feel like their money would matter; after all, in most cases, it was just a few dollars they'd be giving. In their mind what difference would that ever make?

You know what I've learned about money and ministry? Jesus looks at our heart of obedience, not necessarily the amount we give.

Next time you're given the opportunity to sow a seed and you've got a green light in your heart from the Lord to do so, might be a real good idea to not focus on how much or how small the amount. Focus instead on your desire to honor the Lord with your money.

When it comes to what we do with our money, He's watching.

Today's Word is Luke 21:1-3

"And He looked up and saw the rich putting their gifts into the treasury, and He saw also a certain poor widow putting in two mites. So He said, " Truly I say to you that this poor widow has put in more than all;"

OCTOBER 14

GOD LOVES GERMAN SHEPHERDS

Sometimes I encounter people who are absolutely convinced that God doesn't really care too much about animals. When I meet these people, I'm reminded of an account in the Word that shows just the opposite. God does care about our pets and animals.

One of the plagues that Pharaoh and the Egyptians experienced was hail. Twenty-four hours before God sent the hail, He sent a warning to the people to gather their livestock and their animals out of the field where the hail was going to be sent. He went so far as to tell them that their animals would die if they weren't brought in.

Let's make this personal. Our family really enjoys German Shepherds. Through the years, we've had several Shepherds, and each one has had a special place in our hearts. Probably one of my personal favorites was Lucy. We had her for eleven years. I still remember the day our oldest daughter, Ellie, and I picked Lucy out and brought her home.

Through the years Lucy became more and more a part of our family. One day Lucy became very sick; and within a few days, our Vet told us we had no choice but to put her down. He said that not doing so would be cruel. So, Lori and I prayed and got the peace that it was Lucy's time to go.

Sometimes I think it's important to be reminded that God is love, and that love is for everyone and everything He has created; yes, even German Shepherds named Lucy.

Today's Word is Exodus 9:18-19

"Behold, tomorrow about this time I will cause very heavy hail to rain down, such as has not been in Egypt since its founding until now. Therefore send now and gather your livestock and all that you have in the field, for the hail shall come down on every man and every animal which is found in the field and is not brought home; and they shall die."

OCTOBER 15

WIRED FOR GREATNESS

Do you see yourself as God sees you? That's a question that I ask teenagers every single time that I speak in a school. I ask that question for one simple reason - years ago the Holy Spirit led me to do so.

He took me over to the Book of Judges and instructed me to read about the life of Gideon. God saw Gideon's potential as a great leader long before Gideon recognized it.

It's no different with this generation of young student leaders I meet every week on the road. The potential you have is already deposited in your heart. You're wired for greatness. Here's the deal, though. Just as the case with Gideon, you're first going to have to see and believe what He sees and believes when you look in the mirror before you'll ever do all that you're called to do for God.

Here's a little something I'm learning after decades of working for God: He knows exactly who He wants to carry out, what He wants accomplished, when He wants it.

Our responsibility is to trust and obey.

Today's Word is Judges 6:12

"And the Angel of the Lord appeared to him, and said to him, "The Lord is with you, you mighty man of valor!"

OCTOBER 16

IMMEDIATELY

I want you to please do me a favor. As you read the next part of this devotional, in your mind's eye, put yourself in the following situation:

You and several of your closest friends are professional fishermen; fishing is how you make a living for you and your family. The fishing business is all you've ever known.

One day you're casting a net into the sea. As you do, someone you've never seen or before met walks up to you and says, "Follow Me, and I will make you fishers of men."

And then, to make matters more bizarre, you waste no time in following the instruction that you've just heard; you immediately leave your nets and follow Him.

What I've just described really happened. And you know what? It's happening every single day to young people all over the world.

Jesus is showing up in the lives of teenagers, knocking on the door of their hearts, and inviting people just like you to FOLLOW HIM in living a life of faith.

Maybe today you know exactly what I'm talking about, or maybe you haven't yet heard that knock. Either way, take it from some Fishermen who saw Him up close and personal. When He shows up in your life and says, "Follow Me," doing so IMMEDIATELY is the right answer.

Today's Word is Matthew 4:19-20

"Then He said to them, "Follow Me, and I will make you fishers of men." They immediately left their nets and followed Him."

OCTOBER 17

IT' S REAL

Peer pressure is real, especially among teenagers. Maybe you know all too well just how real peer pressure not only can be, but also literally is.

The thing about peer pressure is that the more a person either feels ganged up on or even threatened to go along with something that he or she does not want to be a part of, the more pressure that person feels to conform and go along with everyone else. That's a horrible feeling, and is one that carries with it guilt, anger, and condemnation.

The Bible paints a clear picture of peer pressure when in the book of John, we see where Pilate was cornered by a mob of people. These people pressured him into giving the "green light" to move forward with the crucifixion of Jesus.

Pilate initially resisted their pressure, then something very telling occurred. The people started increasing their pressure on him by saying, "If you let this Man go, you are not Caesar's friend." At that moment the peer pressure won out, and shortly thereafter, Jesus was crucified.

Maybe today you're experiencing peer pressure in your life. If so, here's what you can consider doing: go to God, go to an adult, and go to bat for yourself.

Today's Word is John 19:12

"From then on Pilate sought to release Him, but the Jews cried out, saying, "If you let this Man go, you are not Caesar's friend. Whoever makes himself a king speaks against Caesar."

OCTOBER 18

WHAT WOULD YOU SAY?

Have you ever thought about the last words you will speak on the earth? Ever considered the last sentence you'll ever share with whomever is with you when your life comes to an end?

I had never even thought about the last thing I might say to someone at the end of their life until I was reading in the book of Acts and saw the final sentence Jesus spoke to His Disciples before He was received back up into Heaven. When I read what He said, it was like a light bulb going off. I suddenly realized that unless Jesus comes back for us before we take our last breath, each of us will have the opportunity to share a final thought with whoever might be with us at that moment.

The last thing Jesus ministered to His team focused on their mission after He was gone. Think about that. Of all the subjects He could have covered with them, He was led to focus on their receiving power and then to be His witnesses throughout the world - witnesses that would share the message of the Gospel with people from all walks of life.

How about you? If you knew your life was going to end at a certain date and time, what would you say and to whom would you like to say it?

Today's Word is Acts 1:8

"But you shall receive power when the Holy Spirit has come upon you; and you shall be witnesses to Me in Jerusalem, and in all Judea and Samaria, and to the end of the earth."

OCTOBER 19

LIVING IN THE FOG

Ever heard of a "spiritual term" known as the FOG? Fog is a spiritual term??? Actually, the letters F O G in this instance stand for the FAVOR OF GOD.

Favor is a spiritual force that is as real as rain. It's available to people of all ages, all nationalities, and most of all, it's made available to us as a gift from God.

Through the years I've seen so many examples showing that favor follows faithfulness. Favor isn't something you or I can earn; it is something, however, that we can pray for and receive.

Favor and grace walk together. You really can't have one without the other.

According to the Bible, favor is a shield. The devil hates the favor of God because he knows he can't stop what happens when favor shows up in the life of a Believer who has asked God in faith for His favor to flow into their life.

Next time you are facing a seemingly impossible circumstance in your life, irrespective of what the facts may say, get with God. Remind Him that because of what Jesus has done for you that you're now the righteousness of God in Christ Jesus; and as such, you qualify for His favor.

Ask God to give you favor; and as He does, you too will be living in the FOG.

Today's Word is Psalms 5:12

"For You, O Lord, will bless the righteous; with favor You will surround him as with a shield."

OCTOBER 20

GET THE WORD OUT

I share with students that our ministry never charges anyone anything. Instead, the harvests we receive from our sowing financial seeds into others are what funds us.

Sowing and reaping ... it's a Kingdom principle.

When I began speaking in schools in January of 1993, the Lord gave me Matthew 10:8, and in that Scripture, I saw that I was never to charge a fee. By my not charging a fee for our ministry, I can always stand before any audience and let them know that I'm not there to take from them, but am instead there to give to them.

One day, though, I was having a particularly tough financial time and went to the Lord about what I was facing. As I was praying, I heard this sentence deep in my heart, "If you'll focus on getting My Word out to the people, the money to do so will come in." Immediately I got what He was saying.

Since that day I've been to thousands of schools; and in those schools, I've met a lot of teenagers who've shared with me that they also have a desire to be in full-time ministry but just had no idea how to get the money to do what was in their heart. Maybe I'm describing how you're feeling right now.

Whether you charge or don't charge, whether you're on the road or are local, whether you're a speaker or an author, one thing remains constant. When it comes to ministry, God wants our focus to be on getting the Word out.

Might be a good idea for you to take some time and ask the Lord how you can get His Word out. As you hear back from Him, be ready for the journey of the lifetime.

Today's Word is Matthew 6:33

"But seek first the kingdom of God and His righteousness, and all these things shall be added to you."

OCTOBER 21

HE MUST INCREASE

If time allows at the end of our assembly programs, we build in about ten minutes for questions and answers. These ten minutes can go in any number of directions but almost without fail, someone in those audiences asks if I have any advice for students who feel "called".

That's one of my favorite questions to answer, because the answer I'm typically led to share comes from John 3:30. This answer is short, in fact it's only a seven-word response; but when adhered to, these seven words will change any of our lives.

John 3:30 tells us that, "He must increase, but I must decrease."

What's that mean to you and me? If we really want to grow in God, it means we must put our agenda down and pick up His. We must put down all the distractions the enemy throws our way and choose instead to pick up the Word of God. It means that we must grow out of a lifestyle of being self-consumed and grow into a life of being consumed with His will and desire for our life.

Want to be used by God to reach the world with the Good News? It all begins with Him increasing and you decreasing.

Today's Word is John 3:30

"He must increase, but I must decrease."

OCTOBER 22

THE BREEDING GROUND FOR MIRACLES

I meet many teenagers who ask me what they've done to cause them to not be hearing from God like they once did. My response is, "Maybe it's not what you've done; maybe it's what you haven't done." Here's what I mean.

What's the most recent instruction the Lord has given you to do? Have you obeyed that instruction, or have you set it aside?

As I have shared in an earlier Devotional, one of my favorite people in the Bible is a guy named Ezekiel. He wrote a book in the Bible; and in that book we see how his relationship with God developed to such a point that one day God put him in a valley full of dry bones and asked him a question. While in that valley, God also gave Ezekiel some instructions, one of which was to prophesy (to speak) to those bones. His obedience to an instruction that made no sense caused a miracle to occur.

Maybe today it's your time to go back to an instruction you've earlier received from the Lord, an instruction you've not yet obeyed. Whether it makes sense or not, go ahead and take a step of faith.

Consider this. Your obedience is the breeding ground for miracles.

Today's Word is Ezekiel 37:7

"So I prophesied as I was commanded; and as I prophesied, there was a noise, and suddenly a rattling; and the bones came together, bone to bone."

OCTOBER 23

NEVER UNDERESTIMATE INTERCESSION

Abraham was a mission-minded man. When God gave him a mission, Abraham was on it.

The more you study the life of Abraham, the more you see the depth of relationship he had with God. This relationship becomes even clearer when we see how Abraham interceded for the saving of the righteous who were living in a wicked city called Sodom.

If you read what happened, Abraham went to God in prayer six consecutive times; and each time, Abraham lowered his expectation. He initially interceded and asked God if He would not destroy Sodom if there were fifty righteous people living there. Five times of prayer later Abraham was down to asking God if He'd spare the city if only ten righteous people called that city home.

You know what happened? God answered Abrahams' prayer of intercession by agreeing that if there were only ten righteous people found to be living in Sodom, He'd spare them from the destruction of the city.

When the Holy Spirit puts someone or something on your heart, take it seriously. Take time to pray and listen. Could be that you're the one who's being called to intercede on behalf of someone or something. Your prayer of faith may very well be the difference maker someone or something is in need of right now.

Today's Word is Genesis 18:24 and Genesis 18:32

"Suppose there were fifty righteous within the city; would You also destroy the place and not spare it for the fifty righteous that were in it?"

"Then he said, "Let not the Lord be angry, and I will speak but once more: Suppose ten should be found there?" And He said, "I will not destroy it for the sake of ten."

OCTOBER 24

BUILDING A FIRE

Today let's look at the life of Paul; specifically, the time in Paul's life when he became shipwrecked on an island named Malta.

The Bible reveals that it was a cold and rainy day, and Paul was building a fire. While he was handling the wood to build that fire, a snake came out of the sticks and fastened onto the hand of Paul.

When the natives of that island saw the snake hanging onto Paul's hand, they immediately assumed that Paul was no doubt a murderer; and though he had escaped from the sea, he couldn't escape justice; so, the snake had bitten him.

But here's where it gets interesting. The people then saw that Paul just shook off the snake from his hand, and it ended up in the fire. They took note that Paul had suffered no harm. At that point the natives immediately changed their minds and reasoned among themselves that Paul must be a god.

In a manner of probably two or three minutes the opinion of people migrated from the Apostle Paul being a murderer to a god. And you know what? Neither description was correct.

Paul was simply living by faith; and as he did, he got the attention of people.

Don't give in to popular opinion. Don't just assume someone is a certain way. Take time instead to get to know that person or that situation. As you do, it might surprise you who or what God brings into your life.

Today's Word is Acts 28:3-5

"But when Paul had gathered a bundle of sticks and laid them on the fire, a viper came out because of the heat, and fastened on his hand. So when the natives saw the creature hanging from his hand, they said to one another, "No doubt this man is a murderer, whom, though he has escaped the sea, yet justice does not allow to live." But he shook off the creature into the fire and suffered no harm."

OCTOBER 25

DEMONSTRATED LOVE

How do you demonstrate your love for someone in your life? Do you tell them? Do you share your love in a note or poem? Maybe in a song? Or perhaps you express your love by buying something for that special someone.

All the above are terrific, but do you want to know how God demonstrated His love for you and me? He did so by giving us His very best gift - His only Son.

The Bible puts it as plainly as it gets; "While we were still sinners, Christ died for us."

Think about that. With no guarantee at all that we'd even accept His sacrificial gift of love, God took the first step. It was a step of faith and one that allowed His Son to die for our sins. Our choice is to respond to that demonstrated love by receiving Jesus as our Savior.

For you and me and every other person who will ever live, the price has been paid. Blood has already been shed.

How can we in turn demonstrate our love to Him? We don't have to die for anyone. Our opportunity is to live. By living life according to the Book and sharing this inexpressible gift with a dying world, we demonstrate our love to Him.

Start where you are. Believe God for an opportunity to share the love of God with someone who needs to know they're loved.

Today's Word is Romans 5:8

"But God demonstrates His own love toward us, in that while we were still sinners, Christ died for us."

OCTOBER 26

CLOTHES GET BURNED, FEET GET SEARED

The Book of Proverbs is a book full of common sense and wisdom. One of the cool facts I get to share with students is that Proverbs, by Divine design, has thirty-one chapters. That's one chapter each day. I think it's obvious that the Lord desires us to hang out in Proverbs every single day of our lives.

I really enjoy getting teenagers to look at Proverbs chapter six. In verses 27 & 28 of this chapter, we're asked two plainly stated questions. If you have any common sense at all, you'll quickly agree that the answer to both questions is "No."

As students join me in looking at these two verses, I engage them in conversation relating to sin. Just as we can't take fire to our bosom and our clothes not get burned, and we surely can't walk on hot coals and our feet not be seared, it's no different with sin. We can't sin and think we won't have the results of sin in our lives.

Sin carries with it a penalty. Sure, we can repent and plead the blood of Jesus, be cleansed, and move forward. But the Bible tells us that the wages of sin is death.

Here's what I then share with students. When you're tempted to sin, don't fall for the trap. That's the time to remember that just as sure as clothes get burned and feet get seared, sin carries with it a cycle of death.

Today's Word is Proverbs 6:27-28

"Can a man take fire to his bosom, and his clothes not be burned? Can one walk on hot coals, and his feet not be seared?"

OCTOBER 27

QUICK TO LISTEN

Recently I ministered in five public schools over the course of a day and a half. At the conclusion of our assemblies at each of these schools, students stood in lines to share some of their stories with me. It was at the last school on this trip that I met a fifteen-year-old young man who touched my heart.

He asked to talk, and I took some time with him. I'm so thankful I did; because as I listened to what he had to say, his story so ministered to me.

As we talked, I learned that this freshman in high school had attempted suicide sixteen times over the course of five years. His most recent attempt had resulted in his being airlifted to a hospital in another city; and while in the emergency room of that hospital, he died twice on the table and was twice brought back to life.

He showed me his arms where he had sliced himself with razor blades. Seeing his arms, I asked him why he had cut himself. I've been ministering to students for a long time but wasn't ready for his response to my question. He said, "When he cut himself and saw his own blood, then he knew at least his heart was working."

I then ministered what the Lord prompted me to say and gave this student one of our ministry's YOU MATTER bracelets. We talked a few more minutes, and then my new friend had to get to his next class.

I share this account from the road with you because today, I really believe the Lord needs you to know that sometimes the greatest ministry service you and I can ever offer someone else is to simply listen to what someone God puts in our lives needs to say.

Why is listening important? People need to be heard.

Today's Word is James 1:19

"So then, my beloved brethren, let every man be swift to hear, slow to speak, slow to wrath;"

OCTOBER 28

BEAUTIFUL FEET

One of the most forever time-stamped days of my life occurred when I was twelve years old. It was a Sunday morning, and I was at church. The service had just ended, and I was peering over the balcony when I made eye contact with Mr. Joe Parks.

Mr. Parks was a renowned musician, a writer of Gospel music, and our families went to the same church. That Sunday morning as I was peering over the balcony, Mr. Parks, who was seated on the floor level below, looked up at me, smiled, and seemingly out of nowhere said, "Be ready Dean, God might just call you into ministry."

When I heard his sentence, I just stood there with no idea how to respond. But over the next weeks, Joe Parks' sentence rang clearly, over-and-over in my mind. It was about eight years after that Sunday morning that the Lord revealed Romans 10:14-15 to me, and my life slowly began to make sense.

Maybe today is your day for your world to be rocked. Could be that right now, right here, it's God's timing for you to hear someone say to you, "Be ready, God might just call you into ministry."

Before you make any response to what you've just read, take a few more seconds and read what the Word says in Romans 10:14-15.

If you have a witness in your heart to what you're reading, maybe you, too, have "beautiful feet".

Today's Word is Romans 10:14-15

"How then shall they call on Him in whom they have not believed? And how shall they believe in Him of whom they have not heard? And how shall they hear without a preacher? And how shall they preach unless they are sent? As it is written: "How beautiful are the feet of those who preach the gospel of peace, who bring glad tidings of good things!"

OCTOBER 29

DANCE ANYWAY

Today I'd like for you to get a visual of a King who loved God so much that he publicly danced before the Lord with all his might. In fact, this King's love for God produced such a thankful heart for all that He had done for him and his kingdom that the King not only danced with all his might, but he was also leaping and whirling before the Lord.

Now let's say that same King is married, and his wife sees him coming into the city, bringing with him the Ark of the Lord and all the people. She sees her husband out front dancing, leaping, and whirling around; and as she sees all this, she despises her husband in her heart.

What I've just described really happened. The King was King David, and his wife's name was Michal.

What I've often been led to consider and question is this. Instead of despising her husband, why wasn't Michal down in the streets with him, praising God?

Guess what? If you're one who takes a stand for God, you're in excellent company. Thousands of students have done so before you and thousands more will after you.

But know this: not everyone is going to embrace your beliefs or applaud your faith. That's ok. Take a stand anyway.

You really must look no further than King David. His wife despised him; he danced anyway.

Today's Word is 2 Samuel 6:14-16

"Then David danced before the Lord with all his might; and David was wearing a linen ephod. So David and all the house of Israel brought up the ark of the Lord with shouting and with the sound of the trumpet. Now as the ark of the Lord came into the City of David, Michal, Saul's daughter, looked through a window and saw King David leaping and whirling before the Lord; and she despised him in her heart."

OCTOBER 30

FEARFULLY & WONDERFULLY MADE

One of my favorite truths to share with teenagers is that every one of them is an original. The Bible tells us that all of us are "fearfully and wonderfully made". How cool is that?

I especially enjoy sharing this truth with students who have a tough time believing that what I'm saying applies to them. After all, they think, "What's so wonderful about me?"

Maybe you wrestle with that question as well.

Consider you. The real you. Your characteristics, your look, your creativity, your sense of humor, your compassion, your athleticism, your heart. Before you were born, your Heavenly Father carefully, purposefully, and strategically thought through and carefully planned all of that which makes you, uniquely you.

Don't fall for the lie of the devil. He spends his time lying to teenagers; trying to get them to buy a bunch of lies. When given the opportunity to do so, he causes them to see what's not there; to hear what's not being said; and in many instances, tries to get them to choose death over life.

Let's settle something right now. The Word of God is true. God has never lied for one, simple reason. He can't. He is Truth; and therefore, it's impossible for Him to lie.

Knowing that God speaks only truth, you might want to settle this in your heart right here, right now: you're an original; fearfully and wonderfully made by God Himself.

Today's Word is Psalms 139:14

"I will praise You, for I am fearfully and wonderfully made; marvelous are Your works, and that my soul knows very well."

OCTOBER 31

ONE MORE NIGHT WITH THE FROGS

You might recall that because Pharaoh continually refused to let Moses lead six million people out of Egyptian captivity and into the land of promise God had for His people, God intervened and sent ten plagues into Egypt. One of these plagues was frogs. Frogs were everywhere. They were in bedrooms, in kitchens, in family rooms, on the streets, at the market; everywhere you could see, you saw frogs.

At each occurrence of a new plague, God sent Moses into Pharaoh's "office" to have the Children of Israel released.

It was during one of these meetings that Moses and Pharaoh had a conversation that is one of my all-time most intriguing moments in the Bible. During this conversation, Moses plainly asked Pharaoh when he wanted him to intercede on his behalf regarding the removal of all the frogs that were in Egypt. You would probably think that Pharaoh would say, "Now, immediately!" But no, he instead said, "Tomorrow."

Can you imagine? Standing before you is God's representative and he's asking you when you want this plague out of your life. And the answer you give is, in essence, "Give me one more night with the frogs."

Take this example to your life. Right now, Jesus, your Advocate with the Father, is standing before you saying, "When do you want this 'something' out of your life?" Do you want it out now, or do you want "one more night with the frogs"?

Today's Word is Exodus 8:9-11

"And Moses said to Pharaoh, "Accept the honor of saying when I shall intercede for you, for your servants, and for your people, to destroy the frogs from you and your houses, that they may remain in the river only." So he said, "Tomorrow." And he said, " Let it be according to your word, that you may know that there is no one like the Lord our God. And the frogs shall depart from you, from your houses, from your servants, and from your people. They shall remain in the river only."

NOVEMBER 1

YOU'RE NOT A FOOL

The word "fool" carries with it lots of meanings, but Webster's defines it as, "A silly or stupid person; a person who lacks judgment or sense".

Did you know that in the book of Psalms, the writer plainly tells us that it's the fool, the silly or stupid person who lacks judgment or sense, who says in his heart that there is no God? That's a strong statement, but it's true.

Now if you're reading this and you're not yet too terribly convinced of the reality of God in your life, don't misunderstand what I'm saying and don't let yourself get offended. I'm not saying that you're silly or stupid. I am suggesting, however, that you're lacking some sense as it relates to your embracing Who He is and what He's done for you.

Here's the great news about lacking sense: it can change. But it can only do so when we embrace change.

I often share with teenagers when speaking with them that I'm not there to talk them into something; because if I can talk them into something, someone much more articulate than me can come right behind me and talk them out of it. Therefore, I'm not about to try to talk you into having some sense about a relationship with the Lord. Instead, I'm going to invite you to simply ask God to show up in your life.

Whether you yet believe, or you don't, isn't the point of this devotional today. The point is simple. As God shows up in your life and world, because His presence is undeniable, you'll no longer be able to say that there is no God.

After all, you're not a fool.

Today's Word is Psalms 14:1

"The fool has said in his heart, 'There is no God.' They are corrupt, they have done abominable works, there is none who does good."

NOVEMBER 2

HE'S WITH YOU

Do you remember back to your earliest days of life when maybe at nighttime, with darkness all around, fear would creep in? Maybe you remember crying or screaming, and nothing you did made the fear go away. Yet, when your mom or dad, maybe an aunt or uncle, or possibly one of your grandparents would come into your room and pick you up, hold you close, and gently speak to your spirit, that fear would just melt away.

What happened? What caused the fear to leave? Someone you loved and trusted came to where you were; and as that someone was with you and they comforted you, your confidence overcame the fear.

Now come forward to present day. Did you know that Someone much greater than fear is with you right now, wherever you might be? And no matter what you're going through or even what you've done that might be causing fear to rise up in your life once again, the Bible plainly tells us to not fear. Why is this? Because the Lord is with us.

Just like years ago, when you were picked up out of your baby bed and held closely by someone who loves you, today, Jesus wants to reach down to where you are, pick you up, and hold you close.

As you invite Him into your circumstances and let Him do that which only He can do, you, too, will better understand why He commands you to not fear.

Remember, He's with you.

Today's Word is Jeremiah 46:28

"Do not fear, O Jacob My servant," says the Lord, "For I am with you;"

NOVEMBER 3

THE SECRET THINGS

There have been many times a teenager has walked over to me after an event and, with the deepest of sincerity, asked me about something that's happened in their life or in the life of their family; something that's either been tragic or an occurrence that has caused much pain.

As students ask me, I'm asking the Lord. Most of the time, He brings a verse to my heart that brings some answers and peace to the student, but there have also been times when I haven't gotten any direction from the Lord at all.

In those times my answer is usually, "I don't know. I'm just not sure why that happened. Sometimes it's a mystery, and we won't know the big picture of what happened until we get to Heaven and can have a talk with the Lord about it." And you know what? I've learned that teenagers so appreciate the honesty. They'd rather hear me say, "I don't know" than give them some "spiritual, religious answer" that brings more confusion than peace.

And it's always at this point that I remind those students of this truth: none of us has all the answers, but I know the One who does.

Maybe today you find yourself wrestling with something that brought you or your family a lot of pain; and for whatever reason, you just don't understand how or why it happened. Look at a Scripture in Deuteronomy 29 and trust that God really does know what's best; even during those times when the secret things that belong to Him, He keeps to himself.

Today's Word is Deuteronomy 29:29

"The secret things belong to the Lord our God, but those things which are revealed belong to us and to our children forever, that we may do all the words of this law."

NOVEMBER 4

WE'VE BEEN ADOPTED

I've met a lot of high school students who were adopted. I always so enjoy meeting young people who've been adopted because it reminds me of what God did for you and me – He literally adopted us into His family as His children by what Jesus did for us on that cross.

Through the years I've learned a few things about being adopted: when a person is adopted, that person is chosen.

When a person is adopted, he or she suddenly belongs to a family. And

When a person is adopted, he or she has full legal rights to the family name.

It's no different with our being adopted by God. Today, as a child of God, we:

Have been chosen by God Himself. We belong to His family. And we have full covenantal, legal rights to the family name.

Remember, when God looks at you today, He does so with a smile on His face. Why? Because you're His kid, and parents smile at their kids.

Today's Word is Ephesians 1:5

"having predestined us to adoption as sons by Jesus Christ to Himself, according to the good pleasure of His will,"

NOVEMBER 5

THE POWER OF THE GOSPEL

Among today's generation of young people there is a growing number of teenagers who not only want to hear the Word but also want to operate in the power that comes with it. They are hungry to see the demonstration of the Holy Spirit in and through their lives and settling for the ordinary just no longer interests them.

They've heard about revival services where blind eyes are opening, and deaf ears are suddenly hearing. They've heard about looking at x-rays where once there was a cancer and after someone prayed for the patient, that cancer no longer exists.

Teenagers are telling me that they don't just want to hear about what God is doing somewhere else; they are hungry to see Him do it in and through their own lives.

What an exciting time to be alive! For thousands of years people have believed for the supernatural power of God to be a part of their lives. I believe that time has come and now is.

So how can you get in on the action? Get to know the Word of God. Really get to know it. Make it so much a part of you that one day as you're walking down the street, someone will walk up to you, seemingly out of the blue, and say, "I see the Spirit of the Lord all over you; will you please pray for me? I need a miracle." You then hear from the Lord, pray in faith the Word He gives you, and move on to your next power-packed assignment.

The days of just talking about miracles are over. Now is the time to live by the power of the Gospel.

Today's Word is 1 Thessalonians 1:5

"For our gospel did not come to you in word only, but also in power, and in the Holy Spirit and in much assurance, as you know what kind of men we were among you for your sake."

NOVEMBER 6

A FIGHT WORTH FIGHTING

What is it in your life today that the devil is trying to steal, kill, or destroy?

I believe the Word of God makes it plain exactly what the devil is fighting so hard to remove from our lives. Here's a hint; at the root of our calling, our assignment, and all we have or can have from God is a five-letter word that works by a four-letter word.

FAITH is what triggers God to move on our behalf, and faith works by LOVE.

In the book of Jude we're encouraged, we're exhorted to contend for or to fight for the faith. God has always known that our faith in His Word is the difference maker. He's also known that for us to keep the faith, it's a fight. But you know what? It's a fight worth fighting.

When I say, "Fight," I don't mean a physical knock down and drag out. No, what I'm talking about is a fight in the realm of the Spirit.

Maybe today you realize that you haven't been contending earnestly for the faith; you haven't been spiritually standing strong against a defeated enemy. Ok, let's do something about that.

How do you fight the devil and win? Same exact way that Jesus did in the wilderness. Every single time the devil came against Jesus, the Lord simply, yet emphatically, responded to the enemy, "It is written."

Want to beat the devil and contend for the faith? Say what the Word says.

Today's Word is Jude 1:3

"Beloved, while I was very diligent to write to you concerning our common salvation, I found it necessary to write to you exhorting you to contend earnestly for the faith which was once for all delivered to the saints."

NOVEMBER 7

IT'S ALL ABOUT TIME

Recently my wife, Lori, and I and our three teenagers spent four days at Disney in Orlando, Florida. For years prior to doing so, we'd talk about taking our kids on this trip; but at that point in our lives, I never could get too excited about it.

Part of my lack of excitement was my just not wanting to go to Disney with three kids who were 5, 6 & 7 years old. But more than my just not wanting to go, I really believed it wasn't time for us to go. After all, when you do go to the "happiest place on earth", it certainly needs to be the right time. Right?

As we experienced Disney and made some unforgettable memories, I was so thankful we had waited for God's timing, the exact time that was right for our family. Timing was everything.

How about you and your life? Over in the book of Ecclesiastes, we're told in chapter 3 that there's a season, a time, for every purpose under Heaven. To me the most important word in that verse is the word "time".

If you know much about the Bible, you must know that God's timing is perfect. Whether you're believing God for a boyfriend or girlfriend or to provide you with a car, even to save someone in your family; or on a lighter note, you're waiting on your mom and dad to take you to Disney ... whatever you have on your heart, know that God sees your heart and as long as your desire lines up with His will, in His time, watch your dreams come true.

Today's Word is Ecclesiastes 3:1

"To everything there is a season, a time for every purpose under heaven:"

NOVEMBER 8

ALL ACCESS PASS

Years ago, the Lord showed me that part of my assignment in ministering to teenagers is helping them understand that we were not created to be reliant on ourselves but instead on Him. We were never engineered to go it alone. He knows us. He knows what we will face and how we will handle successes and obstacles along life's way. More than I can say, we need His total involvement in every aspect of our lives.

In the decades that I've been talking with students about their letting God into their lives, many wrongly believe that if they have God in their lives, all the fun will automatically go away. That's just a lie from the devil.

One of the neatest times of ministry on the road occurs when I invite teenagers who have allowed Him full access into their lives to join me on stage and testify about what they're experiencing with God fully invested in their hopes and dreams.

Oh, how I wish you could see the looks on the faces of those students who haven't yet given God full access. As their friends talk from stage and share the fun they have in living a life that pleases God, you can see their interest levels rising.

Want to do something today that'll pay off in your future? Take a step of faith and invite God into your life, into every portion of your life. Give Him an ALL-ACCESS pass and watch what He does with what you give Him.

Today's Word is Isaiah 41:13

"For I, the Lord your God, will hold your right hand, saying to you, 'Fear not, I will help you."

NOVEMBER 9

HE'S ALREADY THERE

The Bible spells it out pretty clearly that none of us knows what will happen tomorrow. In fact, if you actually take time to read the Word, it says that tomorrow is promised to no one.

Since we don't know exactly what's going to happen in every one of our tomorrows and none of our tomorrows are promised to any of us anyway, what are we supposed to do about planning for our future?

I've spent a lot of time thinking about all of this; and as I have, here's what I've learned. I don't necessarily know everything that tomorrow holds, but I do know Who holds tomorrow.

So, Lori and I make plans according to what we believe He shows us to do when we simply get in His presence and listen.

Maybe today you're feeling unusually uncomfortable about life and your future. Can I give you something to consider? Look to the One who holds all our tomorrows in His hand. As you do, you can do so with tremendous confidence; because when it comes to the future, He's already there.

Today's Word is James 4:14

"Whereas you do not know what will happen tomorrow. For what is your life? It is even a vapor that appears for a little time and then vanishes away."

NOVEMBER 10

ONE WORD FROM GOD

When you read the Bible, do you really read it, or do you blow past words and meanings of those words in the context in which they were written?

I enjoy asking students about their time in the Word, because for the most part, the teenagers I meet and talk with are honest people. I know they're honest because of the oftentimes raw answers they give me.

When I read my Bible as a teenager and even into my early twenties, I did so not from a heart of love but rather from a heart feeling obligated to do something. Back then, I felt like I had to read my Bible so I would be spiritual. But you know what? I wasn't being spiritual at all; I was being religious.

And then one day my reading the Word went from obligation to desire, and it did so when I saw, really saw, one verse.

The verse I saw was the very first verse in the Bible. My take on the Bible changed when I read and the Holy Spirit allowed me to see and begin to understand the first four words of the Bible: "In the beginning God ..."

Those four words changed my approach to life. The words jumped off the page and landed deep into my heart. Why? Because the reality of a living, creative God came alive in my life, and suddenly, I had to know Him and His plans for me.

Maybe today you too can relate to just turning pages in the Bible. If so, that's ok; don't beat yourself up anymore. Ask the Holy Spirit to bring the Word alive to you. As He does, get ready to blast off!

As my spiritual father taught me so many years ago; one word from God can change your life forever.

Today's Word is Genesis 1:1

"In the beginning God created the heavens and the earth."

NOVEMBER 11

WELCOME TO THE TEAM

If a teenager who believes he or she is called into full time ministry is in the audience where I've just ministered, many times those teens will come right up and begin asking me questions.

And almost without fail one of their first questions is, "Can you give me those verses again that you quoted that had to do with your calling?"

Many, many years ago the Lord showed me the absolute critical importance of my finding myself in the Bible. And so I went on a journey that today I wouldn't trade for any amount of money. Here's what I discovered.

I'm called to Ezekiel 3:10 & 11 with a mandate of Proverbs 24:11 with a message of Job 33:4; all for the purpose of 2 Timothy 4:5.

Since the Holy Spirit showed me those verses that allow me to do what I've been called to do, and we know that God is no respecter of persons, I can assure you that He'll show you the Words from the Word that you'll need to launch out and fulfill what He's called you to do in your life and ministry.

But know this. It takes time, diligence, and persistence.

So, you're called into full time ministry? Might want to look at the instructions found in 1 Timothy 4:12. As you do let me be one of the ones to welcome you to the team.

Today's Word is 1 Timothy 4:12

"Let no one despise your youth, but be an example to the believers in word, in conduct, in love, in spirit, in faith, in purity."

NOVEMBER 12

OBEDIENCE WINS

When you find yourself suddenly in a storm of life and you're not too sure what to do, take some time and read the first chapter of the book of Jonah.

Jonah was a Preacher who didn't like his assignment, so he disobeyed the instruction of the Lord. His disobedience put a ship-full of workers in danger of death and ultimately landed him in the belly of a great fish.

Tucked away in the first chapter of Jonah is a life-lesson that when the Holy Spirit showed it to me, our ministry was forever changed.

Not everything God asks you to do is going to be your favorite thing to do. When you know it's an assignment from the Lord, do it anyway.

Just because we don't want to do something does not excuse us from being obedient.

Look at your life. Are you in a storm? Can't seem to figure out how you got there? Consider stepping back and taking inventory of some of your recent decisions. As you do, you might just see where you ignored or altogether disobeyed an instruction from the Lord.

Remember, obedience wins.

Today's Word is Psalm 119:105

"Your word is a lamp unto my feet and a light to my path."

NOVEMBER 13

ARE YOU THE ONE?

Are people refreshed when you show up? Ever thought about it?

As you're thinking, the following example, one that I've shared in an earlier devotion, is one I'm often led to share during assemblies. It might help you answer my question.

Let's say it's a Monday morning and you and several of your friends are walking down the hall to your first period class. As you're heading to class, you walk past one of your teachers.

Depending upon your reputation at your school, there's a pretty good chance that when your teacher sees you that Monday morning, he or she is possibly thinking, "Oh dear Lord, they're here this morning." or "Oh thank the Lord, they're here this morning." See the difference? One's a refreshing thought while the other, well ... not so much.

In the book of Philemon, the people of the church had great joy, because one person had refreshed the hearts of people.

Today, you can be that one person who's used by God to refresh others.

Be ready. Be available. Be obedient.

Today's Word is Philemon 1:7

"For we have great joy and consolation in your love, because the hearts of the saints have been refreshed by you, brother."

NOVEMBER 14

DON'T DOUBT IN THE DARK

Do you know that there's a place in God He's reserved just for you? You access this "place" through prayer and worship. The Bible refers to it as the "secret place of the Most High".

When you pray and enter the Secret Place, you go into a protective place of love where you'll hear from God in a way that you're not likely to hear from Him anywhere else.

Many times, people receive specific direction, timing, and confirmations while hanging out with God in the Secret Place. Because of this, I encourage students to take the time to journal what they hear in their hearts as they have these appointments with God in this Place.

Why journal? Because anytime we receive a Word from God, the Bible warns us that IMMEDIATELY the enemy comes to steal. By writing it down, your direction, timing, and confirmation can't be stolen from you, if you take a strong stand of faith and refuse for it to be taken from you.

Trust me on this. The enemy is a liar, and he'll try his best to convince you that you really didn't hear or receive what you did hear and receive while in the Secret Place of the Almighty. When he lies to you, it might be helpful to remember ...

Don't doubt in the dark what you know you heard in the light.

Today's Word is Psalms 91:1

"He who dwells in the secret place of the Most High shall abide under the shadow of the Almighty."

NOVEMBER 15

YOU'LL BE FILLED

Have you ever played sports on a day that was so hot you could have fried an egg on the sidewalk? Let's say you have; and on that day, you ran out of water before you finished the competition. Remember that feeling?

Maybe it was a game of soccer or tennis or maybe you were doing a long-distance run. Whatever you were doing, can you remember how you were so thirsty that just a few sips of water would have made the difference? Remember back to how you were desperately seeking fluid? How your very soul was craving, longing for water, but there just wasn't any?

Got the picture? Good. Now take that same exact feeling of absolutely, positively needing water and transfer it to you now needing the Word of God.

That thirst for the Word is where I believe God wants all of us to be. Here's the good news. If you hunger and thirst after righteousness, guess what happens? Yep, you'll be filled.

Today's Word is Matthew 5:6

"Blessed are those who hunger and thirst for righteousness, for they shall be filled."

NOVEMBER 16

A BRAND NEW YOU

Have you accepted what Jesus has done for you? Are you a born- again Believer? If so, everything you've ever done wrong in your life has passed away, and now all things in your life have become new.

When we make Jesus Lord of our life, He comes into our heart and takes up residence. We literally become what the Bible calls a "New creation". The blood of Jesus washes away a sin-stained lifestyle, and we get to start all over with a clean slate.

Sound too good to be true? Maybe so, but it is the truth.

No matter how far you might have drifted from God, regardless of what you might have done or with whom you may have done it, nothing, and I do mean nothing, is too powerful for Jesus to forgive.

Maybe you're thinking, "But you don't know what I've done." I don't have to. He does, and as quickly as you repent, He forgives and He forgets.

Remember, in Christ, you're a new creation. Old things have passed away; you're a brand new YOU.

Today's Word is 2 Corinthians 5:17

"Therefore, if anyone is in Christ, he is a new creation; old things have passed away; behold, all things have become new."

NOVEMBER 17

CONVINCED WITH ABSOLUTE CERTAINTY

In your life today is there anything about which you're persuaded?

To be persuaded is to be convinced with absolute certainty. So, if you are persuaded, what are you convinced about in your life with absolute certainty?

In the book of Romans, the writer of this book, the Apostle Paul, is persuaded about nothing being able to separate us from the love of God.

Paul goes so far as to give us a list of the things that can never separate us from this love: neither death nor life, angels nor principalities, things present nor things to come, height nor depth, nor any created thing - now that's a list. What's Paul saying?

Nothing, nothing, nothing will ever be able to separate you from the love of God.

My prayer for you is that you really believe this promise of no separation. When you do, the confidence of God will take up residence in your heart; and when that happens, your life will never be the same.

Today's Word is Romans 8:38-39

"For I am persuaded that neither death nor life, nor angels nor principalities nor powers, nor things present nor things to come, nor height nor depth, nor any other created thing, shall be able to separate us from the love of God which is in Christ Jesus our Lord."

NOVEMBER 18

STAND STILL

Life is busy. That might just be the understatement of the day.

When I was a teenager, I thought that I had lots going on, but now that I'm constantly around this generation of teenagers who come from all walks of life, I've realized that they could be on the go literally 24/7 and still have plenty yet to do and experience.

While being busy and productive are not bad qualities at all, we sometimes in our busyness miss out on some neat moments with God. Know how I know this? Because there's been times when I've been so busy working for God; that in my busyness, I've missed what God was trying to get me to either see, do, or experience.

So how do we fix this challenge of being too busy all the time? You can start by turning over to the book of Numbers and looking at what Moses did and said when he had to hear from God.

Moses' instruction to the people was, "Stand still, so I may hear..."

Guess what? The very next sentence in that verse tells us exactly what happened. When the people got still before the Lord, then the Lord spoke to Moses.

It's no different with you today. Maybe life has become too busy and maybe you haven't been hearing from the Lord as you once did. If so, take a page from the playbook of Moses: Stand still.

Today's Word is Numbers 9:8-9

"And Moses said to them, "Stand still, that I may hear what the Lord will command concerning you." Then the Lord spoke to Moses, saying,"

NOVEMBER 19

DON'T OPEN THE DOOR

One of the subjects that I often address from stage is the always ever-popular subject of sex before marriage. Every time I do, I see two distinct looks on the faces of teenagers. One look is that goofy smile teenagers get when they're a little uncomfortable with their surroundings, and the second look I see as I scan the audience is the look of shame/regret. Both looks usually are telling me a story, but it's a story I've heard thousands of times before from young people all over America and in nations around the world.

And it's to those young people in the second group from the above paragraph that I was led to write today.

First things first. The Bible is very clear. "You should abstain from sexual immorality."

Secondly, if you're reading this devotional and you've already given in to the temptation of sex before marriage, remember, there is now therefore no condemnation to those who are in Christ. Don't be condemned; ask Jesus to forgive you; then forgive yourself; and finally, consider changing your choices.

You see, Jesus forgives us for every single sin we commit. Truth is, sin is sin. Whether it's a perceived big sin or a perceived white lie; in God's eyes, sin is sin.

Abstaining from sex before marriage is a choice, and it's a commitment that can be difficult to keep. That's why we have the Holy Spirit. If you go to Him and just talk with Him as you'd talk with your best friend, He'll not only listen, He'll show you in the Word how to stay on course.

Resisting temptation is no easy accomplishment on your own. With the Holy Spirit in your corner, however, when that temptation comes knocking, He'll be right there with you to help ensure you don't open the door.

Today's Word is 1 Thessalonians 4:3

"For this is the will of God, your sanctification: that you should abstain from sexual immorality;"

NOVEMBER 20

YOU DIDN'T CALL YOU

One of my favorite descriptions of the Lord is "faithful". Know why it's one of my favorites? Because of what it means.

Faithful is defined as, "True to one's word, promises, vows". To me, that definition perfectly describes who He is and why He is so trustworthy.

Might help to think of it like this. When He calls you to do something for His Kingdom, you can be assured that His faithfulness to you in that calling is as sure as the day is long.

But you know what? Many young people have shared with me that once they've discovered what He had called them to do, they've initially felt totally ill-equipped to fulfill what was in their heart for the Lord.

At this point I share with these students that just as God is faithful to them, they in turn must also demonstrate their faithfulness to Him and His calling on their lives.

Start from where you are and be faithful to do what He shows you to do. As you learn more and more about just how faithful God really is, your desire to emulate His faithfulness by you being faithful to Him in the fulfilling of this call will grow every day.

Remember, you didn't call you; God did.

Today's Word is 1 Thessalonians 5:24

"He who calls you is faithful, who also will do it."

NOVEMBER 21

KNOCKING KNEES

Have you ever seen something that so freaked you out that when you saw it your hips were loosened and your knees knocked against each other? I've had some moments where fear was not just swatting at the door, it was banging, but I've never had knocking knees.

In the Book of Daniel, we're introduced to King Belshazzar. He was having a dinner party one night, and one thousand guests were in attendance.

The more the King and his guests partied, the more dangerous their evening became. Here's why. The Bible is very clear that we are to have no other gods before the One, True God. As the evening progressed, the Bible reveals that perhaps inhibitions began to decrease, because the guests were all suddenly praying to the gods of gold and silver, bronze and iron, wood, and stone.

The very next verse in Daniel tells us that the fingers of a man's hand suddenly appeared and wrote on the wall of the king's palace. King Belshazzar saw the part of the hand that was writing on the wall, and what he saw was a game-changer. The king's countenance changed, his mind was troubled, and his knees knocked.

What's that got to do with you today? After all you're probably not praying to the gods of gold and silver, bronze and iron, or wood and stone. But do you have other gods in your life?

Maybe it's the god of fashion, the god of popularity, the god of the media, the god of money. Anything that takes your focus off the Almighty God for any sustained length of time qualifies as becoming a god in your life.

Want a suggestion? Keep your focus on Him and keep those knees from knocking.

Today's Word is Daniel 5:6

"Then the king's countenance changed, and his thoughts troubled him, so that the joints of his hips were loosened and his knees knocked against each other."

NOVEMBER 22

YOUR PRAYER IS HEARD

Thousands of years ago there was a priest in the Bible named Zacharias, and he was in full-time ministry. One day while he was in the temple, he had a visit from an Angel.

During this visit, the Angel revealed why he had been sent to visit Zacharias. His prayer had been heard, and his wife, Elizabeth, was going to have their first child; they were to name this child, John. That's a significant series of announcements, but here's where it gets interesting. After telling Zacharias to not be afraid, the very next words out of the mouth of the Angel were, "Your prayer is heard."

Those four words tell us that Zacharias had been praying for a son.

If you read on further in the first chapter of Luke, you'll see that even after having an encounter with an Angel, hearing that his prayer had been heard and would soon be answered, Zacharias (a full-time priest) began to question what he had heard instead of celebrating the miracle. He went so far as to ask, "How can this be?"

How about you? Do you get surprised when God answers your prayers, or do you have confidence that when you pray, He answers?

Prayer is serious business, and we should always expect serious results.

Don't be surprised when God answers your "tough" prayer requests.

Remember, He is God.

Today's Word is Luke 1:13

"But the angel said to him, "Do not be afraid, Zacharias, for your prayer is heard; and your wife Elizabeth will bear you a son, and you shall call his name John."

NOVEMBER 23

WORDS IN RED

One of the lessons I really enjoy sharing with teenagers is this: if you really want to live for God, no matter where you live and regardless of your background, His Book is readily available and is quite literally a Manual for living the God-kind of life.

Many times, a young person will tell me that the Bible makes no sense whatsoever to them. At that point, I encourage them to go get their Bible, get alone, open to the book of Matthew, and from the books of Matthew through John (known as the four Gospels), begin by reading only the words in red.

I explain that words in red in the Bible are words directly spoken by Jesus, reminding them that without exception, Jesus says what He means and means what He says.

In the book of Acts, for example, we see where Paul refers to a sentence the Lord said in those four Gospels. Jesus plainly taught anyone who would ever have ears to hear this truth:

Want to be blessed? Give. You see, the words in red say, "It is more blessed to give than to receive."

If you take the time to invest in the Word, the Word will get into your daily living. When this happens, the Words in red will literally become not just words, but they will become your way of life.

Today's Word is Acts 20:35

"I have shown you in every way, by laboring like this, that you must support the weak. And remember the words of the Lord Jesus, that He said, 'It is more blessed to give than to receive.'"

NOVEMBER 24

THE TRUSTWORTHY

When the Lord finds someone, especially a younger someone, that He can trust to not only listen to Him but who will also obey Him, the Lord has a history of revealing Himself and His Word to the trustworthy.

If you take the time to read throughout the first three chapters of the book of 1st Samuel, you won't have to read too far before you realize the instances where God spoke to people during that time of history were rare. They were rare, not because God didn't have something to say, but it may have been rare because He couldn't find anyone who was listening.

Then a young man named Samuel comes along. Samuel's very life was the result of a promise; and as such, Samuel grew up literally living in church, working for the Priest.

Early in his life Samuel established himself as someone called by God; and because of his commitment to his call and his commitment to the Word he heard, Samuel was established as a Prophet of God; and all Israel knew it.

Want to be tapped on the shoulder by God to do some amazing things with and for Him? Follow the example Samuel set: hear, obey and be committed to the Word.

Today's Word is 1 Samuel 3:21

"Then the Lord appeared again in Shiloh. For the Lord revealed Himself to Samuel in Shiloh by the word of the Lord."

NOVEMBER 25

GOD'S PLAN, GOD'S RESULTS

Ever felt like you were facing an insurmountable challenge; and instead of this challenge going away, it seemed to only grow worse? Could be the challenge of an identity crisis, or the challenge of overcoming a bad reputation, or maybe it's the challenge of trying to live for God in an ungodly environment.

Feeling overwhelmed and under-qualified is how I imagine a military leader named Gideon might have felt when he faced his enemy. You see, for quite some time leading up to this battle, Gideon wasn't too terribly sure if God was with him as He had been with previous leaders who had led the children of Israel. In fact, on one occasion, to bolster his confidence, God made sure that Gideon had an Angelic visit.

Now to make things even more God-dependent for Gideon, the Lord told him that his army was too big and to decrease his numbers. And so, in one moment, 22,000 soldiers were released from Gideon's army. A few minutes later 9,700 more soldiers were sent home ... leaving Gideon with an army of 300.

But you know what? 300 was God's number; and because Gideon did it God's way, with God's plan, he got God's results.

Maybe today that seemingly insurmountable challenge that you're facing isn't so insurmountable after all. Get with God. Listen for His voice of instruction and, maybe like Gideon's 300, you too will soon have a testimony in your life of seeing God doing what He does.

Today's Word is Judges 7:7

"Then the Lord said to Gideon, "By the three hundred men who lapped I will save you, and deliver the Midianites into your hand. Let all the other people go, every man to his place."

NOVEMBER 26

A VOICE OF COMFORT

When I first began speaking in schools, after an event, I'd usually be given handwritten notes from students who had just heard our message of hope. On my way to the next city or back home, I'd read those notes and almost without fail, at least one of those students had shared something with me that really ministered to me personally, something that touched my heart.

It's more emailed messages than handwritten notes these days; but irrespective of the form of communication, it's the message that ministers to me. It's the fact that a student will take time from his or her school life and sit down and write something of how our ministry has affected their life.

No matter how many notes we get, I am always humbled by what students share.

You see, we all need to be encouraged, and Jesus knows this. I believe that's why He puts it on your heart and on mine to maybe send a note, to write a card, to pick up the phone and make that call.

Everybody needs somebody to recognize worth in his or her life; somebody who will take the time to be a voice of comfort in the life of someone else.

Maybe today it's your turn to be that somebody for somebody else.

Today's Word is 1 Thessalonians 4:18

"Therefore comfort one another with these words."

NOVEMBER 27

A THANKFUL HEART

During this time of the year, across the United States, families are gathering around tables full of turkey, dressing, green beans, cranberry sauce, and pies, celebrating Thanksgiving. It's a time we've set aside to express our gratitude for God, our families, and our nation.

When I speak in schools leading up to the Thanksgiving break, I'm always led to challenge students to go deeper than the surface when it comes to having a thankful heart.

How about you? What are you truly, genuinely thankful for? We could begin with the very air you breathe. Let's start there and make a list of those things and, yes, maybe even those people that we perhaps sometimes take for granted.

For several very personal reasons Thanksgiving is probably my favorite time of the year. During all that'll be going on today, sometime during the day, the Lord will tap me on the shoulder and lead me to go for a walk; just Him and me.

I'll do so; and as we walk, I'll begin to thank Jesus for all He's done for me. All the times that no one but He and I even know about, but times that consume my heart with gratitude.

Maybe today you, too, will be tapped on the shoulder and asked to take a walk with your Heavenly Father. If so, I encourage you to go and go with a thankful heart.

Today's Word is Psalms 107:1

"Oh, give thanks to the Lord, for He is good! For His mercy endures forever."

NOVEMBER 28

THE SEED YOU PLANT

What is a "corrupt" word? Why's it important to know what it is? It's important, because in the book of Ephesians we're clearly commanded to let no corrupt word proceed out of our mouth.

The word corrupt is defined as, "Lacking integrity, crooked, perverted, wicked, and tainted". That's a serious list of which I want nothing to do with. How about you?

My goal for this book of devotions is to always point all of us back to the Word. In the Word, we're taught that words are seeds. We're also taught that seeds produce after their own kind.

If you don't want a harvest of corrupt communication in your life, a harvest that's comprised of lacking integrity, crooked, perverted, wicked, and tainted, then do what the Word of God says. Make sure that you do not let any corrupt word proceed out of your mouth.

It's your choice. The seed you plant determines the harvest you receive.

Today's Word is Ephesians 4:29

"Let no corrupt word proceed out of your mouth, but what is good for necessary edification, that it may impart grace to the hearers."

NOVEMBER 29

WHAT YOU NEED TO SEE

Do you ever find yourself wondering what God does all day, every day? With billions of people walking around, driving around, and flying around, how does He keep it all together?

How He does what He does really isn't our business. Why He does it, however, is. God's motivation has been, is today, and always will be, love.

Sometimes His love covers our eyes, so we don't see what's going on around us, and yet at other times His love causes our eyes to open and see what was before hidden.

In the book of 2nd Kings, we are offered an example of God opening the eyes of the servant of Elisha. And when He did, the servant saw what Elisha had already seen - a mountain full of horses and chariots of fire all around.

When Elisha's servant was allowed to see into the Spirit realm, what he saw brought him peaceful confidence. God knew what he needed, and He knew when he needed it.

It's no different in your life today. Maybe you, too, need your eyes opened, or maybe you need them to be closed. Whichever the case, remember that God loves you so much that just like He did for Elisha's servant, He'll let you see what you need to see when you need to see it.

Today's Word is 2 Kings 6:17

"And Elisha prayed, and said, "Lord, I pray, open his eyes that he may see." Then the Lord opened the eyes of the young man, and he saw. And behold, the mountain was full of horses and chariots of fire all around Elisha."

NOVEMBER 30

FAR FROM CAMP

When the Children of Israel made God angry enough to want to destroy them, Moses had to distance himself from them so that he could position himself to meet with and hear from God. To do so he literally took his tent, and the Bible says that he pitched it outside the camp, far from the camp.

Once he got where God wanted him to be, Moses could then talk with and hear from God.

I meet so many students who share with me that they have a desire to hang out with the Lord, but they just don't how to do it. Maybe you can relate.

You know what I share with them? It's not about "doing"; it's much more about "being".

To "be" with God doesn't mean you have to necessarily move and set up camp somewhere else. It does mean, however, that maybe, just maybe, you'll have to re-position your heart to be receptive to what the Lord is saying in the times in which we're living.

Maybe today the "people" that Moses had to move away from is a metaphor for other things in your life. Maybe it's moving away from a certain style of music. Could be that God wants you to move away from a certain attitude. Do you understand?

Moses had to get far enough away so that he could connect with God. Perhaps today it's time for you to distance yourself from that "something" that for too long has prevented you from having what God wants to have with you.

Today's Word is Exodus 33:7

"Moses took his tent and pitched it outside the camp, far from the camp, and called it the tabernacle of meeting. And it came to pass that everyone who sought the Lord went out to the tabernacle of meeting which was outside the camp."

DECEMBER 1

DRAWN AWAY

In the natural, temptation and yielding to temptation is at an all-time high among teenagers. In all the years that I've been on the road speaking with teens, I am encountering more students these days who are dealing with really "grownup" situations in their lives; situations that began as a temptation, were given into, and resulted in sin.

What's the root of temptation? That's an easy one to answer. We find the answer in the book of James where we're told that each one of us is tempted when we're drawn away by our own desires and then enticed.

Our own desires. That's the root of temptation. Seems to me that when our desires change the ability to be tempted will change proportionately.

So, here's the million-dollar question. How do our desires change? They begin to change when we ask God to show us how to fill the void that our once self-centered desires tried to fill but miserably failed.

This is important to know. God never tempts us; that's instead the mode of operation of the enemy.

Tired of being tempted and giving in to the temptation? Begin by submitting to God and His will for your life. When you do, He'll do His part.

Today's Word is James 1:14

"But each one is tempted when he is drawn away by his own desires and enticed."

DECEMBER 2

DELIGHT YOURSELF IN THE LORD

Would you like to know the surest way to receive the desires of your heart? The answer is found in the Book of Psalms: delight yourself also in the Lord.

That's it. When you delight yourself in the Lord, He'll give you the desires of your heart.

What happens, though, when your desires don't show up in your life? Is that on you or is it on God?

The short answer is, it's on us when our desires don't materialize into our lives (remember, God never fails).

So, what could conceivably cause our desires to fail to materialize into our lives? It's a combination of our knowledge of God, our depth of relationship with the Word, and our ability to hear the voice of the Holy Spirit when He speaks to us.

We can convince ourselves that we're delighting ourselves in Him; but if the desires of our heart are always selfish desires, God loves us too much to give us what He knows we either don't need or can't handle.

That's when we must be honest with ourselves and take a deep, introspective look into our hearts. As we do, and as we yield to His desires for our lives, suddenly we won't spend all our time trying to get something for ourselves. No, when we are deep with God, His Word will lead us to what we're to believe for. Then the Holy Spirit will ensure that whatever "it" is, finds its way into our life.

Want the desires of your heart to be met? Delight yourself in the Lord.

Today's Word is Psalms 37:4

"Delight yourself also in the Lord, and He shall give you the desires of your heart."

DECEMBER 3

DON'T LET THE PAST ROB YOU

I've got some terrific news to share with you today! If you're spiritually bound at all, you're getting ready to be set free.

Over in the book of Isaiah we're given an instruction that isn't difficult to understand. The Bible tells us to, "Not remember the former things, nor consider the things of old."

The former things. Things of old. Those two descriptions are obviously talking about the past. Since God instructs us to not hang out and dwell on the past, why do so many young people ignore this instruction and continually rehearse their past mistakes and choices?

One reason is they haven't fully understood the necessity of trusting God and obeying His Word.

When God tells us not to remember something and then tells us to not even consider something from our past, He means it. He knows what'll happen if we stay glued to our past versus moving forward in faith.

Maybe the devil has beaten you up over past mistakes. Ok. Have you repented? Have you asked Jesus to forgive you? Then let's get going.

When I talk about this subject in chapels, here's how the Lord usually leads me to close. Do not let your past rob you of the future God has for you.

Today's Word is Isaiah 43:18

"Do not remember the former things, nor consider the things of old."

DECEMBER 4

LOVE HIM & FIND OUT

Ever really considered what God, the Creator of the universe, Who's capable of doing what He wants, when He wants, for whomever He wants, has prepared for your life?

Did you know that the Bible talks about what He's prepared? It has, and here's how it's described.

"Eye has not seen, nor ear heard, nor have entered into the heart of man the things God has prepared..."

Think about the number of "off the chart" brilliant/creative people who are on the earth today; yet despite their gifts, the Bible tells us that no eye, no ear, no heart has ever even conceived what God has already planned. To me, that's staggering.

But there's a prerequisite to you experiencing the plan of God in your life, and this condition is found in the last five words of the same verse that I referenced above. The five words are, "for those who love Him."

When you love God, you'll honor His Word, and you'll obey His instructions. When God sees your obedience, guess what? He has no problem whatsoever releasing His plans into your life.

Want to see what God has planned for your life? Love Him and find out.

Today's Word is 1 Corinthians 2:9

"But as it is written: 'Eye has not seen, nor ear heard, nor have entered into the heart of man the things which God has prepared for those who love Him."

DECEMBER 5

LIVING IN YOUR HEART

Let's say that a few years from now you have become a real estate developer, and you buy and pay for a tract of land. On this land, you decide to develop a residential neighborhood. But before you begin selling the lots and building the homes, you first go over to that property, walk all over it, you survey it, and then you choose the portion of that property that you are going to build your new home on.

You get to pick your lot because it's your property.

It's the same with your Heavenly Father. The Word tells us that the earth is the Lord's and the fullness thereof, meaning, it's all His. Because He owns it all, He can certainly choose where He wants to live. Agreed?

Here's where it gets interesting. He's chosen to not dwell in temples made with hands. Instead, God lives in your heart.

Think about it. You must be pretty amazingly special for God, Who could live anywhere He wanted, to take up residence in your heart.

Next time you're not feeling all that special because you've perhaps listened to a lie of the enemy, take a minute to put life into perspective. If you're a Christian, consider Who's living in your heart.

Today's Word is Acts 17:24

"God, who made the world and everything in it, since He is Lord of heaven and earth, does not dwell in temples made with hands."

DECEMBER 6

LET THEM FLOW

Ever been going along in life and you hear a song that takes you to a memory? How about seeing someone whom you hadn't seen in a while and seeing them causes you to relive an emotional time-stamped occurrence in your life? How about when you're suddenly very mindful of a person who means something truly special to you and, in that moment, you feel tears running down your face.

This happens to me quite a bit. These days it happens more and more as I'm leaving an event at a school. The more you invest your heart into a person or a situation, the more of your emotions are likewise invested.

Remember Joseph in the Old Testament? We've talked about it earlier in this book. His brothers sold him into slavery, and he was thrown into jail; but through it all, God knew there was a day coming when there'd be a reunion, and tears would flow.

Sometimes your body just needs to let the tears come. I don't know all the medical or psychological reason why tears are important, but I do know this: just as Joseph saw his brother Benjamin and couldn't control his tears, there will be times in your life when you'll sense the tears are getting ready to flow. Know what the Lord says? Let them flow.

Today's Word is Genesis 43:30

"Now his heart yearned for his brother; so Joseph made haste and sought somewhere to weep. And he went into his chamber and wept there."

DECEMBER 7

A MISSION TO FULFILL

When God has you on a mission and your faith is developed to the point that you're committed to that mission, nothing the devil can do or attempts to do will stop you from accomplishing it.

But please know that he will certainly try to stop you. Look at the life of Paul. The enemy tried to stop him by beating him; by ensuring he was shipwrecked; had him imprisoned; and the devil was behind the time he was lost at sea for several days. None of these distractions, however, took Paul's focus off his mission.

At one point along his journey, Paul was experiencing so much resistance from the enemy that God sent an Angel to him. Among other things the Angel shared with him was this one sentence that became a constant message Paul was hearing: "You must be brought before Caesar."

It's no different in your life today. God has assigned you a life mission. Sure, there will be resistance; count on it. But more than the resistance, count on the Word of God coming out of your mouth in faith deflecting every fiery dart shot your way.

Maybe you're in some warfare right now. Go back and read what the Angel spoke to Paul. As you do, be encouraged because you, too, have a mission to fulfill.

Today's Word is Acts 27:22-24

"And now I urge you to take heart, for there will be no loss of life among you, but only of the ship. For there stood by me this night an angel of the God to whom I belong and whom I serve, saying, 'Do not be afraid, Paul; you must be brought before Caesar; and indeed God has granted you all those who sail with you."

DECEMBER 8

ON THE RUN

Teenagers share with me that they feel like they're being attacked by the devil, and they're not too sure how to make him stop. They then tell me that overall, they're good people, with good hearts toward the Lord, but nothing they do seems to make the devil exit their lives.

I'm then usually prompted to ask them an obvious question. "What are you doing that's not working?"

If you're being attacked, beaten up, and harassed by the enemy; but what you're doing to stop him isn't working, open your Bible, turn over to the book of James, and follow two plainly printed instructions:

Submit to God and resist the devil.

Plain and simple. Submit to God and His way of doing and being right, resist (stand strong against) the devil, and watch what happens. The devil will have no choice but to flee from you.

Years ago, I learned that the word "flee" in this verse actually means to, "turn and run in terror".

What will happen when you submit and resist? You'll turn the tables and put the devil on the run.

Today's Word is James 4:7

"Therefore submit to God. Resist the devil and he will flee from you."

DECEMBER 9

THE ULTIMATE AUTHORITY

As a born-again young person, you're called to answer to a Higher Authority. This does not mean that you're not submitted to authority in your life, you are. It just means that as a Christian, we must always obey God.

I'll give you an example. When I minister in public high schools, I'm typically not allowed to give a public invitation for salvations. Because I'm under the authority of that local school and its Principal, I stay within the boundaries that have been set. But I always share my testimony, and near the end of my time with these students, I let them know that if they want to talk after our assembly, I'm certainly available.

Know what happens? Without fail, once the assembly is over, students stand in line for usually up to thirty minutes to share some of their stories with me.

How does this happen? It's the direct result of obeying God.

In your life today, might be a really good idea to make sure you're submitted to your authority, both here in the earth and to the ultimate Authority.

Today's Word is Acts 5:29

"But Peter and the other apostles answered and said: "We ought to obey God rather than men."

DECEMBER 10

HIS COMMITMENT

One of the most treasured lessons I've learned from the Lord is His unyielding commitment to take care of His kids.

I remember when all three of our kids were under five years old. Those days had many trying hours, and life was seemingly one challenge after another.

I specifically remember one afternoon. I had driven up to my office and I was on my phone, talking with one of our Partners. I was having an unusually hard day - nothing was going right, and I needed a miracle.

When I hung up the phone with that Partner, I just lost it and sat there in my car, crying harder than I'd cried in years. The pressure was too much.

Once I regained my composure, the Lord began to gently remind me of all the times He'd shown up in our lives and ministry, albeit not in my time, but certainly just in time. He took me down a list of occurrences, and sure enough, at each stop along the way, His commitment to take care of us, to provide for us, and yes, to bless us, was simply undeniable.

Not long after that moment, I saw a verse in Deuteronomy that again reminded me of how He takes care of us every day.

Maybe today you know what that evel of pressure feels like - maybe you know it all too well. If so, may I suggest that you take a few minutes and ask the Holy Spirit to take you on a stroll down memory lane?

As you do, I imagine that like me, you will realize He's ensured that your "Garments did not wear out on you, nor did your foot swell ..."

Today's Word is Deuteronomy 8:4

"Your garments did not wear out on you, nor did your foot swell these forty years."

DECEMBER 11

STRENGTHEN YOURSELF

I recently got a text message from a friend of mine, and in it he asked me to give him a call. I called him later that day and from the instant he answered his phone, it was obvious he was not having the best of days.

He briefly shared with me what had gone wrong that day. He went on to say that he'd called a bunch of friends, but no one had answered. Then he shared one more item of interest with me: he told me that even though his day had been what it had been and despite the fact that none of his friends returned his call, somehow, he was feeling better.

When I heard him say that he was better, without giving my response any thought, I heard myself saying, "So you encouraged yourself today." No sooner had those words left my lips, I had a verse of Scripture on my heart.

The verse is found in 1st Samuel, and it's the account of David being greatly distressed because the people he was leading were talking about stoning him. Instead of starting a first-class pity party for himself, David chose instead to strengthen (to encourage) himself in the Lord.

Maybe today hasn't been the best of days in your life or could be that tomorrow has more than enough challenges waiting for your full attention. Whatever the case, I'd like to encourage you to do what the only guy in the Bible who's referenced as "having a heart after God" did when he had some tough times - purpose in your heart to strengthen (encourage) yourself in the Lord.

Pray, sing, dance, shout, believe - when you do, you'll find yourself encouraged.

Today's Word is 1 Samuel 30:6

"Now David was greatly distressed, for the people spoke of stoning him, because the soul of all the people was grieved, every man for his sons and his daughters. But David strengthened himself in the Lord his God."

DECEMBER 12

UNTO HIM

What's your motivation for doing what you do? That's a question I ask teenagers to answer but before answering it, I ask them to get "gut honest" with themselves.

Why "gut honest"? Because motivation is a big deal to God. Know why? Motivation goes to the heart of the matter. Our motivation reflects our heart.

The Bible tells us that, "Inasmuch as we do something for someone else, we're doing it for Jesus."

Whether it's sitting next to the not-so-popular student at lunch, or maybe it's going by the florist and buying a daisy for your mom, or still yet, maybe it's sending a note of encouragement to someone the Lord puts on your heart. Before you do any of this, though, take the time to first check your motivation.

When your motivation is correct, your heart is as well.

Remember, when you do it unto someone else, you're simultaneously doing it unto Him.

Today's Word is Matthew 25:40

"And the King will answer and say to them, 'Assuredly, I say to you, inasmuch as you did it to one of the least of these My brethren, you did it to Me.'"

DECEMBER 13

TO THE ENDS OF THE WORLD

One of the principles from the Word that the Holy Spirit often leads me to minister to students is the principle of starting where you are and growing into where He wants you to be.

For example, I share that before I ever ministered overseas, I was first ministering in my hometown. Before I ever shared our YOU MATTER Campaign in an arena with sixteen thousand students in attendance, I first shared our Campaign in a juvenile detention center with seven students. Before I was ever led to write this 365-page daily devotional, I first wrote a fifty-page booklet about discovering your destiny.

The Word gives us this principle in the book of Acts when Jesus tells His disciples (and us) that they (and us) would be His witnesses in Jerusalem, Judea, Samaria and to the ends of the world. See how the outreach grows? It does so as we grow in our faithfulness to the Word, to the call, and to His instructions in and on our lives.

Are you called to a traveling ministry? Want to travel the globe and share the Good News? Then start where you are and obey His seemingly small and insignificant instructions. When you do, get ready. Soon you'll be heading to Jerusalem, Judea, Samaria, and to the ends of the world.

Today's Word is Acts 1:8

"But you shall receive power when the Holy Spirit has come upon you; and you shall be witnesses to Me in Jerusalem, and in all Judea and Samaria, and to the end of the earth."

DECEMBER 14

SUFFICIENT

Did you know that every trial you'll ever go through has a beginning, middle, and an end? No matter how difficult or distraught a certain situation might appear to be in your life right now, nothing temporal lasts forever. That's a fact.

Because of this fact, I strongly encourage teenagers to grow through their circumstances, knowing that there's a beginning, a middle, and an end. Part of this "growing" is learning to ask for and receive the grace of God.

No matter what comes your way, God knew it was coming before it ever arrives. And because He knew it was coming, He prepares you. Your responsibility is to follow His directions, walk in love, learn through the process, and receive His grace.

Maybe right now as you're reading these words, you're going through an unusually tough season. Take a minute; pause, and then pray. Ask the Lord to give you the grace to not only get through this season but also the grace to learn some life lessons as you come through this time.

Remember, His grace is sufficient.

Today's Word is 2 Corinthians 12:9

"And He said to me, "My grace is sufficient for you, for My strength is made perfect in weakness." Therefore most gladly I will rather boast in my infirmities, that the power of Christ may rest upon me."

DECEMBER 15

WELL DONE

For years now the Holy Spirit has repeatedly led me to share the following sentence with teenagers in high schools and conventions: "Although the Lord allows me to speak with thousands of students each month; no matter how many are in the crowd, I always have an audience of one."

An audience of one. Do you get it? You see, when we hit a home run in what we're called to do, the applause of man will never overpower the approval of God; and likewise, even when we fall short of our best for Him, the applause of an audience will never overpower the loving mercy of God.

My goal as a minister is to successfully accomplish everything I believe He's called me to do and to do it to the best of my ability. When this happens, the two words I'm looking to hear from Him are, "Well done."

How about you? Do you look for the applause of man or the applause of God? Do you seek the approval of your peers or are you desiring Heaven's stamp of approval?

My prayer for you today is that as you do whatever you do for the Lord, you'll do it in a way that'll cause you to hear your Heavenly Father say, "Well done."

Today's Word is Luke 19:17

"And he said to him, 'Well done, good servant; because you were faithful in a very little, have authority over ten cities.'"

DECEMBER 16

READ IT, BELIEVE IT & SPEAK IT

As I have been writing these daily devotionals, I've had a slogan come to my heart, and today I was led to share this slogan with you: When it comes to the Word of God, read it, believe it, and speak it.

Sounds simple, doesn't it? Almost too simple, as if there was something missing. But I truly believe that the Word works for those who don't over complicate it. It works for those who read it, believe it, and speak it.

I have no idea how many teenagers have shared their love for God with me; and today, I hope that you, too, count yourself among those who really do love Him. Want to take your relationship with the Lord to an even deeper level? Grab your Bible, ask the Holy Spirit to lead you to where He wants you to be in the Word today, and then follow the slogan: read it, believe it, and speak it.

Today's Word is Mark 5:36

"As soon as Jesus heard the word that was spoken, He said to the ruler of the synagogue, "Do not be afraid; only believe."

DECEMBER 17

PLAIN TALK WINS

There was a day when Jesus was talking with His disciples about where He'd come from, about where He was soon returning, about the disciples having sorrow, and then joy.

Apparently, His disciples just weren't getting it because several verses later, Jesus plainly told them He was leaving the world and returning to His Father.

When His disciples heard that sentence, their response proved that they then understood what He was saying.

I believe Jesus was showing all of us an example to follow: plain talk wins.

Your friends who maybe aren't yet living for God may not understand the King James Version of the Bible. But I sure believe they'd understand your ministering to them about the true meaning of forgiveness. They'd get your plainly talking with them, in their language, regarding what forgiveness is all about and how they can receive forgiveness right there, right then.

Plainly talk the Word to and with your friends. As you do, remember, plain talk wins.

Today's Word is John 16:29

"His disciples said to Him, "See, now You are speaking plainly, and using no figure of speech!"

DECEMBER 18

KNOW THE TRUTH

What's the best way to get rid of a lie? Introduce the truth.

No matter what the circumstance is that you may be facing as you read this devotional, the truth of the Bible will always defeat a lie of the devil.

Too many young people have fallen for the lies of the enemy. The devil is hitting this generation with lie after lie; lies such as, you don't love God, you're not as passionate about the Lord as you once were; you're not really called, after all, look at what you did last weekend. Lie, lie, lie.

It's time to stop buying what the enemy's selling. The truth of the Word is a free gift. It being free, however, doesn't reflect its value. It's free, because it's for everyone; but to make it available to every person who'd ever live, it cost Jesus everything He had and all He was.

For you to stop buying the lies of the enemy, you must first know the truth. To recognize the truth that's in the Word, you must know what the Word says.

And so today let's attack the lie that the enemy has been sending into your mind. Want to stop buying the lies? Then know and speak the truth.

Today's Word is John 8:32

"And you shall know the truth, and the truth shall make you free."

DECEMBER 19

YOU'RE BLESSED

I've begun showing my age when talking with teenagers, because I've begun sharing with them that I've been speaking with teenagers longer than any of today's teenagers have been alive.

I share that little nugget of truth with them to get more of their attention. I then share with them that this generation of teens is spiritually seeing and experiencing more than any generation before them in the history of the world.

I remind today's students of what the Bible says concerning what they are seeing and hearing. I ask them to look at Luke chapter 10 where Jesus spoke privately to His team. During this conversation, He plainly explained that the eyes and ears of His disciples were blessed because very powerful people had desired to see and hear what His team was daily seeing and hearing, but were unable to.

If you're a born-again Believer, you're on His team. As a member of the team, if you're tuned into His frequency and are obeying His promptings, guess what? Your eyes are seeing and your ears are hearing what others before you have neither seen or heard.

Please take where you are seriously. For whatever reason, in His infinite wisdom and timing, God chose you to live in a day and time such as this.

Remember this the next time the enemy comes lurking around: you've been chosen to see and to hear ... you're blessed.

Today's Word is Luke 10:23-24

"Then He turned to His disciples and said privately, "Blessed are the eyes which see the things you see; for I tell you that many prophets and kings have desired to see what you see, and have not seen it, and to hear what you hear, and have not heard it."

DECEMBER 20

HOPE IN GOD

Know what the answer is to a soul that feels down and depressed? To a heart that feels uneasy and has a lack of peace? Hope in God.

Hope is a feeling that what's wanted can be had. When God is your source, hope springs alive in your heart and in your life. When this happens, your believe machine turns on.

Suddenly, with hope now in the equation, what once seemed impossible and unattainable, is now very much possible and within your reach.

Maybe this all sounds too good to be true, because maybe right now you're just feeling lost or down. You know what? God's Spirit is your Helper. He knows how you feel, and He knows how to lead you to the truth that'll set you free!

What's your role in all of this? Turn your heart toward the Lord and hope in Him.

Today's Word is Psalms 43:5

"Why are you cast down, O my soul? And why are you disquieted within me? Hope in God; for I shall yet praise Him, the help of my countenance and my God."

DECEMBER 21

A SPIRITUAL FARMER

One of my favorite verses in the Bible only has five words in it, but those five words show us how to grow and develop our faith as we live a life pleasing to the Lord.

In this one verse, we learn:

1. Who we are.
2. What we are to do.
3. The identity of our power in Him.

Each of us is called to be a "Sower" - one who sows seed. That's who we are.

When prompted by the Lord to do so, we each have the assignment of sowing the seed of faith, sowing seeds. That's what we're called to do.

The Word of God is the key - that's the power we have in Him; it's the seed we sow.

So, whether you live on a farm in the country, in an apartment on 5th Avenue in New York City, or in a suburban home, guess what? If you live for God, wherever you live, you're a spiritual farmer - one who sows the Word.

Today's Word is Mark 4:14

"The sower sows the word."

DECEMBER 22

DECENTLY & IN ORDER

When teenagers begin their high school experience, very early in the school year I often am given the opportunity to speak to these freshman classes. I always look forward to having time with them, because high school is such a brand-new experience.

When our daughters, Ellie and Meg, were in 8th grade, they and their buddies made it clear to my wife and me that the 8th graders "ruled" Middle School. Once they graduate from Middle School, however, these same students are now finding themselves on the bottom of the High School "food chain". What to do?

One of the most valuable nuggets the Holy Spirit has taught me that I now so enjoy sharing with students is the nugget, the lesson, of doing everything decently and in order. I especially am led to share this truth with younger students. Why? Because when an incoming ninth grader learns early on in high school that there is an "order" to what they are experiencing, their high school days can be some of the most enjoyable and meaningful days of their lives.

In His Word, God has made it very clear for all of us, young and old alike, that His mandate for each of our lives is that all things need to be done decently and in order.

God knows what He's doing, and He knows why He wants us living in a certain way. Pay attention and be obedient: let all things be done decently and in order.

Today's Word is 1 Corinthians 14:40

"Let all things be done decently and in order."

DECEMBER 23

TOOLS OF THE TRADE

When my grandfather was alive, I so enjoyed spending time with him. One of my favorite things to do with Pap (my grandfather) was to go downstairs in my grandparents' home and play pool (billiards). I have no idea how many hours of pool he and I played through the years, but I know we played a minimum of three to four games each time we'd play.

On more occasions than I care to admit, just when I "knew" I had beaten him, he'd peer over his glasses, his nose would spread across his face, he'd smile, and then Pap would make a shot that I had never even dreamed was possible, much less makeable.

I'd then ask him where he'd learn to play pool like that. I remember that after he told me about growing up playing pool, he'd get serious with me and tell me about the electrical trade he'd learned and then talked with me about what it took to operate some of the electrical companies he'd owned.

My dad is the same way. He honed his skills in the construction and real estate development trade. People in those industries knew of my dad's people-personality and of his commitment to getting projects completed on time and under budget. His tools of the trade served him and our family well.

How about you? Maybe you haven't yet discovered God's calling for your life, but did you know that you still have tools for your own trade? What trade is that? The trade of living a life governed by the fruit of the Spirit.

Might be a really good idea if today you open your Bible to the book Galatians, and once there, read about and receive the tools of the trade provided to you by the Holy Spirit.

Today's Word is Galatians 5:22-23

"But the fruit of the Spirit is love, joy, peace, longsuffering, kindness, goodness, faithfulness, gentleness, self- control. Against such there is no law."

DECEMBER 24

REACT OR RESPOND

Want to be known as someone who has great understanding, or would you prefer to be known as the guy or girl who lives lacking understanding and does so in a continual state of being foolish?

That's not a trick question, and I sure hope it doesn't take you long to ponder your answer.

If you want to have great understanding, the Bible says to be "slow to wrath." How does you being slow to wrath qualify you for great understanding?

Might have a lot to do with you understanding the difference between how you either react or respond to situations that come and go in your life.

It's very easy to react to something that angers you, and in your reaction, you're maybe not too slow to become wrathful. But as you grow in the Word and as you submit to the Holy Spirit, you'll move from reacting to responding. As you respond, your response is based on what the Word says and how the Holy Spirit leads, causing you to be slow to wrath and, as such, you'll have great understanding.

It's your choice: react or respond. One produces foolishness, the other great understanding.

Today's Word is Proverbs 14:29

"He who is slow to wrath has great understanding, but he who is impulsive exalts folly."

DECEMBER 25

THE REASON FOR THE SEASON

Merry Christmas. Merry Christmas. Merry Christmas.

Wow! Christmas Day is here. Teenagers all over the world are waking up, making a beeline to the Christmas tree, and are ripping into packages. What a day!

But you know what? In addition to the gifts under the tree, there's one gift that is freely available to every single person all over the world - this gift isn't a thing, though, no, it's a Person.

Over two thousand years ago, in a smelly, crowded stable, the King of Kings and Lord of Lords was born. Today, we celebrate the birth of this King. His name is Jesus.

There's no greater gift you or I will ever receive than the gift of eternal salvation that brings with it the opportunity of a lifetime - a personal, real relationship with the Lord.

During all the hustle and bustle that almost always accompanies Christmas, I believe you'll be well-served if you take some time today and think about the birth of a Baby who grew to be a King, who then died a death He didn't deserve, then to be resurrected as the One, true Lord.

Sure, Christmas is a wonderful time of the year. But it's truly only wonderful when we consider Who makes it so very special.

His name is Wonderful, and He is the reason for the season.

Today's Word is Isaiah 9:6

"For unto us a Child is born, unto us a Son is given; and the government will be upon His shoulder. And His name will be called Wonderful, Counselor, Mighty God, Everlasting Father, Prince of Peace."

DECEMBER 26

HE'S EVERYWHERE

He's everywhere. He's with you in sad times, in happy times, in life and in death. He's with you on a date night and He's with you when you're sitting home, all alone, wishing you were on a date. He's with you on the athletic field, in the dance studio, in the art class and as you walk along the beach. He's everywhere.

The Bible asks the question, "Where can you go from His Spirit or where can you run from His presence?" The short answer is, "Nowhere." Why? Because He's everywhere.

Are you starting to pick up on today's theme?

God is omnipresent, meaning, He's everywhere at the same time. But how? How could He possibly be there with you and simultaneously be here with me and yet, at the same time, with every other person alive on the planet? You might think that's impossible but not so. Remember, all things are possible with Him.

Why is it important to understand that you can't go anywhere where He's not going to be with you? Because maybe, just maybe you know that anywhere you go, you take Him with you. That understanding might cause you to only go where He leads you to go.

I encourage students to see the Holy Spirit for who He is - a friend who STICKS closer than a brother. Where you go, He goes.

Today's Word is Psalms 139:7

"Where can I go from Your Spirit? Or where can I flee from Your presence?"

DECEMBER 27

THE LIMB MOVED

A dear friend of mine named Johnny Gresham called me this morning and shared a story with me that when I heard it, I also heard the Lord say, "Take note. This is for teenagers."

Johnny explained to me that one day recently he was down at his farm doing some work. The next day he noticed a squirrel at his farm running back and forth along a tree branch. The squirrel was ticked off. Something wasn't the same, and this change was affecting his life.

You see, the day before Johnny had done some tree trimming and a particular branch had been cut back by six feet. Just so happened that that branch served as the squirrel's landing pad as he flew from one tree to another. My friend then told me that he watched as in a moment of frustration and determination, that squirrel got a running start and leaped from one tree to the other. This time, however, because the limb had been shortened, there was no place for the squirrel to land; no place that is except for the ground.

The squirrel did hit the ground, and Johnny said he watched as the squirrel then just walked away. That squirrel took his landing pad for granted. He just assumed it would always be there.

What does that have to do with you today? Don't take life for granted. Appreciate every day you're given to live, because life is truly that, a gift. Be thankful.

Stay close to the Lord; and as you do, if someone moves your limb, you won't be caught off guard. Instead, you'll just adjust, and God will provide a place for you to come in for a safe landing.

Remember; make the choice that no matter what, you're going to maintain a heart full of thanks.

Today's Word is Psalms 100:4

"Enter into His gates with thanksgiving, and into His courts with praise. Be thankful to Him, and bless His name."

DECEMBER 28

WATCH

The Bible tells us to "Watch" because we know neither the day nor the hour in which Jesus is returning for His church. Watch for what?

Watch how we live life; watch where we go, watch with whom we go; watch the words we say, watch the compromises we're tempted to give into. But above all else, watch for His soon return and live accordingly.

Let's go a step further. What if you knew with absolute certainty that today, let's say five hours from right now, you'd hear a trumpet blast, look up toward the east, and suddenly you'd see Jesus riding toward you on a white horse? What would you do differently over these next five hours? Who would you call? Whose forgiveness would you ask? To whom would you say, "I love you?"

Why put off until tomorrow that which you could and maybe even should do today?

However you look at your life and the return of Jesus, whether He comes back in five hours or in five hundred years, you and I are one day closer to our end of time.

What should we do? According to the Bible, we should watch.

Today's Word is Matthew 25:13

"Watch therefore, for you know neither the day nor the hour in which the Son of Man is coming.

DECEMBER 29

ASTOUND THE DOUBTER

One of my favorite "moments" in life happens when I hear someone say the following sentence as it relates to faith and living a life of faith, "There's no way that can happen." When I hear those words, I automatically know to start watching for what we call a miracle.

Why is this? Because nothing is impossible with God. I'm fully convinced that when God hears someone say that sentence, He takes great pleasure in showing anyone who has ears to hear and eyes to see that just because it sounds or looks impossible from the human perspective, hang on; His approach to life is way beyond human limitations.

You see, I genuinely believe that one of the characteristics of true faith is that when called upon, Bible-based faith produces results that astound the doubter.

How do you inspire a doubter to consider becoming a Believer? By showing that person the reality of God and His Word.

Maybe today there's a "Doubter" in your life. Want an idea to consider? Don't just talk about faith, live faith. As you do, believe God for the supernatural to become more and more a part of your life.

As this happens, guess what else will happen? Doubters will become Believers.

Today's Word is Romans 10:17

"So then faith comes by hearing, and hearing by the word of God."

DECEMBER 30

TRADE TROUBLE FOR PEACE

What is it this year that has troubled you? As you come to the last couple of days of the year, can you glimpse back over your shoulders and see what has troubled you on and off over these past twelve months?

Maybe it's an attitude; perhaps it was a sickness. Could be that a painful divorce took place in your family, or maybe so far this year in school just wasn't what you thought it could have or would have been like for you.

Whatever "it" was that troubled you, I'm going to offer you a suggestion. Obey the Bible when it says, "Do not let your heart be troubled."

How's that even possible? It's possible as you invite and receive the peace of God into your heart. Remember, the peace I'm talking about is a guard, and it's readily available to you right here, right now.

Ready to get rid of that troubled, sinking, dreadful feeling in your gut? Reach out and receive by faith the peace that Jesus has for you.

Today's Word is John 14:27

"Peace I leave with you, My peace I give to you; not as the world gives do I give to you. Let not your heart be troubled, neither let it be afraid."

DECEMBER 31

BEGINNING & END

Is it difficult for you to imagine that in a few short hours we'll close the book on another year?

Later tonight there will be gatherings and parties and celebrations in all shapes and sizes. And while those gatherings will come and go, there's one thing that I hope you'll hang on to as this year gives way to a brand new one.

My prayer for you is that you'll hang on to the power of hope - the genuine, true hope that comes directly from the Word of God.

No matter how you spend this New Year's Eve, soon this year will be forever gone, and the experiences of a brand-new year will be fast approaching.

Here's something you might want to consider. How you leave this year may very well determine how you enter next year. Want a suggestion? Leave this year in the presence of God. Not in a religious manner but, instead, in a faith manner.

By doing so, you're giving God first place in your life. Sure, He wants us to enjoy our friends and family today and tonight, but just remember to include Him in the celebration. After all, He's the One who gave us this year to live.

Ok. That's it. Have a terrific New Year's Eve.

Sometime tomorrow I hope you'll pick up this book, turn to January 1, and let's begin the process of our spending the next year together, being daily reminded from the Word of God that yes, whoever you are, wherever you are, in Him, YOU MATTER!

Today's Word is Revelation 22:13

"I am the Alpha and the Omega, the Beginning and the End, the First and the Last."

PRAYER OF SALVATION

If you would like to give your heart to Jesus and begin a relationship with Him, it would be my honor to introduce you to my best Friend.

Repeat this prayer out loud, and as you do, know that all of Heaven is about to blast off into a serious party - all because of you and the Covenant you're entering with God to make Jesus the Lord of your life.

"Father, in Jesus' name, I repent for the sins I've committed. I ask you to please forgive me. According to Your Word, I believe in my heart, and I say with my mouth that Jesus died for me; that He paid the price for my sin on Calvary, and that you raised Him from the dead.

Father, today I know and confess that Jesus is seated right beside You, at your right hand. He's talking with You about me. Jesus, come live in my heart. Be my Savior. From this moment on, I'm Yours and You're mine. Let's hang out together. This is settled. I'm a Believer, in the name of Jesus. Amen."

Now that you're a Christian, take the next steps. Get a Bible that you understand and read it, every day. Ask around, search online, find you a Bible-believing church that preaches the uncompromised Word of faith and get plugged in.

If you would like to share with us that you prayed this prayer today, we'd really like to hear from you. Reach us at dean@deansikes.net.

God bless you.

www.deansikes.net